brasil arquitetura

brasil arquitetura

Francisco Fanucci
Marcelo Ferraz
Cícero Ferraz Cruz
Luciana Dornellas
Julio Tarragó
Roberto Brotero
Juliana Ricci
Francielle Lopes
Keli Lobo

editorial staff

Abilio Guerra
Fernanda Critelli
Silvana Romano Santos

graphic design

Victor Nosek

photographic essays

Nelson Kon
Daniel Ducci
Leonardo Finotti

image research

Juliana Ricci

brasil arquitetura

projects 2005/2020

Francisco Fanucci | Marcelo Ferraz

editors

Abilio Guerra

Marcos Grinspum Ferraz

Silvana Romano Santos

critic essays

Abilio Guerra

Guilherme Wisnik

Marta Bogéa

projects texts

Francisco Fanucci

Marcelo Ferraz

São Paulo, 2020

Romano Guerra Editora

edições sesc

cultural support

Fundação Baía Viva
dpot – mobiliário brasileiro
Bassim Trabulse + Reinaldo Kalil
Gusmão Planejamento e Obras
Flaibam e Junqueira
Isabella + Henrik
Penha Vidros
Gabriela Soares + Fernando Rodrigues
Cerâmica Fachinetto
Lume Organização de Eventos Ltda
Associação Gaúcha Municipalista
Gabriela Amaral + Juliano Arruda

Editors' Note

Brasil Arquitetura was created in 1979 by Francisco Fanucci, Marcelo Ferraz, and Marcelo Suzuki when they were young architects and had just graduated from the School of Architecture and Urbanism at the University of São Paulo – FAU USP. The trio became a duo after Suzuki left the firm in 1995.

Their work is known and recognized in Brazil and abroad by the versatility displayed in dealing with a great diversity of institutional programs for museums, cultural centers, theaters, marketplaces, and schools, not to mention community housing and family homes. Even as they base their operations in São Paulo, the firm's partners have managed to make their marks in a range of urban situations all across Brazil, with such antipodean examples as the Socioambiental Institute in the small town of São Gabriel da Cachoeira, in Amazonas, and the Praça das Artes project in cosmopolitan São Paulo.

Beyond their multifaceted practices, several interventions executed in preexisting buildings assured the firm public recognition of their expertise in the field of renovations, a perception that is enhanced by the excellence of the resulting cultural facilities, which have become urban landmarks in the cities where they were implanted. Such projects as Cais do Sertão, in Recife, the Rodin Bahia Museum, in Salvador, the Bread Museum, in Ilópolis, and the Central Mill Theater, in Piracicaba, have rehabilitated obsolete and forsaken buildings to rework them into today's standards and practices.

From the point of view of concept, shape, and materiality, the work of the team led by Fanucci and Ferraz is characterized by the synthesis of contemporary action and a commitment to Brazilian modernist tradition. A particular characteristic of their work is the ever-present concern they show in highlighting the civil, cultural, and climatic features of each locality, which are translated into ethical and aesthetical values in their work, for instance, in the preservation of the natural environment and in the various forms of reinterpretation of traditional constructive elements.
This meaningful and accomplished career has earned the firm referential status and also a previous publication (Cosac Naify, 2005), in which projects and works dating back to their foundation in 1979 were reviewed. Now, in celebration of their forty years of activity, this new publication coedited by Romano Guerra Editora and Edições Sesc São Paulo reviews the firm's projects from the period between 2005 and 2020. The quantity of bibliographical references in the texts conveys the vast critical acclaim regarding Brasil Arquitetura, befitting the greatness of their body of work, prominent in the context of Brazilian architecture today.

Romano Guerra Editora
Edições Sesc São Paulo

Contents

Left, Castaman Mill, Arvorezinha, 2008; top, Roman House, reference drawing for Bread Museum's logo, Arvorezinha

Lessons by the Stone

Marta Bogéa

This essay seeks to recognize in the settings proposed by Brasil Arquitetura the "education by stone," which will constitute both the "concrete fleshing-out" of the architectural artifact to endure the time of the form and the stone that "ingrains the soul" to also endure in memory, the very reason for the existence of this same architecture.

It begins, thusly, in the cadence of João Cabral de Melo Neto's poetry – "A educação pela Pedra" (Education by Stone, in the free translation)[1] –, to peruse the ways in which the architects form strategies that enable them to "attend to the stone, capture its voice" in the malleable aspect of the material, while, at the same time, searching for that "stone of birth", which ingrains the soul of the landscapes.

Two forms of iconographic documents entangle the weft being woven here: The photographs taken by Marcelo Ferraz and Francisco Fanucci in their travels and the constructive designs and (especially) details that make up the work plans elaborated for each of their construction sites. Among the images that portray and frame those places, wrapped around so many other sites/landscapes traversed by the architects, as well as drawings that concoct their transformations, the wording of this text was constructed.

The Aged Marketplace, the Old Infirmary and Their Renewed Landscapes

In a cold and sunny month of June, in 2019, I was in Jaguarão, visiting with Marcelo Ferraz. The vast landscape echoed with the familiar and imaginative descriptions that surrounded those places – the pampas, a region that blurs the borders between Brazil, Argentina and Uruguay.

In the small town, spread along the Yaguarón River, one can see and cross into Uruguay, via a bridge called Barão de Mauá. Almost everyone in the town has family ties to both sides of the river, Brazilians and Uruguayans. In addition to Portuguese and Spanish, they speak a number of expressions which are their own, terms that were spun across time by this peculiar and intricate brand of cultural constitution.

Moreover, they are *frontier folk*. Such a trace denotes the inevitable field of negotiation, by one and the other, the negotiation of knowing oneself to be one and the other, or, yet, one in the other. If culture identifies itself in the recognition of otherness, in Jaguarão, a cultural peculiarity – this twofold condition – is constitutive of its people.

The political and geographical borders were not able to dissolve this common ground because the shared landscape and way-of-life lead to certain common denominations which, in turn, allocate themselves as determined ways of being.

These are, for instance, variations of their own language, registered by Aldyr Garcia Schlee, a local writer and translator of Portuguese and Spanish, in the *Dictionary of the Culture of the Pampas*.[2] The words retrieved by Schlee from texts of important interpreters of the reality of the *pampas* in Brazil, Argentina, and Uruguay compose the lexicon, as evocations of both languages.

The judicious dictionary sheds light on the distinction between regionalist allegory and the effective value of each local expression in its uniqueness, an important challenge in our present time, so fond of worldisms, generic languages, and unified settings. From the inevitable charms of approaching the world to the disenchantment of losing ourselves, each of us, in the

Bodegão's interior at Vila Borghetto, typical local furniture and fish preparation for Holy Week, Anta Gorda

pasteurization of a falsely unified world – which makes us lose the particular vibration of discovering one another in the difference of otherness, so often, in those sparks –, we reinvent ourselves.

One of the most admirable traces of the work of Brasil Arquitetura springs out of this tenderness. The architects peek into otherness. And they do it with genuine curiosity and grace, by looking closely, by gathering themselves around the sites, by joining in with people and sharing their stories. They do not look at them "from outside and above, in a superior and extrinsic perspective, translating them artificially into the terms of highbrow urban norm."[3] Those are the same qualities attributed by Schlee to define the literature that is interesting to him, the literature that allowed him to concoct their dictionary.

Both Schlee and the duo of architects manage to escape the trappings of allegory and mimesis, in search of what can best be described as translation; and, in the case of the architects, also, juxtaposition and contamination.

I inhabit this landscape, at least imaginarily, ever since the time when, intrigued, I first saw the project for the Pampa Museum, in our preparations for the Território de Contato (or contact territory, in free translation) exhibition, in 2012.[4] It lingers in my memory, besides the beauty of the old infirmary ward in ruins, the photograph of a signpost/arrow that held no inscription and oscillated in various directions; more windsock than arrow, it swings in the wind. It doesn't point to any particular place, as it could point to all of them. In the same manner, it does not point to what it aims to signify, since its area of inscription is hollow. This signpost/arrow seems to be a curious metaphor for an apparently placid landscape, which is thickened by the inevitable ambiguity of its particular situation. Beyond the iconography that constitutes a certain framing of the sites, I was there myself for a few days, to visit two projects of the firm in Jaguarão: The renovation of the Municipal Market and the construction of the Pampa Museum.

The market is finalized today, although it remains closed, awaiting for its power connection and its proper opening; the museum, on the other hand, is still under construction, an interrupted work in progress, a condition so disconcertingly Brazilian that turns buildings into ruins even before they can be completed.

My interest in these two particular projects, among the vast production of the firm, was piqued by the opportunity to visit two working sites of such distinct architectural gestures in the same small town. The contrast between the two was already perceptible in the documents I had previously seen.

The Municipal Market is an admirable original construction, which came to be known to Ferraz by a larger photograph of the city, during one of his visits to the mayor's office for meetings regarding the Pampa Museum. His keen eye saw the value in the edifice. Later, he sought to visit it.

The market was built between 1864 and 1867. Today, it is recognized as state preservation patrimony to be preserved by

House at Vila Borghetto, façade and detail, Anta Gorda; local grain warehouse

the Institute of Historic and Artistic Heritage – IPHAN. During a long time, it served as a commercial center of basic supplies for the population, but it fell into decay in the last few decades. The market was in precarious working condition by the time the architect first laid eyes on it. It had suffered the typical modifications expected of the competition with the industrial world and it displayed the decline and abandonment of things that are left on the outskirts of newer logics of production. In order to survive, it would need to be reinvented.

The task is usual in the projects of this pair of architects. In a way, it is part of the same condition that prompted them, for example, to recover the mills of the Taquari Valley.[5]

The design project, from 2010, at first sight, is a near nothing. It maintains the recognizable and valorous façade of the old building: The two triangular courtyards, superior and inferior; the same stonework in the lower part; the sequence of blue doors in its terrace; the elegant whitewashed parapet; the sophisticated use of contour that makes it towering enough to see far into the other side of the river.

From up close, after a few perusals, one begins to see where the project intervened most. The first of these architectural gestures is a judicious and attentive redefinition of its rooms, configuring a small variation in that which was originally a continuous similitude. Some premises are enlarged by agglutination. The passageways will now house the necessary equipment for the workings of the new building in a fresh slab that redefines the height. New public bathrooms were built. The stores in the lower street level gained different uses; for instance, cold storage rooms that will give support to the restaurants.

Beginning with the spatial reconfiguration, it was possible to notice a subtle difference: The doors, previously all in blue-painted wood, were now constituted of three different materials. Some maintained the traditional use of wood, but four were replaced by corten steel (particularly those that house the new equipment) and others were overlaid by glass panels. In this manner, beyond the unprecedented uses that the building received, the new setting is stablished and becomes evident through the choice of materials.

The superposition of the glass will allow restaurants and bars to host lively nights (in the way nights are lively in small towns). It is possible to imagine feeling quite comfortable in one of those shops after dark, gazing at the river, protected from the chilling winds of the *pampas*. The old market had no need for this peculiar imaginable situation; it had the daytime uses of an open-market, it was a place of movement, not of contemplation.

The change of usage seeks new connections, a condition of re-existence that would allow us to reconsider the old market, with its altered goods and modes of trade. The project is a *near*

Examples of typical Serra Gaúcha houses

nothingness, yes, which chose to prioritize the integrity of the old market, in the interest of transforming, mainly, to preserve. Above all, it is the usage that is altered. The features of its form remain, although slightly changed by the unprecedented materiality that converges on the material found there.

The procedure is quite different from the one designed for the renovation and transformation of the old infirmary ward.

The Pampa Museum inherits an important feature of its former matrix, the military infirmary ward built in 1880-1883 to treat the wounded of the frontier wars, a building far enough to be protected and inevitably close enough to the conflict to shelter the soldiers. That inherited feature is the quadratic design around its central courtyard. This endows the construction with a certain logic of fortification. By architecture, it defines the clear distinction between the inner sheltered space and the outer open space.

The building is consolidated as a typical defensive structure, with a central courtyard surrounded by a sequence of rooms and a peristyle corridor facing the inner yard. Its completeness was compromised by the collapse and removal of the stones on one side of its quadrature. The ruin that was found by Fanucci and Ferraz was only a part of what it had been. Its majestic, defensive presence had been compromised by this open flank, undermining the once clear arrangement of being either in the ward and safe or out of the ward and exposed.

The primary gesture of design, an evidence of the understanding and respect for the ancient artifact, was to reconfigure its completeness. For this effect, and without the innocence of wanting to recapture a lost age, the authors adopted concrete to restore the corner, redacting the built form and imprinting a visible adjustment through new material.

From there, one of the most recurring traces in the entire complex edification begins to appear: A kind of record keeping, by using new couplings with unprecedented materiality. The couplings, then, reshape that which was in a state of collapse. This gesture also encompasses different scales: It goes from the detail of the sealing of the windows to the decision to construct two new buildings – the auditorium and a new pavilion, which will hold the administrative offices, eventual parties and temporary exhibitions.

In the reconstruction of the windows, a pattern of detail guides the transformation: The small gutter and drop outlet adjust and vary according to the soundness found in each porthole.

Castaman Mill
Town of Arvorezinha

The renovation of the set of buildings in the Castaman Mill and in the surrounding area will represent another important step in the preservation of the cultural landscape of Italian immigration in Rio Grande do Sul, which has some of its most notable traces in the mountainous region of the Taquari Valley. It will also be a decisive step in the implantation and consolidation of the Route of the Mills, a cultural and touristic route designed with the purpose of revealing and preserving the roots that provide documentation and testimony to an important chapter in the formation of the Brazilian people. With a contemporary approach that fosters economic growth and regional development, this project is perfectly fitted to a new concept of preservation, the so-called cultural landscapes, which envision the natural and human environment as the unified protagonist of these sceneries.

Route of the Mills' map; Hugo Castaman and Amábile Itália, couple owner of Castaman Mill, Arvorezinha

In the newly built units, the contour lines of the design deserve some attention. The ensemble is still today a majestic presence in town. Located in the highest part of the settlement, known as Cerro da Pólvora (or Gunpowder Hill, in free translation), it is possible to see it from Rio Branco, the Uruguayan city across the river. The new pavilion was placed at an intermediate level, so that the old ward could still have a view of the river. The clear axis that organizes its almost exact symmetry (since the partitions on each side are distinct) aligns with the axis of the central door of the old building. An internal terrace keeps the view of the landscape open. It unfolds onto the doors, which seal the new unit of cyclopean concrete, designed to receive temporary exhibitions.

With the task of restructuring the new set and the added areas of the old edifice, one finds a beautiful pillar of corten steel – could it be an involuntary homage to the cruciform pillar by Mies van der Rohe in the German Pavillion in Barcelona? There, the steel is stainless and reflexive, here, opaque and adherent; there, a single piece unit, here, decomposable. Both are elegant designs of a slender colonnade that radiates movement more than it defines a uniform mesh.

The conversation I had with Fanucci, during the writing of this text, in the midst of many sketches and in face of my recollection of Mies, revealed him to be knowledgeable about the rigorous detailing process developed by the architect. In this context, it is important to highlight that Fanucci, in his formative years and in the early years of his partnership with Ferraz, collaborated with architects who were his professors, like Abrahão Sanovicz and Joaquim Guedes, two names commonly associated with the construction and rigor of the detail. During the same period, Ferraz was collaborating with Lina Bo Bardi. The pleasure in the detail, the attention to particular ways of life, the perceptiveness in relation to the landscapes – even the savvy to choose with whom to collaborate – are all traces derived from these learning years. Since then, they have both shared and honed these exchanged traces.

It is within this mutual confluence that, for example, the path between the old building and the new units is drawn. The path

Castaman Mill, ensemble perspective, site plan and photos, Arvorezinha, 2008

goes through a wide staircase flanked by flowing water, which, then, flows into a water mirror. This reveals and values the water present in the entire region. It is an elegant detail that ensures the gentle sound of water is heard in the ambiance, through an employment of graduate falls, which sonically animates the environment. An effect obtained by rigorous constructive detail.

The project highlights important natural elements that are very prevalent in the local environment. These were neglected by the original building, but here they become protagonists. The geography of the place is also constituted by a section of flagstone, part of it composed of large intact stones, and another part that is fragmentary, of easy decomposition. Across the entire region (not only here, it is important to say) water emerges. In the high ground, a small lake is formed, as a result of water springs and a certain configuration enabled by a small quarry excavation. From this vantage point, one might notice a sort of natural auditorium, which did not escape the perception of the architects, perhaps in remembrance of the majestic quarry that holds the beautiful auditorium proposed by them in the competition of the Pure and Applied Mathematics Institute – IMPA, in 2015. It is worth to recall the terms of that memorial:

> The auditorium of the new IMPA will crown the whole ensemble. Immersed in the quarry, at times introspective with black curtains, at times extrovert and integrated with the exterior, it will be the greatest stage for the slate blackboard, the irreplaceable tool of mathematicians. From the stone to the stone.

Beside the open amphitheater, which, in a way, was already present on site and became defined only by the addition of the tiered seats, the will of the rock shall present itself in exuberance in the new auditorium placed as if in the bowels of the earth. Kept in the same level as the interior terrace, the small auditorium was built by the cutting and removal of parts of the stone; the space left was turned into a precinct.

Water falling from the moisture that springs from the walls will be collected through a special gutter designed between the natural walls and the floor. The strong presence of the stone makes it worth the effort of construction and the almost offense

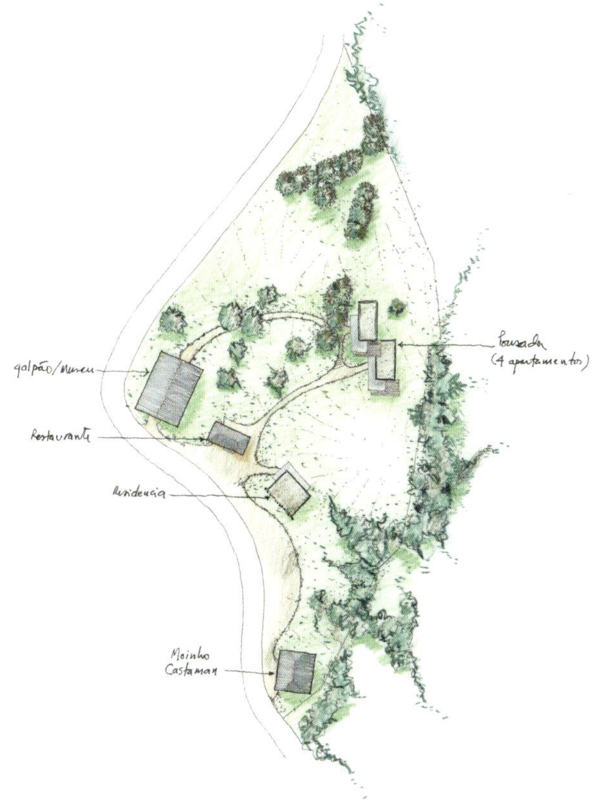

it represents to the original landscape, transmuted into poetic pertinence: "Its cold resistance, to what flows and flowing, to be malleable", according to the rhythm of João Cabral de Melo Neto's poetry.

In this small auditorium, the architects came up with an unexpected room, almost a magical and imaginary site. Visiting the place, even among the incomplete museum installation, one can't help but desire that, once the building is inaugurated, at least from time to time, it might be possible to turn off all the machinery designed to showcase periodical films and allow the bare architecture to be displayed with no other artifice but itself.

A water current, seen from high above, traverses the central terrace in the form of a small creek in an artificial riverbed. Along with the ground fire pit, they pay a lovely homage to a well-known and celebrated architectonical picture of the city of São Paulo, the *São Francisco River* and the central fire place in the socializing spaces of Sesc Pompeia, from 1898, a project by Lina Bo Bardi and a team of architects which included Marcelo Ferraz. That which is pure artifice in the Sesc building – fireplace and riverbed – emerges re-naturalized in the scenery of the South: Ground fire and a creek that speeds away the water sprung from stone.

Imagined between the given landscape and the unprecedented setting, in the Pampa Museum, at least two time periods in the life of the place converge and collide: The old infirmary ward is still noticeable and imaginable in its integrity, still experienced as a ruin – for it remains relatively stable, without the illusory return to a time when it was intact; simultaneously, one gathers evidence of the new Pampa Museum, into which the ruin converges, its amendments added to the new outline.

In this sense, it is a very distinctive project from that of the Municipal Market. In the former, there's collision, in the latter a continuity in connection. These two designs allow us to verify, in close proximity with experience, something that might be perceived across the entirety of the firm's production. More than a unique method or a single manner of performance, it is the insightful attention to each case that gives rise to its possibilities of transformation. And, if the particular diction of the authors is noticeable, it is also clear that in each project this diction is expressed in indelible dialogue to what the architects discover in each place.

During the conversations that fostered this text, Fanucci recalled the book of stories by Aldyr Garcia Schlee, *Uma Terra Só*. He shared with me the cover photo where the old market of Jaguarão is seen, the river and Uruguay on the opposite margin.

Castaman Mill, internal photos, Arvorezinha, 2008

The epigraph is "here, there is but one land, there is but one people, either on this side or on the other."[6] He also sent me this beautiful and brief section of one of the stories:

> Pretend
> that all is true
> pretend
> that we remember
> everything that might have been
> everything that was
> and everything that was not
> there and here
> hither.[7]

"Pretend that everything is true, pretend that we remember...", a delicate intertwining of fact and fiction, recollection and imagination which translates so well the poetical fleshing-out carved *in the stone* by Fanucci and Ferraz, here, in Jaguarão and in so many others "there."

Imagined Settings, Brazil Among So Many Brazils

The Brazil of Brasil Arquitetura holds many Brazil(s) more. The ample variety of sites where their vast production can be found is surprising. In each of them, it is possible to recognize the authors, while, at the same time, we have a sense of unfamiliarity gathered from the particularities of their process of renovation and thorough enjoyment of the landscapes they will work on.

On the one hand, they ensure that whatever comes to pass is a product of the history of the place, in line with the local community. On the other, they do this without concealing themselves, for they act as active participants who contribute to the development of each place.

They seek to recognize and contribute. They certainly disrupt the path in which things were headed, as any outlander will do. On equal measure, however, they strengthen local values that, as a natural tendency, seem to be left unremarked by those who have always lived there. Attentive to local lore and conscious of their position as visitors, they search for ways of escaping generalist or superficial solutions and to inhabit each of these localities by getting closer to the people and by giving the landscape they seek to decipher their full attention.

Ferraz and Fannuci create an interesting confrontation between the possibilities enabled by the past – and only because of that able to succeed in the future – and the dynamics of present life. They do so by electing each community as their own, in line with the perspective presented by Luisa Bonesio in the text entitled "Habitar a terra e reconhecer-se nos lugares" (inhabit the land and recognize oneself in places, in free translation):

> to partake in the situation, to inhabit there, across extensive time, in a project of fidelity to the place founded not over a natural community of autochthonous people and their

Castaman Mill, perspective, Arvorezinha, 2008

São Marcos Church, Arvorezinha

> territory, but over the election of a place to which one attends, participating in an elective community that one inhabits only in the measure that a person decides to be one of those who take care of the place – it comes alive as a necessary element in a sense of relationship, symbolic and affective investment, and responsibility for future designs.[8]

In this sense, each place integrates a certain site of production, not a generality of self-referential authorial solutions. Not only in the vast territory of our country, but even in certain regions – as, for example, in the southern sceneries to be found – one can differentiate the proposal for the Mission Museum, in São Miguel das Missões, from the projects related to the Route of the Mills or even to the two proposals for the city of Jaguarão.

They renew Jaguarão, attentive to the frontier and the river: In the Pampa Museum, in the majestic and ruinous infirmary, they consolidate fragments by interjecting concrete-stone into the native rock; in the aged marketplace, they reassert its beautiful and prosaic setting.

In São Miguel das Missões, in the company of Carlos Eduardo Dias Comas, they remain attentive to the sophisticated intervention by Lúcio Costa and take it a step further, in the same key, but now articulating the perimeter of the preservation site and the city around its edges, part here, part there, with a central plaza that asserts both the ensemble and the local practices, even when they are disjointed. In the Route of the Mills, they create a network that even today continues to sprawl out, irradiating novelties, but preserving and renewing striking buildings, impacting their surroundings.

The proficiency of materiality is repeated – for example, of concrete or leveled slabs, roof gardens, present in the inception. They are also renewed through the use of wood in the magnificent mills as well as in the simpler houses. Both the local landscapes and some of the memories associated with them are shown in the works – metaphorical houses – since "the house inhabited is also the house dreamt of, the house we have left and the house we will return to, the house of our forefathers and the house of our children, ultimately, the house that time buries and the one that time renews."[9]

If, on the one hand, with forty years of existence, traces indicate an unequivocal and consistent authorship – which means that the firm can be identified in their works by the procedures that they employ –, on the other hand, these recurrent traces are less visible in the forms than in the methods. They present certain gestures that echo in these places, but that appear in shifting materiality. There, the singularity of gestures and the material employment that reverberate in each site call one's attention.

A double movement is enacted: On one side, things native to the place are framed and valued; on the other, gestures unfamiliar are presented and installed. They seek to demonstrate

Castaman House, façade, doors, kitchen/canteen, window, and shed, Arvorezinha, 2008

the generous commitment of an architecture that does not fail for omission in sharing the best it can present for the benefit of the continuation of life as it is where it acts.

Ferraz and Fanucci do not treat landscapes as allegories, facts for nostalgia; they recognize charms that they seek to highlight. An unexceptional conversation with Ferraz during our trip together confirms this hypothesis. We were passing by a certain house in Jaguarão, which has some excessive graphic work of design. In the face of my astonishment and discomfort, he pondered, conceded that it was a tad peculiar, and he spoke of his desire to understand the reasons for the beauty that lies in each situation so he could, then, evoke them. It was curious how that demonstrated his eye to me, tracking the scenery, noting the imagery with curiosity, and editing it, by cut, by frame, by detail.

As if they were the "travelling seaman" narrators of Walter Benjamin,[10] Ferraz and Fanucci travel gathering images that will be foundational to other projects. Some of them remain visible, plotted in consonance with the new venue, like the wondrous artisanal luminaire seen in some lot of the region and rebuilt in the terrace of the Bread Museum, in Ilópolis, or the new guardrail designed from the collection of protective guarding in wood installed in the local houses.

However, it is important to recognize the fact that this harvest would not be very fruitful if it didn't unfold within the laborious and detailed process of molding the material. The figure to emerge here is that of the craftsman as understood by Richard Sennet,[11] to whom the skill to perform a well-crafted piece of work will require of the craftsman a dedication well beyond that of the simple task.

Castaman House, details, Arvorezinha, 2008

The judicious development of the designs that engineer these constructions reveals a careful performance of craftsmanship. Although we've come to know the projects in their most general features, observing the details of the designs, we realize that each step of this procedure is configured through an inexhaustible honing of the language; the same gesture, the improvement through review, and the fresh qualities given by the singularity of each material and each landscape come to fruition.

The willingness to recognize whatever complementary virtue lies in the reiterated desire to remain a duo and the time spent together in common authorship has certainly impregnated both of them with what most naturally resides in the other. One of them is more clearly a traveling narrator, the other one more visibly a craftsman.

Once, when I asked whose watercolor drawings were those I saw, they both replied: "The drawings are Chico's, the watercolors are Marcelo's. It is always like this!" This short, almost anecdotal story demonstrates that not only do they produce within their complementarity, they enjoy it greatly. It also demonstrates that the ability of one relies on the know-how of the other.

Between the intervals of each other, their team sails on, always greatly valued. And, accepting the challenge to press on and renew one another, both of them seem to know how to preserve a continuous and desirable dialogue, even in continuous and desirable distance. This is vital for otherness (so intrinsic to the foundation of a duo) to continue to flourish, perpetuating and cherishing the many domains and stories that today are already accessible to all of us by decantation. All of us, who, with interest, observe them as they act.

Notes

1. João Cabral de Melo Neto (1966), "A educação pela Pedra," in: *Antologia Poética*, 12.
2. Aldyr Garcia Schlee, *Dicionário da Cultura Pampeana Sul-Rio-Grandense*.
3. Ibid., 1st volume, XXXIII. Free translation.
4. For more in regard to this, see: Marta Bogéa and Abilio Guerra, "Algo Muito Humano Além de Belo. Exposição Território de Contato, Módulo 1: Cao Guimarães e Brasil Arquitetura."
5. A project recently reviewed by me in the following text: Marta Bogéa, "Imaginar o passado, com saudade do futuro." This ensemble of mills was also very relevant to my initial acquaintance with the firm's production, during the elaboration of the text: Marta Bogéa, "Brasil Arquitetura. Uma partilha das distâncias, construindo convívios."
6. Aldyr Garcia Schlee, *Uma Terra Só*, 7. Free translation.
7. Ibid., 12. Free translation.
8. Luisa Bonesio, "Habitar a Terra e Reconhecer-se Nos Lugares," in: Adriana Verísssimo Serrão, ed., *Filosofia e Arquitetura da Paisagem: Um Manual*, 208. Free translation.
9. José Duarte Gorjão, "O Tempo da Cidade," in: Adriana Verísssimo Serrão, ed., *Filosofia e Arquitetura da Paisagem: Intervenções*, 182. Free translation.
10. Walter Benjamin, "O Narrador," in: Obras Escolhidas, volume 1 – *Magia e Técnica, Arte e Política*. Free translation.
11. Richard Sennett, *O Artífice*.

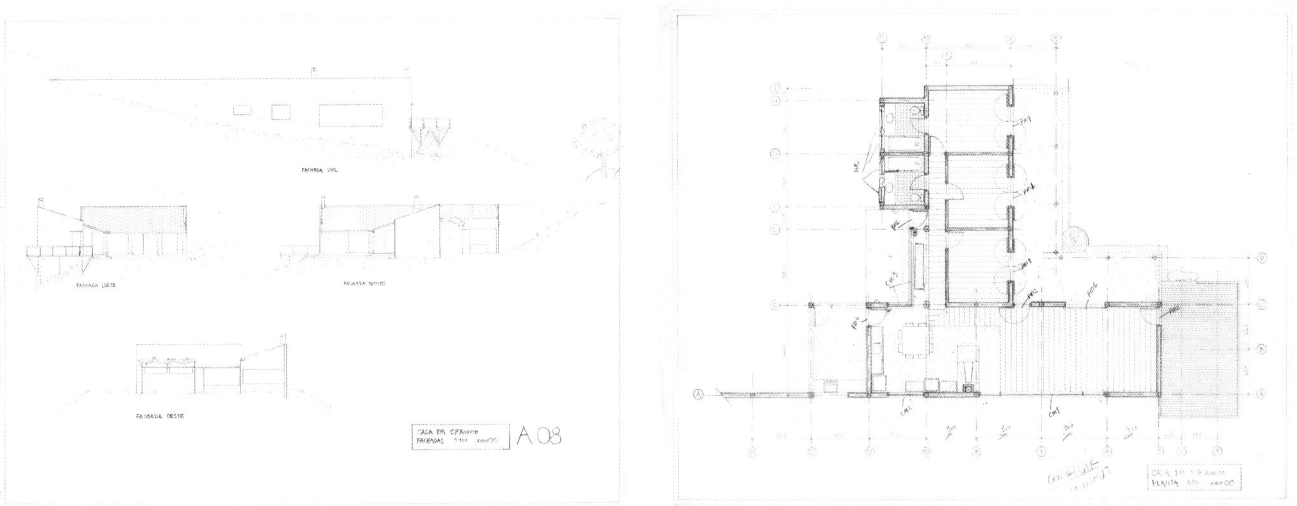

São Francisco Xavier House, elevations and plan, São Francisco Xavier, 1999

The Passageway and the Fold – Marcelo Ferraz and Francisco Fanucci's Rural Homes

Abilio Guerra

Where our sertão remains
Every happy little house
Still neighbors a stream
And still harbors its arbors

Where our sertão remains
Every happy little home
Cooks on the coal cooker
The wood stove's still blown

[...]

Where sertão remains
Every little house is glad
for on the evenings we get our Hail-Mary
And the pleasure of being alone

Casinha feliz, lyrics by Gilberto Gil[1]

1.

In São Francisco Xavier, a district of São José dos Campos, in the Mantiqueira Mountain Range, near the state line of Minas Gerais, there, in a predominantly rural region, lies the Mantiqueira House, a project designed by the architect Francisco Fanucci in the year 2000.[2] Nestled at the top of one of the great hills in the area, the building balances itself on the side of a steep hill, on partially earth-worked grounds. Shaped like an "L," the house is organized in two wings, one of which holds the social and service areas. It has three portholes opened to the South landscape, where one can see tumultuous hills resembling a stormy sea. In the living room, the largest opening – a great tear of transparent glass – has two other windows in its extremities, which can be opened for ventilation. To the left, the fireplace room is connected to the exterior veranda, exposed to the elements. To the right, in the kitchen, with a wood-burning stove and the old-style red burnt cement floor, there is another window.

During our visit, when we were peering out of the kitchen window, an unexpected memory emerged: Fanucci recalled his childhood home in Cambuí, positioned on the high parts of the city, with a window view of the landscape in the background.[3] On the exterior, out of this same side, there is a door-window to the porch, which is equipped with a wood stove for barbecue and pizza.

Of this side, from afar, one can only see its whitewashed wall spliced to the dividing wall,[4] a kind of white horizontal blade, aligned from the top, as it slowly vanishes, from the bottom-up until it is gone, in the ascending terrain. It is similar to an installation of the landscape design by Richard Serra.[5] This grandiloquent façade – which detaches the open view from the valley, full of trees and a creek – is abruptly subsided by the folding of the unit in half, with the private area of the bedrooms turning ninety degrees, in a domestic dialogue with its surrounding. The one side roofs of the two wings are tilted in a convergent manner, sheltering under them the "L" shaped porch, which is connected to rooms and halls by doors. As the resulting external precinct – exposed on a section and concealed on another – is partially closed-off on the other two sides by vegetation, it suggests a courtyard. An image reinforced by the semicircular use of cobblestones over the flat terrain. On the other side of the bedroom wing, next to the hallway, there is a section with bathrooms and an orchard, but, also, another patio is formed, encapsulated on the other three sides by the living room veranda, the steep hill and afforestation.

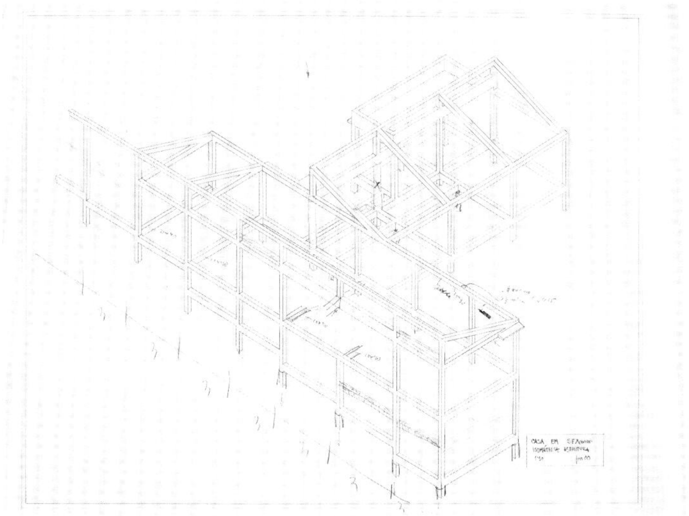

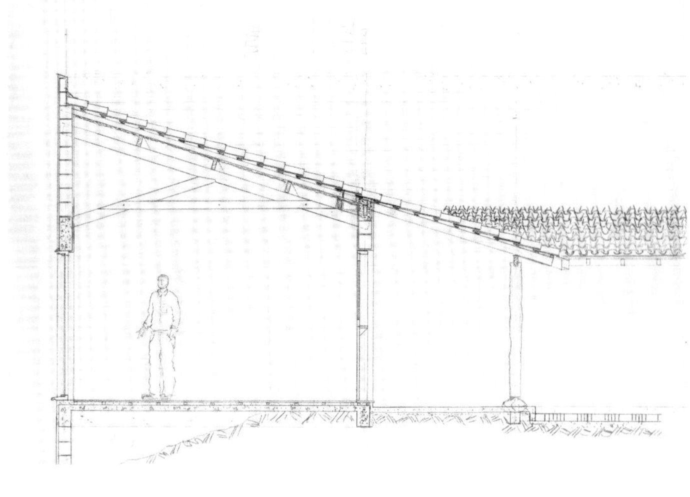

São Francisco Xavier House, structure isometric and section detail, São Francisco Xavier, 1999

2.

On the edge of a plateau, near the top of a hill, the Boa Vista Farmhouse is perched, a house designed by Marcelo Ferraz for himself and his family in the rural town of Dom Viçoso, in 2008. Out of the podium-shaped stone base, the building dashes toward the steep slope. Below, as far as the eye can see, successions of plains form the great hills of the Mantiqueira Mountain Range in the Southeastern region of Minas Gerais, near the borders with the states of São Paulo and Rio de Janeiro. The house – two units in the shape of rectangular cuboids, connected and aligned by a small glass passageway – is arranged longitudinally in relation to the hillside, so that the ambience of both blocks, where the common social areas and the bedrooms are set, reveals the same magnificent landscape. The possibility to gaze out onto this landscape is the manifest reason for choosing this particular site, as the author of the work himself, Marcelo Carvalho Ferraz, has attested.[6]

The stone base, the whitewashed walls, the wood-fire stove, the veranda looking out to the hill below and the porch looking inward, the two small and narrow rectangular windows (in the kitchen and at the end of the bedroom hallway), the view of the cultivated and busy fields below, the grassy yard that gives access to the house, the stone wall that establishes the property's boundaries, the succession of stonework erections built with native rocks, the intimate relationship between the main house and the warehouses of coffee processing and storage, the yards for drying the grains, the homely vegetation resembling untamed undergrowth, which springs up and takes over the exterior upper side of the two functional blocks[7] – in short, the supreme simplicity of the work – all of that suggests the incorporation of local rural elements to the architectural and landscaping projects. An acknowledgment of this initial impression comes from the architect himself, in his book *Arquitetura Rural na Serra da Mantiqueira*, in the form of an observation regarding the rural homes of the place: "When in brickwork, they usually sit on basis of stone."[8]

3.

However, the assertion Ferraz makes about the provincial household puts into question the choice made by both architects for summits. According to his book: "The most adequate place to build a house and the essential surrounding equipment for daily life" is, generally, "at the intermediate level, half-slope, protected from strong winds, near running water, which should be delivered by gravity's work, and also on solid ground, without risk of erosion. The construction of the house must never bring about earthworks. Its establishment should be more of a landing, the terrain should be respected in its original contour."[9] These are recommendations overtly disregarded in both houses.

The appreciation for the ability to gaze – the cornerstone of Fanucci and Ferraz's architectural methods – also moves their designs in the opposite direction of the criteria present in the typical houses of the region, which are dominated by the introspective character of "small and closed boxes."[10] A statement by Fanucci sums up the writings of Ferraz on the matter: "In this manner conceived, the houses seem like the ideal shelter, the protection and coziness those who have spent the entire day working under sun and rain look for. Home is the moment of intimate regathering, of darkness permitted by the kerosene lamp light, of respite for the sight that, from the first rays of the sun until dusk, had its limits set in the blue-green succession of plains that form the great sea of hills."[11]

The architects are aware of how much their projects differ from the region standard of houses. They understand their own houses are occupied by people who live in the cities, who only occasionally visit the premises, and who take the exuberant views they permit as precious things in their days of rest. It is a completely different situation from that of the men and women of the country, who are weary of so many hills, so much green and light, and who would rather rest from work in the coziness of a house sheltered from winds, rain, heat, and from the very

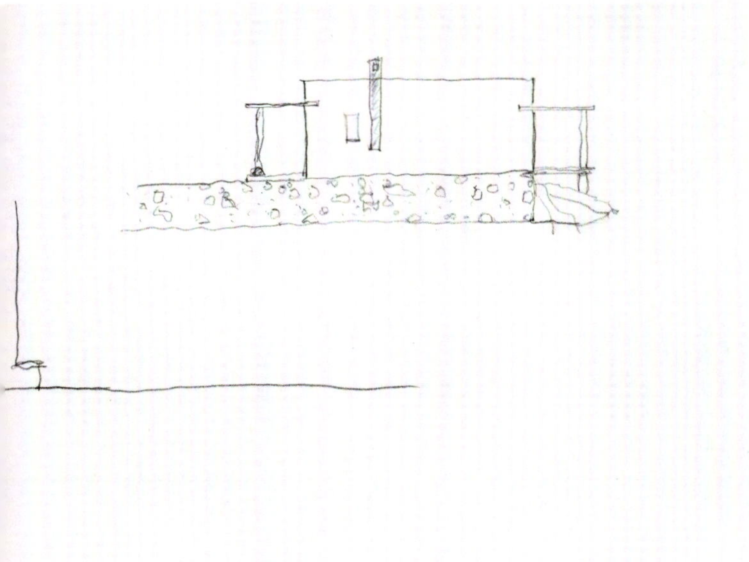

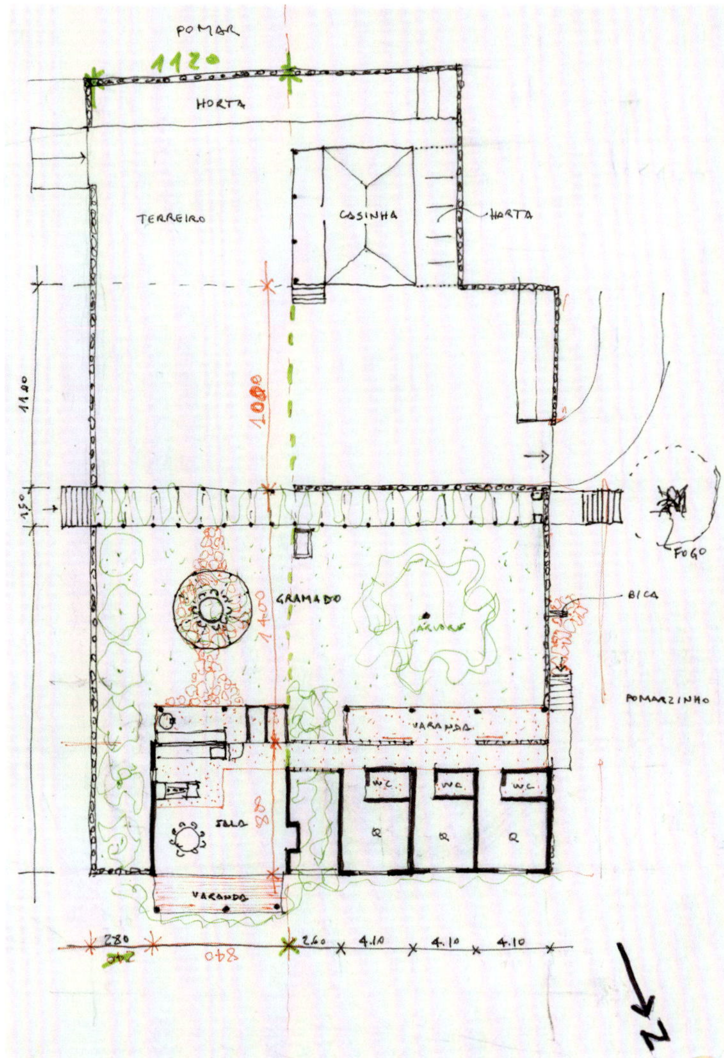

Dom Viçoso House, lateral elevation and site plan, Dom Viçoso, 2010

landscape surrounding them. In the photographs by Marcelo Ferraz, published in his book about the Mantiqueira Mountain Range, one can observe the measured presence of porches, generally small, but many times absent, reaffirming the little disposition countrymen have for relating to the surrounding nature in their few hours of respite.

4.

During the research conducted for the 2012 Território de Contato (or contact territory, in free translation) exhibition, Marta Bogéa and I detected the importance the duo placed on their sketching notebooks, produced during the development of the firm's projects. In them, there are texts, pictures, and drawings that gather a variety of information regarding the place, the landscape, the terrain, the architecture, the objects, and the local culture as a whole: A broad research of regional elements that become direct or indirect references for the project.[12] The research is part of the working process, a phase that precedes the development of project design per se.

Such a procedure is anchored in Brazilian modernist tradition and dates back to the 1920s. In his *Ensaio Sobre a Música Brasileira*, published in 1928, Mário de Andrade asserts that great art has folk culture as a subject and erudite art as an expressive basis. He also raises an alarm not to be misunderstood: "If, in fact, now that we are in a formative period, we are to employ often and excessively the direct element provided by folklore, we need not forget that artistic music is not a folk phenomenon, but a development of it."[13] The modernist project is, therefore, adapted to our land and our people, as a particular method that prescribes the fusion of native elements and imported procedures.

This guiding principle is verified not only in music – as one can tell by "Bachianas Brasileiras," "O Trenzinho do Caipira," "A Floresta do Amazonas," and other works by Heitor Villa-Lobos –, but also in the paintings of Tarsila do Amaral and Di Cavalcanti; in the literature of Raul Bopp, Oswald de Andrade and the same Mário de Andrade; in the architecture of Lúcio Costa; and in the landscaping of Roberto Burle Marx. It is possible to identify in all of them the two aspects foreshadowed by the writer from São Paulo: The initial research of elements from the local tradition (songs, dances, rituals, dress items, household utensils, urban objects, colonial buildings, natural landscapes, native vegetation etc.), followed by an aesthetic composition or arrangement of modern inclination. A curious unfolding of the method are the so-called "ethnographic travels," which have the purpose of gathering knowledge about national landscapes and culture, a practice that has been adopted by several artists and architects.[14]

Cambuí House, sections, first floor and ground floor plans, Cambuí, 1979

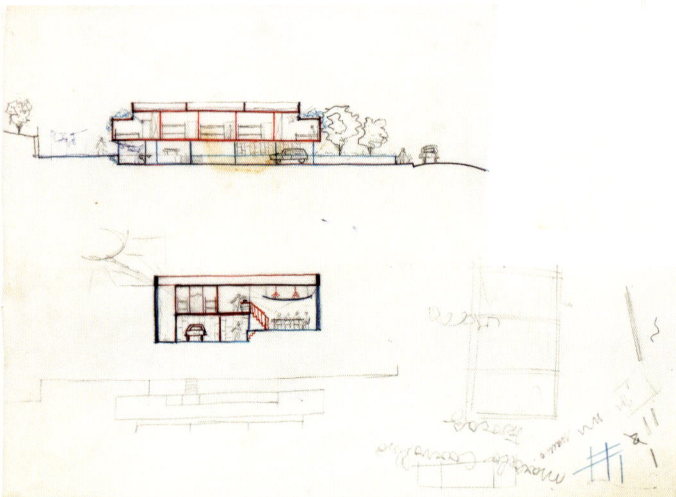

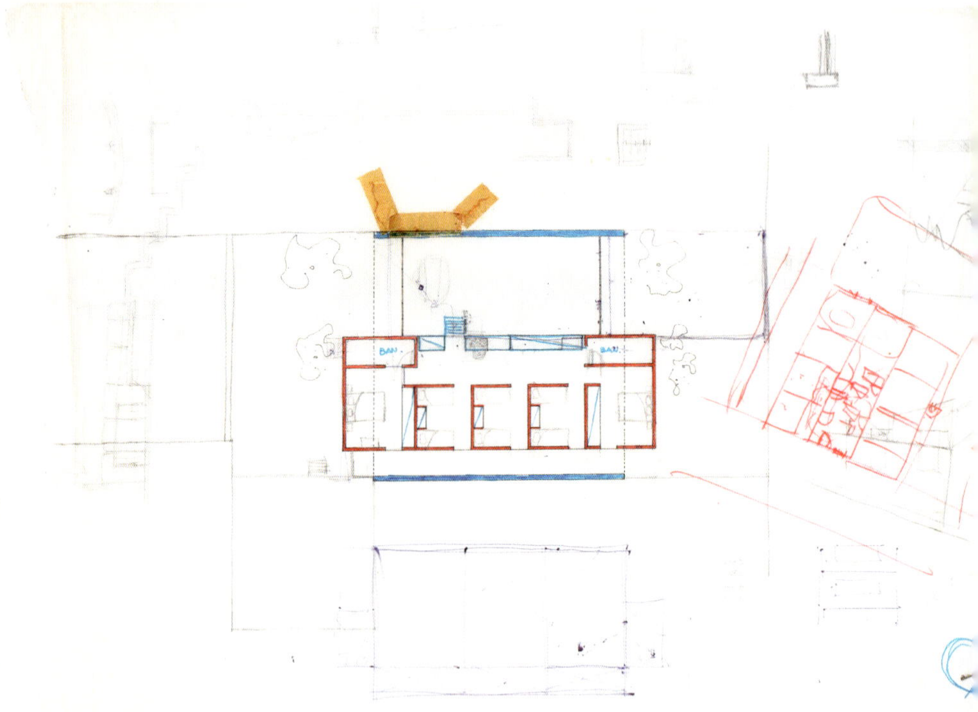

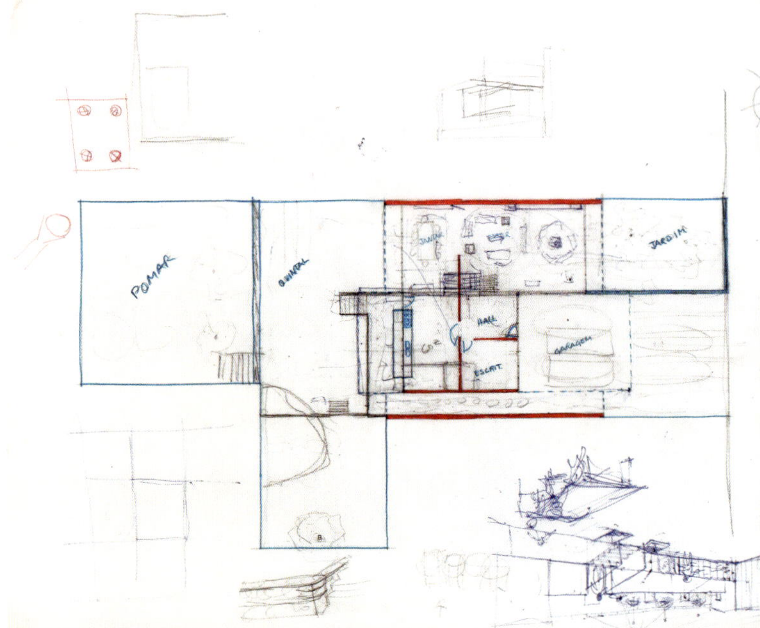

5.

Nevertheless, several project decisions that were adopted (constructive elements, scheduling, spatial arrangement and typology) align both houses with the cultured tradition of urbanity. The functional division materialized into two sectors, the integration that joins social and service areas in a single space, the forthright relation between interior and exterior, and, most of all, the courtship of minimalist art draw the Mantiqueira House away from local tradition. The flat green roofs that cover both blocks, the bathrooms positioned in the central strip and lighted by zenith openings, the great span present in the 8 by 8 meters quadrature of the integrated social area of living room and kitchen, the single bearing of all portholes in the bedrooms and social areas, the functional division expressed in the bi-nucleated scheme of floor plans, these are all indications of the alignment of the Dom Viçoso House to modernist tradition.

At least in the eyes of Ferraz, the abundance of such elements appears not to be enough to dispel some allusions that greatly bother him. Thus, the refusal to construct a more usual roof is justified by the architect as an antidote to the demeaning label of "hillbilly architecture," a label seen by him as a way of "quenching certain things, putting a stamp on it and laying it aside."[15] Attuned to his partner, Francisco Fanucci states that his only regret in relation to the decisions made in the project is having opted for a traditional roof, "a poor solution for the high grounds of a hill, since the wind displaces the tiles." In line with Ferraz, he affirms point-blank: "I would do it differently today; I would employ a concrete slab."[16]

In the text that introduces the houses designed by Brasil Arquitetura in the first book dedicated to the firm, Vasco

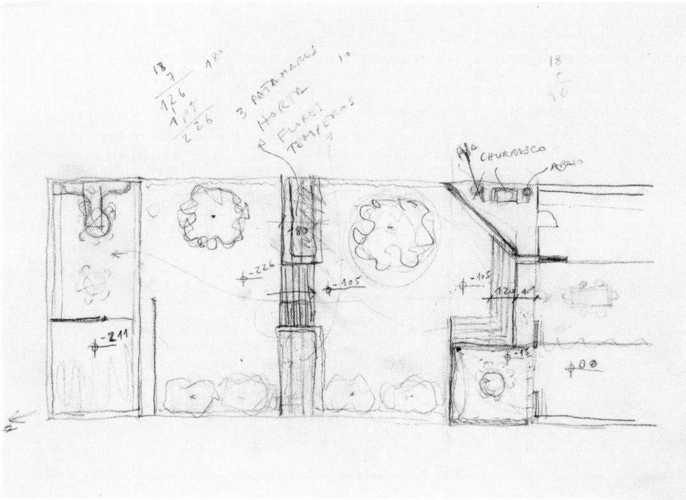

Pepiguari House, sketches of ground floor plan development, São Paulo, 2011

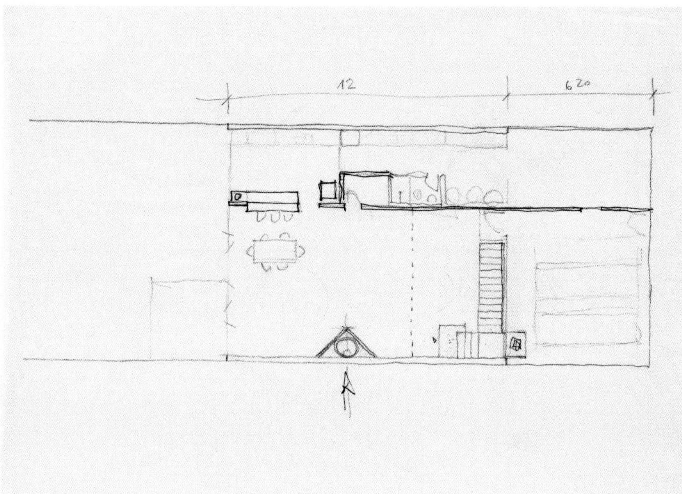

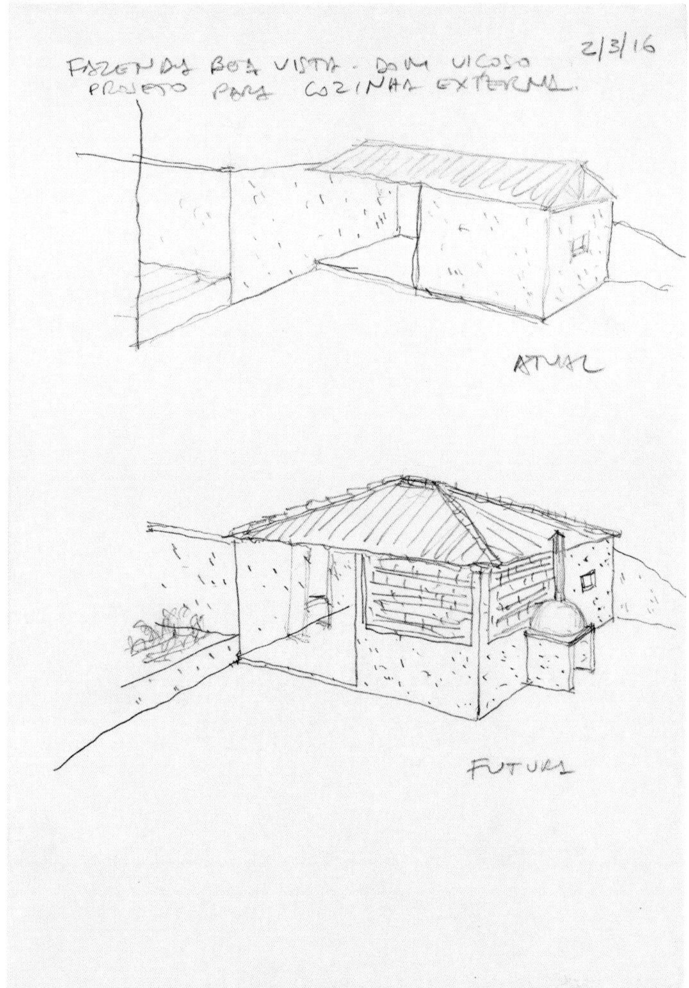

Dom Viçoso House, perspectives, Dom Viçoso, 2010

Caldeira explains the synthesis of rustic and cultured elements they operate: "The residential projects by Brasil Arquitetura have been virtuous sites of experimentation with constructive materials of rustic and semi-artisanal manufacturing, many of them recuperated from Portuguese-Brazilian tradition, many of them modified and adapted; other times, they appear in combination with elements derived from modern erudite culture."[17] Caldeira cites many of these cultivated references, including the Brazilians Lina Bo Bardi, Lúcio Costa, Francisco Bolonha, Alcides da Rocha Miranda, Carlos Ferreira, Vilanova Artigas, Paulo Mendes da Rocha, and Carlos Millan; the Portuguese Fernando Távora and Álvaro Siza; and the further foreign Alvar Aalto, Sverre Fehn, Luis Barragán, Hassan Faty, Geoffrey Bawa, Le Corbusier, and Marcel Breuer. The elective affinities identified by Caldeira suggest the coupling of two traditions: Modern architecture, with its repertoire, especially the use of reinforced concrete; and vernacular architecture, more tied to the land, concerned with the materiality and the constructive detail, drawn to the coziness of living.[18]

Two houses designed by the firm are counterexamples that cause some dissonance from their usual method of formal research. The first one reveals their early education at the University of São Paulo. The second one suggests the return of the prodigal sons to the paternal household. The two of them are boxes of three gray opaque sides – the roof and the lateral façades – and two glazed ones, facing the street and the backyard, a recurrent scheme in the São Paulo school.

The traditional tripartite division – social area, service area, and bedrooms – is accommodated by different designs: Marcelo Ferraz, in a solo project, adopts three middle-levels, with floors built at half height, for his parents' house (Cambuí MG, 1979); meanwhile, the Pepiguari House (São Paulo SP, 2011) establishes itself with a lower social level and an upper private one.[19]

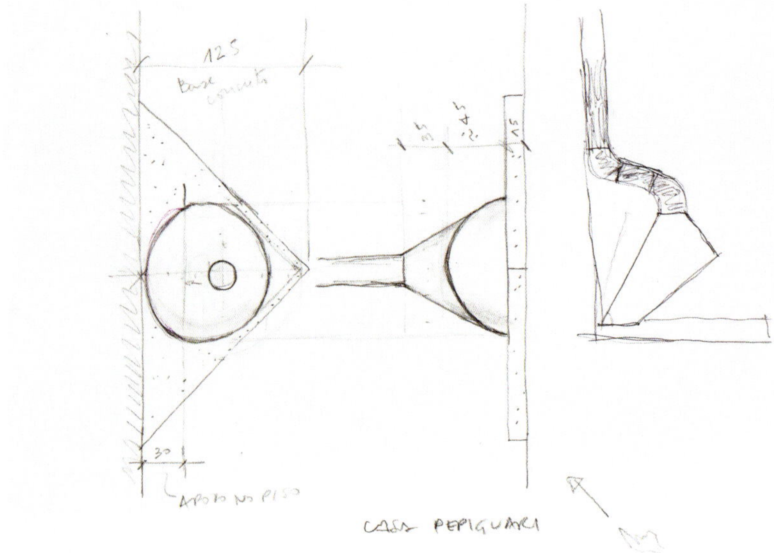

Pepiguari House, fireplace study sketches, São Paulo, 2011

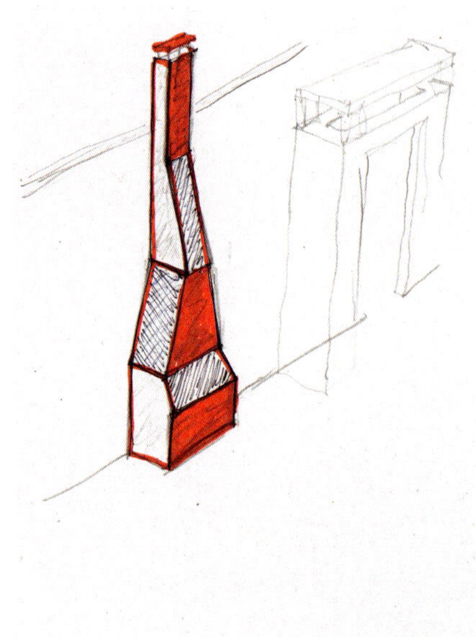

Dom Viçoso House, fireplace study sketches, Dom Viçoso, 2010

6.

The houses of Marcelo Ferraz and Francisco Fanucci are hybrid objects, a sum of constructive elements both local and foreign, a binary opposition that could also be translated into "folk and cultured" or "autochthonous and exotic." The incorporation of these elements has two motivations: The first one, more disciplined and cultural, based on their academic education and intellectual curiosity, a matter already discussed above; the second one, more perceptive and intuitive, is related to experience and memory. About the latter, a clue emerges, surprisingly, in Ferraz's speech. During our trip together, after initially denying the role memory plays in the rationality of his projects – "there is no place for nostalgia in my work" –, the architect freely begins to tell stories about his infancy:

In my childhood, one of the most pleasurable things was bathing in the river where I learned to swim. It was the coolest thing. I would go swimming without telling my mother, but I would dirty myself in the muddy waters and, when I returned, she knew where I had been. Fire was always essential. Every winter, when it was cold in the small town where I lived, there was a bonfire at night. In the abandoned lots beside my childhood home (where the house I designed for my mother is today), my father would light a fire.[20]

Water and fire, natural elements of marked experience in infancy, are very fertile in his residential projects. In both the houses he has designed for himself, they are affirmed; the fire presents itself in its civilized fashion, embedded in the hollowed places of the hearth and the wood stove. In the farmhouse, they inhabit the same common areas of living room and kitchen. The importance of these pieces is emphasized by Ferraz, particularly the significance of the fireplace, present in many of his designed homes, indispensable in his own: "I light it even in summer. Sometimes the fire is not for heat; it is like in a village, the fire is there so people will gather around it. The fire inhabits, it creates spaces."[21] The liquid element is more visually present on the outside, on a small artificial lake of running water, which escapes through an outlet placed on the little stone dike. The reflecting pool is adjacent to the cement walkway that runs close to the tall stone wall, which, in turn, encompasses a grassy garden – a sort of rectangular courtyard demarcated by the support structures, the stone wall, and the house.

At Mantiqueira House, there are three spots for fire: The master bedroom fireplace, positioned in the extreme section of the private wing, is rarely used; the living room fireplace, located in one of the extremes of the social wing, is used occasionally; the wood stove, placed on the fold section where kitchen and living room meet, is used often, almost always as a hearth. Collective living, eventually, can be extended into the other rooms, of cozier furniture, adorned with bamboo chip weft, wooden floors and whitewashed walls – or to the porch, protected from sun and rain. The rooms are for cover, daydreaming, and sleep. From this perfect shelter, one can see or hear external manifestations of nature, which lose their vigor and potential violence for being depurated by the walls and insulation. The sound of running water falling into its stone basin is perceptible at night and lulls the ears of Madalena, the architect's wife. Her ears are tormented by a constant buzzing, but the soothing sound of water affords her comforting sleep.[22] In its natural state, water is another trigger for a story by the architect. Once upon a time, with the sun already gone for dusk, they all heard, coming from the little waterfall embedded in the river's grotto, thundering roar from a mountain lion that descends from the hills on misty days…[23]

Ubiracica House, development sketches, São Paulo, 1996

Anhangabaú Valley contest, sketch, São Paulo, 1981,
architect Lina Bo Bardi and team

7.

Considering their partnership has lasted for four decades, it is only in their own homes, when there's relative autonomy in the decision-making, that it is possible to detect each architect's idiosyncrasies. However, in some measure, the comparison between these projects ends up confirming the duo's intertwining of thought and work. The Mantiqueira House, by Francisco Fanucci, is almost a decade prior to the Dom Viçoso House, but a few years after the book about the Mantiqueira Mountain Range written by Ferraz, which can be understood as a kind of program-letter for both projects. Therefore, understanding the proximities and particularities in the rationalities and predilections of the architects in not a simple thing, due to the entanglement of their experiences over an extended period of time – it is rather surprising how several statements regarding project decisions and architectural works of reference are practically the same. This is a symptom of their communal polishing of images, ideas, and values; as gravel is gradually polished by river water.

Beyond the aspects previously discussed, other communicating vessels are visible among the two rural projects, such as the tree trunks serving as pillars. In the Dom Viçoso House, a series of trunks supports the porch roof. In the Mantiqueira House, a solitary piece of wood holds up two concrete beams. These are choices that point to a shared repertoire of solutions, where one architect's original design is developed by the other's contribution, a common feature in the work of people who share a business for such a long time. According to Fanucci, "the tree trunk idea was, initially, for it to be forked, a trunk that divided itself into two branches, one for each beam."[24] The idea seems to have its inception in the fabulous "trees of steel" by Lina Bo Bardi and crew – Fanucci and Ferraz were a part of the team –, in the Anhangabaú Valley contest of 1981. "As ancient tropical trees," the columns would fulfil a fundamental task: "To give the iron/steel the ingenuous and asymmetrical freedom of nature, set against the regular abstractive scheme of the building."[25] Gathering roots, belonging to the soil, developing natural forces organically, the pillar tree emerges as resistance to an artificial human habitat.

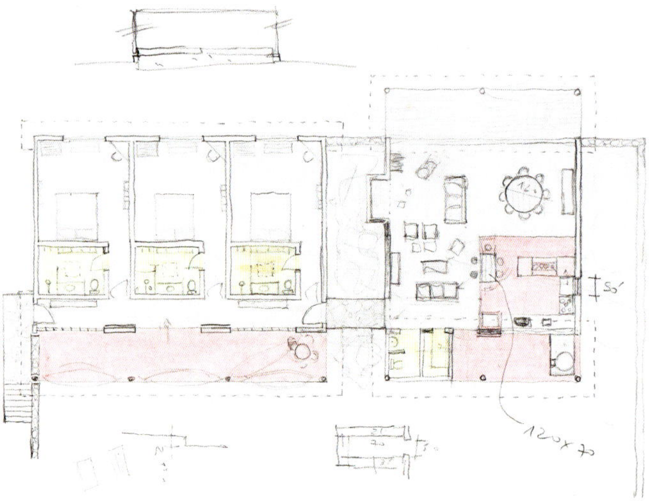

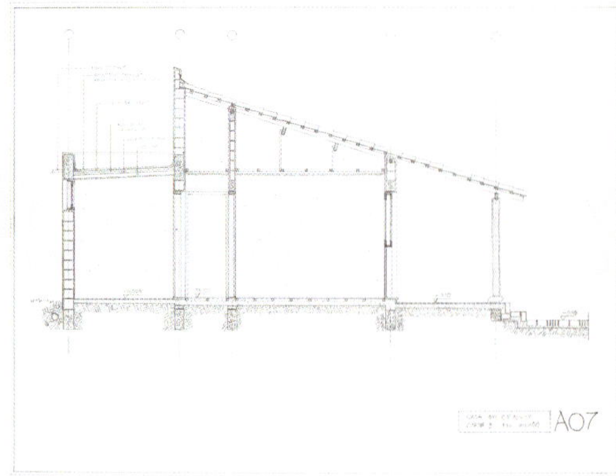

Dom Viçoso House, plan, Dom Viçoso, 2010
São Francisco Xavier House, section and cover plan, São Francisco Xavier, 1999

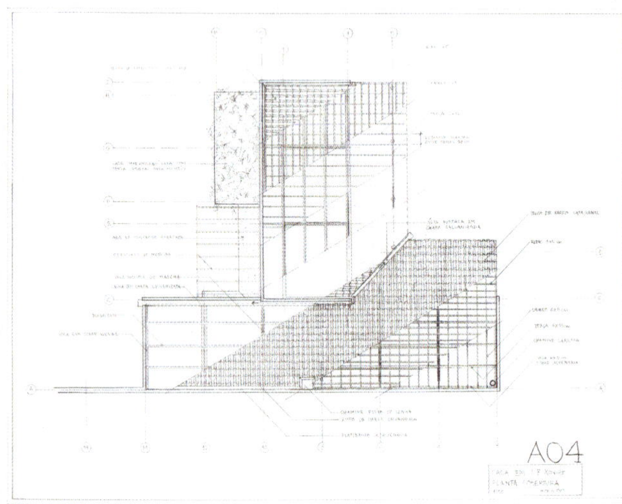

8.

The decisions on how to obtain natural light in the interior of these constructions establish flagrant differences between the two houses. Ferraz comes up with the sophisticated solution of opening a glass slot between the roof slab and three concrete tabs that cover the veranda and the porch (out of the four largest sides of the two blocks, only the one with the bedrooms is left without this protection and is filled with windows that peer out into the landscape): The tabs are supported internally by reinforced steel bars stuck to the superior slab; externally, support is accomplished by tree trunks performing the duties of pillars. The result endorses one of the architect's predilections: "I enjoy light; my house is very bright."[26] In the Mantiqueira House, the three openings towards the main landscape, along with the other doors and windows designed by Fanucci, permit the gradual intake of light, allowing for a more diversified interior lighting during the day. In this case, we can also see the architect's predilections at work: "I prefer gradation and variation of light in the internal spaces."[27]

The distinctive typologies also delineate particular aspects in each house. In the Dom Viçoso House, the two stagnant blocks are connected by a small glass hallway.[28] According to Marcelo Ferraz, "You exit in order to enter, it is so much so that the floor of this passageway is gravel. It is quite beautiful when there's a storm outside and you walk through the rain without getting wet. You cross the stony floor and, then, you are inside again, in another room, with wooden floors. It is a transitory element, a threshold."[29] The passageway, or vestibule, has the psychological function of rooting the resident in his dwelling. The roughness of the floor and the unobstructed view of the natural landscape simulates being outside during the brief stay in the threshold. The glass and the cover of the hall protect the passer-by from the external elements – therefore, the impact is not on the body, but on the spirit, which is startled by the natural forces, only to be appeased, subsequently, by the certainty of being indoors, protected, nestled. To shelter is to comfort the body and the spirit.

At Fanucci's house, right on the fold between the two sections,[30] internally, one finds the kitchen with its wood stove; a vital spot, where people gather to cook meals, eat, drink, talk, and fraternize. Gaston Bachelard warns us that "every corner of a house, every angle of a room, every narrow space where we like to hide and confabulate with ourselves is, for the imagination, solitude, that is, the embryo of a room, the embryo of a house."[31] This is a place of immovability, of extreme refuge, the primordial home that lulls our dreams and reveries. Positioned precisely in this crucial corner of the residency, the secondary kitchen door, which opens out into the service area, with time, has become the primary entrance. According to Fanucci, this was a mistake in the project, resulting from the inability to foresee the place's importance. However, one can assume that intuitively he understood that this was the dwelling place to be preserved. He could not imagine that, for those who arrive, to walk in through this entrance would be to walk directly into the *home*.

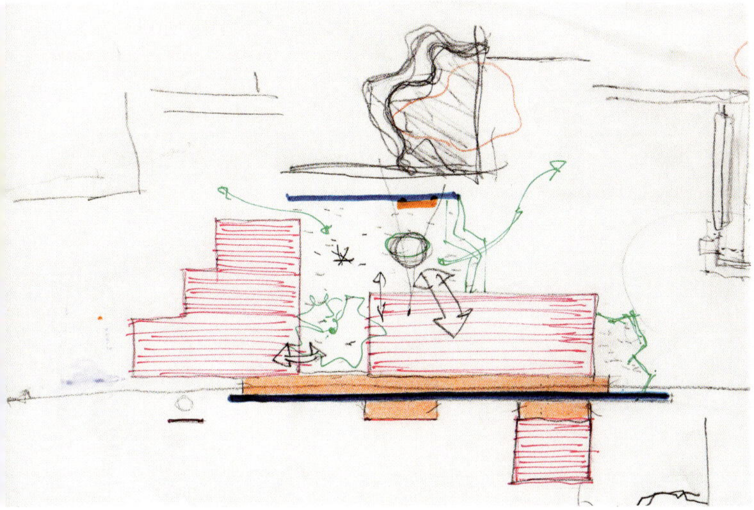

Villa Isabella, development sketch, Finland, 2005

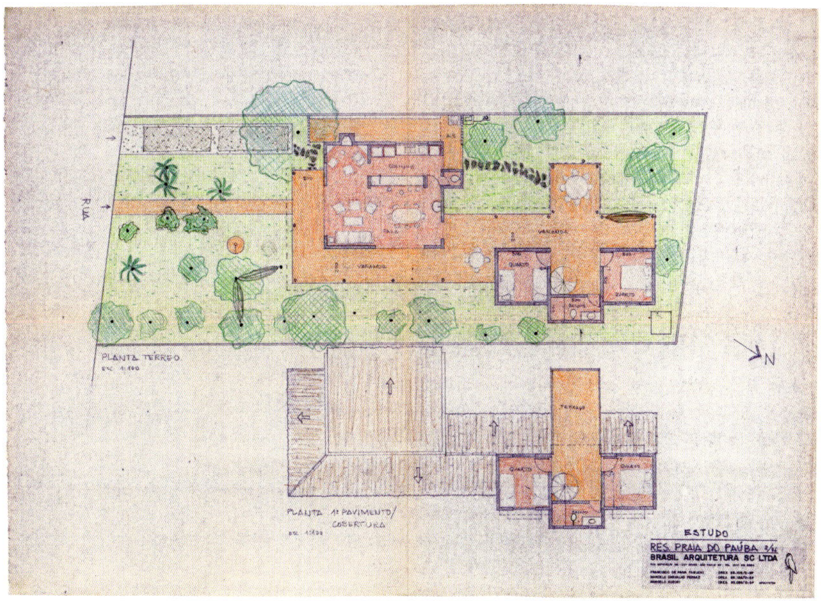

Paúba House, ground floor and first floor (with cover) plans, São Sebastião, 1986

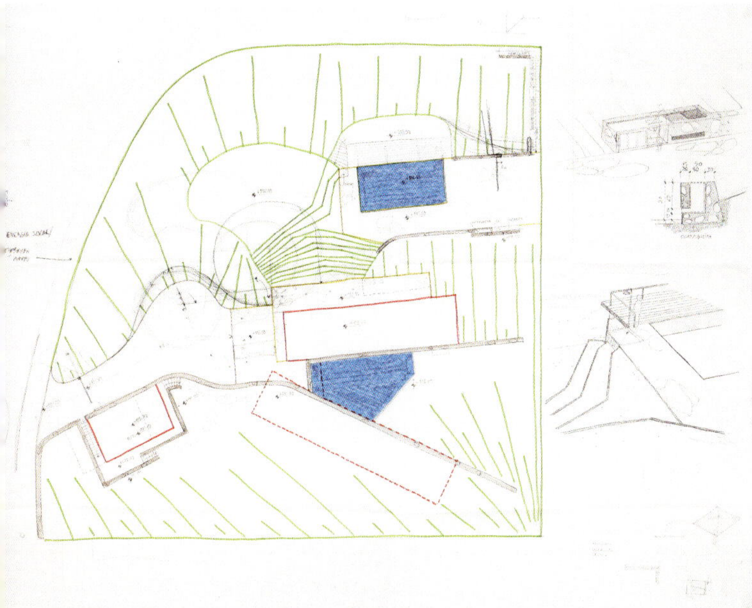

Cotia House, site plan, Cotia, 1998

9.

The houses of Marcelo Ferraz and Francisco Fanucci suggest the image of a primordial shelter that abates the cosmic terror that afflicted our ancestors in the face of incomprehensible nature. The house is an invention that separates us from the natural state, it holds within its walls artificial fire, which, in turn, humanizes our relations, bringing people closer together. According to Bachelard, "this condensed heat, this warm well-being, so loved by men, makes the image jump from the level of the image one sees to the level of the image one lives."[32] And the image one lives – the phenomenon of *being there* – we can identify as the deepest root of architecture, its psychological basis, revealed to us in the desires for refuge, comfort, and intimacy.

Still, these particular historic representations portrayed here are products of specific constructive and artistic imaginations, as we have attempted to show. The green roof, now covered with bushes, is an element of great relevance in the Dom Viçoso House. In the Mantiqueira House, it is a residual effect, employed over the bathroom section, which latches onto the bedroom corridor externally.[33] The apparent ruggedness of the garden roof softens the strict orthogonality of the white walls and concrete slabs. They seem vernacular, but nothing of the sort can be found in the constructions of the *countrymen*. This device by the architects suggests the randomness of contamination by ecological forces – something that is commonly verified in ruins – or a shrewd camouflage of the natural habitat, as with animal homes, especially a bird's nest: "Our home, understood in its oneiric powers, is a nest in the world;"[34] a safe house, the perfect refuge.

According to Bachelard, "memory and imagination are not to be disassociated. One and the other work in their mutual deepening. One and the other constitute, in the order of values, the communion of remembrance and image."[35] In the subject-matter, memory and imagination are usually seen as distinct, and they work on different registries. If it is certain that collective and individual memories are storages supplied with images and experiences vital for creation, they do not seem to constitute a satisfying answer to justify poetic imagination. In art, it is always possible to verify innovation, something that has not yet been experienced.

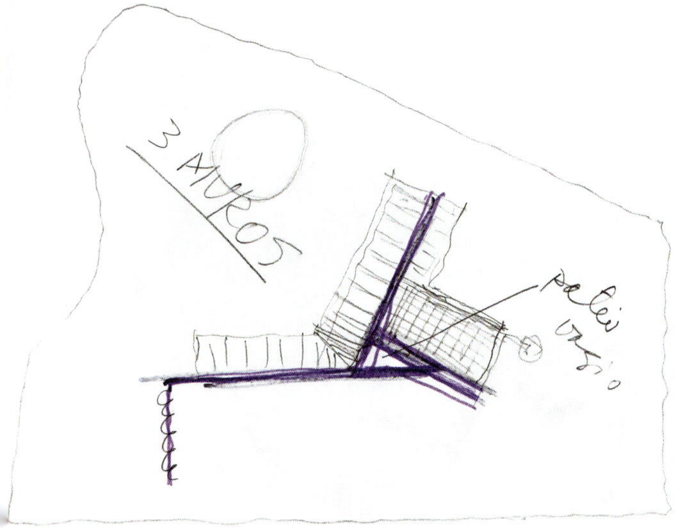

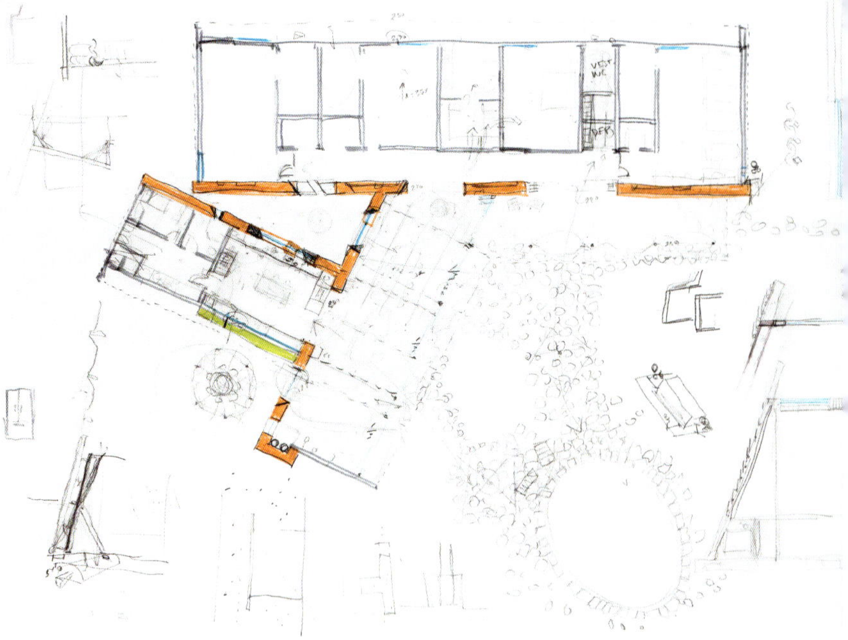

Monte Mor House, site and ground floor plans development sketches, Monte Mor, 2018

10.

Strong images result from the connection between memory and imagination, taken here as embryonic for artistic creation.[36] Full of significance and multiple contents, this connection many times escapes the understanding of the artists themselves. According to Fanucci, "in the act of designing there is much we do without being mindful of what is done." In other words, "to perform architecture is, in a sense, to take this great leap of penetrating an unknown territory, almost intangible, between thought and action."[37] This risk – divination or gamble – Fanucci names intuition. "At times, you have an instinct about a project, that you must pursue it. You don't always have a perfectly logical reasoning for it, you don't always have a technical basis to justify your proposal, but you know that something good might come out of that. It is the time to gamble. And, here, we have a point of contact with the work of an artist, for it is intuition we are talking about."[38] To follow one's intuition is to allow oneself to discover solutions that fuse expression and content in unprecedented fashion, it is to transform a strong idea into an invention, it is to give form to *poetics*.[39]

What we might call the poetics of Brasil Arquitetura always – or, nearly always – involves a propensity to reconcile – to fuse or to amalgamate – architectures of distinct character: A more vernacular, organic, tectonic architecture, largely ingrained in the territory; and another architecture, a more orthogonal and geometric one, more functional, abstract, artificial, and typological. To give examples, it is about joining Vilanova Artigas and Lina Bo Bardi; Carlos Millan and Sverre Fehn; or Marcel Breuer and Lúcio Costa, as it seems to occur in the Dom Viçoso House, bi-nucleated, with its porch and swinging hammocks. To this poetical ambiguity, the childhood and early manhood memories of Cambuí are added. Those are imbued with the experience of close contact with a collective rural memory in a small town of Minas Gerais.

In the aesthetic creation, elements and typologies of two universes are combined – wood stove and reinforced concrete, porches and functional division. Yet, it would be restrictive to base the understanding of the work on such an obvious foundation. Poetic imagination, by summoning deep spiritual energies, overflows the limits of the objective arrangement of these looted elements. In close observation, the feeling of experiencing relevant aesthetical creation will not be absent. They explore the potency of strong concepts – dividing wall, pillar tree, roof garden, passageway and fold, as our examples have shown. The essentiality of the house reveals, in a vigorous and profound manner, how the phenomenological experience of man is a result of artistic creation – in this case, architectural. The final relayed statement by Marcelo Ferraz is of equal simplicity: "To build a home is to enter in the experiment of habitat, that first habitat, of the family nucleus. It's a full project: It's the place where you live, the place where you eat, the place where you study, the place where you suffer. You give existence to a place."[40]

Notes

1. The lyrics were sung by Marcelo Ferraz during one of our interviews. Translated by Caio Romano Guerra.
2. Francisco Fanucci was my host when I stayed in the Mantiqueira House on the 21st and 22th of September, 2019. In the comings and goings of my stay, we talked about the house and his thoughts on architecture. These conversations were not fully recorded, only notes were made. Previously, on the 17th of August, I conducted a recorded interview with Fanucci.
3. Francisco Fanucci, "Interview with Abilio Guerra," September 22, 2019.
4. In residential projects, the wall is present in the Villa Isabella project (Finland, 2005) through the use of dry-stacked rough stones, trespassed by passageways and vistas, allowing for visual and bodily contact with the surrounding woods. It is also present the Montemor House, with three solid wattle and daub walls arranged in a radial shape; in the Tacaruna Cultural Center (Recife PE, 202); in the International Olympic Committee (Lausanne, Switzerland, 2013); and in the Brick Museum (Arvorezinha RS, 2015).
5. I am refering to the sculpture *Pulitzer Piece*, stepped elevation, St. Loius, Missouri, 1971. See: Francisco Fanucci and Marcelo Carvalho Ferraz, *Francisco Fanucci, Marcelo Ferraz: Brasil Arquitetura*, 160.
6. Accompanied by Marcelo Ferraz and our respective wives, Silvana Romano Santos and Isa Grinspum, I stayed at the Dom Viçoso House from the 26th of July, 2019, until the 28th of the same month. During this time, four interviews with the architect were recorded.
7. It is the development of a technique for the enhancement of concrete resistance through water treatment that is typical of architecture in São Paulo. After the first three hours of treatment, the solid concrete slab is covered for a month with a layer of water of 10 to 15 centimeters high, which seeps into the protrusions, becoming a waterproofing factor. Then, the following layers are deposited in sequence: expanded clay to cover the water; geotextile blanket for filtering; sand and dirt, basis for spontaneous vegetation growth. The water level is maintained by an outlet positioned 10 or 15 centimeters high to bleed the water out when it rains a lot; when it does not rain, it serves to prevent complete evaporation, a buoy closes the water outlet to maintain moisture.
8. Marcelo Carvalho Ferraz, *Arquitetura Rural na Serra da Mantiqueira*, 18. Free translation.
9. Ibid., 18. Free translation.
10. Francisco Fanucci, "Interview with Abilio Guerra," September 22, 2019. Free translation.
11. Ferraz, *Arquitetura Rural*, 19. Free translation.
12. Marta Bogéa and Abilio Guerra, "Algo muito humano além de belo. Exposição Território de Contato, módulo 1: Cao Guimarães e Brasil Arquitetura."
13. Mário Andrade (1928), *Ensaio Sobre a Música Brasileira*, 37. Free translation.
14. Abilio Guerra, "Modernistas na Estrada."
15. Marcelo Carvalho Ferraz, "Interview with Abilio Guerra," July 26, 2019. Free translation.
16. Francisco Fanucci, "Interview with Abilio Guerra," September 22, 2019. Free translation.
17. Vasco Caldeira, "Casa Brasilis," in: Fanucci and Ferraz, *Francisco Fanucci, Marcelo Ferraz*, 114-115. Free translation.
18. Patricia Nahas attributes this search for synthesis to the double education the architects received. Taught at the School of Architecture and Urbanism – FAU USP to follow the rigors of the orthogonal concrete box, later, they were converted to the popular ways by the indirect teachings of Lúcio Costa and the fundamental and direct influence of Lina Bo Bardi. Patricia Viceconti Nahas, *Brasil Arquitetura: Memória e Contemporaneidade. Um percurso do Sesc Pompeia ao Museu do Pão (1977-2008)*.
19. Two institutional projects carried out at dates close to those of the houses adopt similar procedures. The Cambuí City Hall (Cambuí MG, 1978) – project designed by the architects Marcelo Ferraz, Marcelo Suzuki, Jose Sales Costa Filho, and Roman Tâmara – and the Work and Workers Museum (São Bernardo do Campo SP, 2010) are gray cuboids on pilotis, with sliced slabs in the intermediate levels of its interior, connected by stairs and bridges.
20. Marcelo Carvalho Ferraz, "Interview with Abilio Guerra," July 26, 2019. Free translation.
21. Ibid. Free translation. At the house Ferraz designed for his parents (Cambuí MG, 1979) and at the Pepiguari House (São Paulo SP, 2011), there are fireplaces and wood stoves. These projects are more in line with São Paulo orthodoxy, but these elements somewhat attune them with the series of residential projects by the firm.
22. Francisco Fanucci, "Interview with Abilio Guerra," August 17, 2019.
23. Ibid.
24. Francisco Fanucci, "WhatsApp Message to Abilio Guerra," October 2, 2019. Free translation.
25. Lina Bo Bardi, Ucho Carvalho, Francisco Fanucci, Paulo Fecarotta, Marcelo Carvalho Ferraz, Bel Paoliello, Guilherme Paoliello, Marcelo Suzuki and André Vainer, "Anhangabaú Tobogã – concurso de projetos, São Paulo, 1981," in: Marcelo Carvalho Ferraz, ed., *Lina Bo Bardi*, 252. Free translation. The solution also resembles the stylized tree pillars of the Bread Museum (Ilópolis RS, 2005), a later project.
26. Marcelo Carvalho Ferraz, "Interview with Abilio Guerra," July 26, 2019. Free translation.
27. Francisco Fanucci, "Interview with Abilio Guerra," September 22, 2019. Free translation.
28. The insulated glass passageway is used at Tamboré house (Barueri SP, 1989), Cotia House (Cotia SP, 1998), Lagoa House (Florianópolis SC, 2016), and Villa Isabella (Finland, 2005). Only with the cover, it appears at Paúba House (São Sebastião SP, 1986), Villa Carolina House (Finland, 2017), the Bread Museum, and the Tacaruna Cultural Center. Uncovered, as a footbridge, it appears at the Rodin Bahia Museum (Salvador BA, 2002). In the original project for the Ubiracica House (São Paulo SP, 1996), the dining room and the office would be in a glass slab running loose over the water mirror, an idea that was abandoned during construction.
29. Marcelo Carvalho Ferraz, "Interview with Abilio Guerra," July 26, 2019. Free translation.
30. The fold and the wall were used together in the Muro Azul House (São Paulo, 1994) to ensure complete isolation of the residence from the neighborhood and to capture the lighting from above, which gives the interior of the house a blue hue. At the Aldeia da Serra House (Barueri SP, 1989), the building's division into three functional blocks gives form to two folds when viewed from the outside.
31. Gaston Bachelard, *A Poética do Espaço*, 286. Free translation.
32. Ibid., 296. Free translation.
33. The green roof also appears in the the Araucaria Museum (countryside of Rio Grande do Sul, 2018).
34. Bachelard, *A Poética*, 264. Free translation.
35. Ibid., 200. Free translation.
36. Something along those lines was said by Fanucci: "One does not control memory, it manifests itself many times without our knowledge. Madalena, my wife, made some embroideries with *favelas* as theme. The other day, returning to São Paulo, as we passed through Guarulhos, she mentioned that those images of the favela had been recorded in her memory and came to mind, without her realizing it, at the time she was designing her embroideries. It had been in her memory, but she only identified the process a posteriori. Of course, there was also her intervention on the image she had in her memory." Francisco Fanucci, "Interview with Abilio Guerra," September 22, 2019.
37. Francisco Fanucci, "Interview," in: Fanucci and Ferraz, *Francisco Fanucci, Marcelo Ferraz*, 178. Free translation.
38. Ibid., 178. Free translation.
39. During the thesis advisement for Patricia Viceconti Nahas, I sensed the role these ideas played in the works of Brasil Arquitetura, but only a decade later did I find the appropriate conceptual basis to formulate it.
40. Marcelo Carvalho Ferraz, "Interview with Abilio Guerra," July 26, 2019. Free translation.

Praça das Artes, photos taken during construction, São Paulo, 2006

The Architect as a Cultural Militant and a Proposer of Questions

Guilherme Wisnik

1.

"Architecture is a dangerous profession because it constitutes a poisonous mixture of impotence and omnipotence." The statement is accurate in the measure that architectural projects act in such scales that, at times, they seem to be on the verge of impacting and transforming the lives of many people, but they almost always come upon constraints that thwart these grandiose dreams. These constraints are such as low budgets, poor execution of works, technical impossibilities, and lack of understanding and support from clients. It is, therefore, a schizophrenic profession, as Rem Koolhaas observes ironically.[1]

Even here among us, in the periphery of global capitalism, the observation is valid. Architecture is a hard profession. It involves the ability of coordinating different sciences and teams, in the context of a nation that values this knowledge less and less; boycotts it, one time after another. Architecture also involves very large emotional investments in desires of transformation, ballasted in a form of systemic thought that articulates distinct knowledge in a world where everything seems to move towards particularism and atomization. To perform architecture in Brazil has been a heroic and idealist endeavor; many times, sadly, an inglorious, tragic, and even quixotic task.

However, the case of Brasil Arquitetura, while generally fitting to this larger scheme, allows us to look a little further, beyond this claustrophobic and pessimistic overview. The context of isolation and incomprehension experienced by architects in Brazil today is much owed to certain incapacity on the part of the architects themselves to rethink their discourses in respect to a world of constant change. It is necessary to search for new forms of action and social insertion of the architectural knowledge. That is – it seems to me – a very distinctive and important characteristic in the production of this particular firm in the context of Brazil and of the city of São Paulo. Marcelo Ferraz and Francisco Fanucci are always searching for newer escape routes in relation to this foretold disaster.

An expressive part of what Brasil Arquitetura has produced in the last decades is due to the propositional attitude embodied by the architects, who do not place themselves as mere technicians equipped to solve the demands that reach them, translating into forms a set of prior requirements. Rather, they act much more as researchers, studying the possibilities of urban and architectural transformation of our cities. They are posers of question and articulators of the means to perform them, following in the footsteps of what Lina Bo Bardi did at Solar do Unhão (1959) in Salvador, when, by her own initiative, the historic complex was restored and transformed into a Museum of Folk Art.

In a context as adverse as ours, architects must constantly open ground in the midst of a society that seems to not require their knowledge for anything. This knowledge, as we have said, is based on systemic articulation, reconstruction of lost meanings,

Praça das Artes, photos taken during construction, São Paulo, 2006

and appreciation of the public and collective dimensions of things. Many of the firm's projects are, then, born out of the architects' own research, their proposals and articulations. This allows for projects which would have never been devised in the traditional conditions of the client-architect relation; such projects as the KKKK Complex (1996), in city of Registro, São Paulo, and the Bread Museum (2005), in Ilópolis, Rio Grande do Sul. These works pave way for a sequence of other – still possible – projects to be incorporated into the so-called Route of the Mills, like the Brick Museum (2016), in Arvorezinha, Rio Grande do Sul.

Constructed in the 1920s to store and process food (specially rice) produced by Japanese immigrant farmers, the warehouses of exposed brick which form the KKKK Complex, on the banks of the Ribeira do Iguape River, were abandoned and deteriorated. Aware of the situation and in dialogue with other researchers, the architects decided to move forward with an initiative to raise funds to restore the buildings and give them a new purpose in the life of the city and region. After many comings and goings, with the support of the local city hall and the state government, they finally managed to complete the work, constituting the Japanese Immigration Memorial of the Ribeira Valley, a historical record of these settlements. To the epochal ensemble, recovered and completed by marquees of apparent concrete, a new unit was added: A whitewashed masonry cube, whose volume respects the ensemble, but whose distinctive finishing gives it the necessary contemporary accent. It was also possible to reconstitute an amicable relationship to the surrounding landscape, by the creation of the Beira-Rio Park, which also serves as a bulkhead for the containment of floods in the city.

Two decades later, in 2018, the possibility of building a unit of the Social Service of Commerce – Sesc in the city was presented. This would incorporate the precious set of buildings, located by an already well-attended public park near the river. To this end, the firm carried out the projects to adapt the older set to its new use and to create a new Sesc building, expanding the historical complex once more. Another construction was designed to house the Japanese Immigration Museum in the vicinities, a fact that attests to the success of the operation started by the architects in 1996.

In the Taquari Valley, in the mountain range of Rio Grande do Sul, the Italian immigrants who had sprung from the Veneto region built, in the 1910s, an expressive ensemble of wooden edifices used as mills in the making of flour and bread. With the economic decline of these activities and the lack of maintenance support in the last decades, the mills were abandoned. The architects, then, engaged in the repair of one of these buildings, situated in the same town of Ilópolis, the Colognese Mill. They suggested to the city hall the restoration of the edifice and the creation of a new use for it. To this effort were added the essential support of the Nestlé company and of the Latin American Italian Institute. Next to it, were designed and built two new elongated pavilions, made of glass, concrete, and wood, to house the Bread Museum and a confectioner school, which modernizes the historically produced knowledge of the region, forming new generations of individuals dedicated to the craft. With this novelty, the mill itself is now back in regular activity as an annex to the museum and the school.

In the same region that constitutes the so-called Route of the Mills, in Arvorezinha, where the ceramics company Facchinetto is located, by the impulse of the previous works carried out in Ilópolis, the opportunity to build the Facchinetto Pottery Museum was presented. Housed in a sloping hillside, the project makes the basalt rock of the grounds emerge in a brute manner within the building. Erected on two floors, the premise stands on concrete slabs and brick masonry walls, with a bare and austere spatiality. Supporting the slabs, uncanny brick pillars stacked at varying angles form expressionist columns that delineate vertical references, addressing the manual and stacking qualities of the composition, central aspects in the history of brick construction.

A similar mode of concern with the background of buildings is present as a fundamental question in the well-known case of Praça das Artes (2006), in the historic center of São Paulo. Commissioned by Carlos Augusto Calil, Municipal Secretary of Culture between 2005 and 2012,[2] the project begins as a satellite annex to the Municipal Theater, extending the building of the city's old Dramatic and Musical Conservatory, located on São João Avenue, as part of the new complex. Over the years, the project gradually changed as it became possible to acquire neighboring lots to add to those initially granted, thus expanding the aggregate. With the support of the Secretary of Culture, this organic process of expansion across the remaining lots on the block became the answer to a strong intentive question that marks the actions of the architects: To perform a thorough urban seam, consolidating, by means of the buildings, the public passageways that connect the Anhangabaú Valley, São João Avenue and Conselheiro Crispiniano Street. And so, in a city block greatly parceled-out into smaller lots, it was possible to achieve an important work of urban integration, through the creating of hollow spaces and the interconnecting of premises, acquiring new public spaces for the city.[3]

In a sense, the project was inspired by a typology very prevalent in the region: The commercial galleries that connect streets across quarters. Or, better yet, by the typology of the open block, such as it is displayed in Centro Comercial do Bom Retiro (1959), by Lucjan Korngold.[4] As Abilio Guerra shows in his analysis of Praça das Artes, the open block model works there as a "piece of adjustment between the classic and modern urbanism that are present in the traditional street and grid as well as in the large concrete platform of the Anhangabaú Valley, designed by Jorge Wilheim and Rosa Kliass."[5] Thus, unlike other striking cases such as the Rock, Califórnia, Metrópole or Nova Barão galleries, the Brasil Arquitetura project – a partnership with Marcos Cartum – had to deal with the lack of a clear perimeter to the building from the start, forced to break away from other neighboring buildings at times or to create friction with the gables and windowless façades on the immediate sides, while leaving empty areas for public circulation and resting with plazas and amphitheaters. The architects were very skillful in exploring the designs of an urban sewing to the maximum, through fragmentation and addition, by perusing the setting. This is what shapes the poetical language of this work. Hence, there are several groupings engineered in Praça das Artes, with different heights and colors, interconnected by unique elements, such as walkways and tunnel ramps, as opposed to being connected by serial systems of circulation.

Praça das Artes, photos taken during construction, São Paulo, 2006

All of this is enhanced by the myriad openings at irregular intervals in the façades of apparent concrete, a form that reinforces the sense of randomness voluntarily sought by the architects, as opposed to a more classic and universalist approach of order, proper to the language of modern architecture. If Oscar Niemeyer explains the variations in the spans of arches in the building of the Mondadori publishing house (1968) in Milan by the will to create a rhythmic shape associated with the syncopated beat of samba, here, Marcelo Ferraz alludes to the irregularities of the scores of electroacoustic composer John Cage. At the same time, it is difficult to avoid thinking of the tangle of windows in the Ronchamp Chapel (1950), by Le Corbusier; nor, evidently, of the irregular openings of the concrete towers of Sesc Pompeia (1977), by Lina Bo Bardi, a project on which Ferraz, still a young architect, collaborated.

In fact, the approximation between Praça das Artes and Sesc Pompeia goes beyond a mere formal matter. It touches on the notion of "citadel," which appears not only in the density and variety of volumes built in these cases but also in the monolithic qualities of the works, which do not distinguish between structure and insulation. It is known that Lina Bo Bardi called Sesc Pompeia "the citadel of liberty," an allusion to a construction that transfuses urbanity into its inner spaces, binding this built-in urbanity to an inventive artistic disposition which creates forms through a process of imagination over the project's brief. If, historically, the citadels were military fortifications, these "citadels of liberty" in São Paulo are, on the other hand, trespassed by the historical democratic process, connecting the towers to the ground by plazas and making them porous to the multiple and imponderable uses that might be enacted by urban population, particularly intense in downtown São Paulo where Praça das Artes is located.

By counteracting the excessive division of land, related to the preponderance of real-estate speculation and of an individualism that permeates the logic of private property, this new urban arrangement situated in front of Anhangabaú Park activates a rich sense of urbanity that, in addition to the dialogue it poses with the aforementioned commercial galleries, promotes an interesting sense of "urban congestion," to cite another phrase by Rem Koolhaas. By the use of these terms, the Dutch architect aims to describe the multiplicity of uses that are made possible in New York City edifices, linking the origins of this phenomenon to the epic tale of the project and construction of the Rockefeller Center complex (1929-1939), which managed to incorporate originally isolated lots into a

larger unit, in a design proper to the truly metropolitan scale of a dense and diverse city.[6] In effect, since it doesn't incorporate all the lots in the block, only a few of them, Praça das Artes is less close to examples such as the Rockefeller Center and the Lever House (1952), also in New York, or Conjunto Nacional (1952), in São Paulo; it is closer to an urban citadel pressed into the guts of an urban block. A more similar example is

Galeria Metrópole (1959), by Salvador Candia and Gian Carlo Gasperini, whose project had to negotiate with the edges of neighboring lots, attentive to the opportunities of pulling closer or away. At Praça das Artes, the whole is not a single volume, integral and legible from all sides. On the contrary, it is a heterogeneous compound with three distinct fronts. It seems to change in its façade with each new viewpoint, proposing an experience of discovery across its spaces, as people are drawn into them, to enter them and to cross them.

Thus, if the terrain found in this block was often irregular and chaotic from the point of view of its size and occupation of the setbacks, the patient process of elaboration and growth that the project undertook was able to metabolize in architecture a sluggishness typical of the logic of occupation and construction in the city of São Paulo, reverting into positive value something that is normally viewed as a flaw. "By adversity we live," used to say Hélio Oiticica, referring to Brazilian social reality in a third world key.[7] With Praça das Artes, the architects operate an intelligent process of urban acupuncture, without denying the sense of monumentality inherent to the briefs and the locale. They interpret the positive sense of terrain vague present in the Dadaist and, later, Situationist metropolitan insights, which, as Ignasí de Solà-Morales explains, envision in the urban hollows a latent potency of transformation.[8] This potency is a non-productive expectation, begetting alternative visions of the city which insinuate themselves as folds, possible, on the actual city. Not by chance, and through a very different formalization, Praça das Artes carries on a popular, transgressive, and spatially vertiginous impetus, very significant as a state of mind in Lina Bo Bardi's project for the Anhangabaú Valley (1981), in which Marcelo Ferraz and Francisco Fanucci participated actively.

Praça das Artes, photos taken during construction, São Paulo, 2006

2.

Fanucci and Ferraz belong to a generation that attended university during the 1970s; a moment in which the hardline reality of Brazilian dictatorship fostered deep fractions in the manner one might view the profession and the teaching of architecture. Laid under suspicion, given the urgency of the political struggle and of the metropolitan questions tied to the outgrowth of the favelas in general informality, the activity of building design was discredited.[9] Despite this context of crisis and exhaustion, Fanucci and Ferraz, like many other colleagues, persisted in the desire to effect architecture, but away from the *militancy of drawing* professed by Vilanova Artigas and his FAU USP group, linked to the ideology of the Brazilian Communist Party – even though Fanucci and Ferraz did study at FAU, the School of Architecture and Urbanism at the University of São Paulo. Lina Bo Bardi, who at that time was living years of limbo and ostracism, came to represent a diverse and richly fertile reference for this dissimilar group, through a connection made by Joaquim Guedes. This influence led to an unusual third path, foreign to the fierce dispute between the disciples of Artigas and Sérgio Ferro, which then dominated the atmosphere of the university and profession across the city.

Born in the rural areas of Minas Gerais, Francisco and Marcelo have a proximity to the agrarian world[10] and have a genuine interest in vernacular culture, an interest responsible for arousing in them an unusual affinity within the context of *paulista*[11]

architecture, an affinity for the investigations of *Brazilianness* introduced, for instance, by the architecture of Lúcio Costa. This desire is clearly stated in the name of their architectural firm. And if, on the one hand, postmodern stances were generally rejected in Brazil, especially at FAU USP, for being associated with North American commercialism or with an excessively erudite culturalism of European matrix, which was considered to be regressive, on the other hand, a certain postmodern *spirit of the time* surely helped them to find in Lina a fundamental model to aspire. One of the main contributions of postmodern attitude to architecture was the critique of an utopian stance, according to which reality is viewed as a blank slate for the planning action *ex novo*. Postmodern

thought opens new ground for a decoding of reality through an anthropological lens of dialogue, which understands otherness (or the existent) as a source of valid discourses capable of teaching us.

Lina, who always rejected the idea of postmodernism and who formed her own conceptions of the world in the pre-Second World War Italy of figures such as Antonio Gramsci, Gio Ponti and Giuseppe Pagano, probably wouldn't agree with this approximation. Nevertheless, for Francisco and Marcelo, who experienced, at a young age, the confrontation between an ideologically charged professional environment and the atmosphere both naïve and libertarian of hippie culture, and who admired a wide range of architectonical models like Rogelio Salmona, Sverre Fehn, and Álvaro Siza, the stark separation between modern and postmodern was no longer productive nor necessary. The danger, of course, would be to turn the arduous devouring of Brazilian folk culture of Indigenous and African roots performed by Lina – in her words, a culture "unpalatable, dry and difficult to digest"[12] – into docile and exotic tropicalism, by an operation of postmodern pastiche. In other words, it would amount to converting the *ugliness*, upheld by the Italian architect as an expression of violence and accusation, into something palatable and pretty; a danger that Ferraz and Fanucci, much like their former associate Marcelo Suzuki,[13] have known well and were able to avoid.

With an understanding that the crude violence of Lina's architecture, which might be associated with Glauber Rocha's aesthetics of hunger, is the expression of a *sui generis* personality and of a precise historical moment, her former collaborators did not seek to copy her designing gestures. Rather, they learned from her a particular way of grasping and processing references. And, with that, they gathered a certain working method set in the desire to be closer to a folk know-how. This is stated in the formal aspects of their work, for instance, in the recurring decisions to interfere in older edifices in a pronounced manner, reworking them with lighter elements and adding new volumes which are clearly distinctive and austere. Apt examples of such interference are the Central Mill Theater (2009), in Piracicaba, and the aforementioned KKKK Complex, instances where one is able to perceive the foundational echoes of Lina's work at Solar do Unhão, in Salvador, and at the Sesc Pompeia building. However, at the same time, in the conceptual and political levels, this same facet is expressed in their choices for researching, proposing and striving to the execute cultural projects related to the recycling of older buildings, coming up with new possibilities that pursue ways of keeping that cultural heritage alive, instead

Praça das Artes, photos taken during construction and Orpheus and Eurydice opera of 2012, São Paulo, 2006

of leaving it to ruin or placing it in the sterile state of museology. This proactive characteristic of Brasil Arquitetura's demeanor in project design is the main particularity of their firm, which allows them to transcend the role of the architect as an autonomous professional designer, leading them closer to an anthropological stance, politically militant by means of its indelible ties to culture. It also outlines their most creative form of non-mimetic assimilation of Lina Bo Bardi's legacy.

When we observe the clients and briefs of the projects executed by Brasil Arquitetura, we can clearly notice the political emphasis of the architectonical gestures, linked to different cultures of left-wing inclination in roots Indigenous, Afro-Brazilian, immigrant, and *sertaneja*;[14] all of them identified with minority practices of survival and resilience against various forms of exploitation and oppression. It is the case of such projects as the building of the Socioambiental Institute (2000), in São Gabriel da Cachoeira; Terreiro Osumarè (2017) and Marighella Memorial (2016), in Salvador; the Igatu Museum (2008), at Chapada Diamantina; the Cais do Sertão Museum (2009), in Recife; the Route of the Mills, in Rio Grande do Sul, among others. A great contribution to this initial characteristic of the firm, related to the reviewing of memory, was the role Marcelo Ferraz played as coordinator of the Monumenta Program of the Federal Ministry of Culture, between 2003 and 2004. The initiative was responsible for the restoration of historical sites all across the country. During the period, a program for regional museums tied to IPHAN was also stablished.

At this point, it is necessary to remember that today the transformation of deactivated industrial buildings into museums and cultural centers is a trend all over the world, with notorious examples like the Museum D'Orsay (1980), in Paris, by Gae Aulenti, and the Tate Modern (1994), in London, by Herzog & de Meuron. The Sesc Pompeia building, designed in 1977 and distant from the eye of the international reviewers, is genuinely at the vanguard of this process. Instead of demolishing the building to construct a new edifice in the Pompeia neighborhood, as was suggested at the time, the conservation and renovation of the complex does not reflect a nostalgic look at the past by Lina, but rather the appreciation of the constructive and tectonic qualities of the original erection with its brick and concrete structures in plain sight. It also denotes a sensible perception of the playful potentiality of the space, derived from visits to the deactivated barrel factory, when children, adults and older folks occupied

the space, played and toiled around it. The architects' attitudes towards the abandoned factory did not fetishize the object. On the contrary, there was an aim at understanding new possible uses that could intersect across its spaces and contemplate a city in transformation. That is a beautiful lesson learned there by Francisco Fanucci and Marcelo Ferraz.

Now, returning to our starting point in the provocative statement by Koolhaas, we might say that the peculiar way in which Ferraz and Fanucci conduct their work situates them outside of the schizophrenic duality between an all-powerful demiurge architect and the depressed, resentful figure of an architect that is powerless. Neither one thing, nor the other, Francisco and Marcelo continuously grasp at opportunities to transform buildings and urban spaces, by searching for new and convincing ways to reinvent forms and requirements, to seduce people, and to sell ideas. Their architecture is guided by militancy, but a militancy of the memory, a militancy for its constant update into contemporary life, for the survival and resilience of explored and forsaken minorities in our violent and unequal process of urbanization. It is a struggle for more dignified and pluralistic cities.

Notes

1. Rem Koolhaas, "Conference," January 21, 1991.
2. Praça das Artes is the most significant architectural achievement of Carlos Augusto Calil's management as São Paulo's Municipal Secretary of Culture, which was characterized by a strong sense of urbanity, understanding architecture and urbanism as essential parts of the idea of culture. Other important measures during that time were the institution of the Virada Cultural event, the renewal of the Municipal Theater and the Mário de Andrade Library, and the expropriation of some important downtown street cinemas, with the aim of recreating São Paulo's Cinelândia. For more information on this, see: Guilherme Wisnik, "Prêmio APCA 2012 – Categoria "Cliente/promotor." Premiado: Carlos Augusto Calil/Secretaria de Cultura da Prefeitura de São Paulo."
3. Focused on the study and practice of music and dance, the Praça das Artes ensemble includes the Municipal Symphony and Experimental Repertory orchestras, the Lyric and Paulistano choirs, the Municipal String Quartet, the Municipal School of Music and the concert hall of the old Dramatic and Musical Conservatory. The dance activities are represented by the City Ballet and the Dance School. In addition to these institutions, the complex also houses a documentation center, the Oneyda Alvarenga Musical Archive, an exhibition gallery, administrative areas, spaces for acquaintanceship, restaurants, cafes, and two levels of underground parking.
4. Abilio Guerra, "Quadra aberta. Uma tipologia urbana rara em São Paulo."
5. Abilio Guerra, "Prêmio APCA 2012 – Categoria "Obra de arquitetura." Premiado: Praça das Artes / Brasil Arquitetura e Marcos Cartum."
6. Rem Koolhaas, *Delirious New York: A Retroactive Manifesto for Manhattan*.
7. Hélio Oiticica, "Esquema Geral da Nova Objetividade (1967)," 101. Free translation.
8. Ignasí de Solà-Morales, *Terrain Vague*, 181-193.
9. See: Cecília Rodrigues dos Santos, "Arquiteturas do Brasil: Brasil Arquitetura," in: Fanucci and Ferraz, *Francisco Fanucci, Marcelo Ferraz*.
10. Francisco Fanucci was born in Cambuí, Minas Gerais, and Marcelo Ferraz in Carmo de Minas, but was also raised in Cambuí. See: Ferraz, *Arquitetura Rural*.
11. T.N.: *Paulista* refers to what or who is natural of São Paulo.
12. Lina Bo Bardi, *Tempos de Grossura: O Design no Impasse*, 12. Free translation.
13. The office was founded in 1981 by Marcelo Ferraz, Francisco Fanucci, and Marcelo Suzuki, who left the partnership in 1995.
14. T.N.: Derived from *sertão*, which refers to harsh, dry regions, away from urban centers and large cultivated lands, the term *sertanejo* includes the people who inhabit this region, their way of life, their food, music etc.

Projects

The 36 projects presented here (selected among works executed, not executed, and currently in construction) refer to the period between 2005 and 2020 and contemplate the variety of commissions and localities that were presented to the firm or were sought out by them during that period. The accompanying texts were produced in varying circumstances, some are memorials from presentations to clients, others were part of public contests in architecture, and there are also texts that were used for specialized publications. They were all adapted to serve the purpose of this book, while also maintaining the spirit of their original source material.

Socioambiental Institute – ISA

São Gabriel da Cachoeira, Amazonas, 2000

São Gabriel da Cachoeira is a town of about 45 thousand inhabitants, mostly indigenous, of 22 different ethnic groups living there together. Located a thousand kilometers Northwest of Manaus, it is in the Amazon region near the borders between Brazil, Colombia, and Venezuela. The establishment of the head-offices of the Socioambiental Institute – ISA in the city, between the densest urban fabric and the banks of the Negro River, was designed precisely to highlight the possibility of instituting a gentler and friendlier relationship between human occupation and the environment, between urbanity and nature.

It constitutes an effort to counterpoint the recurrent practice, so common in riverside cities, of building edifices with their backs turned to the river, using it solely as domestic sewer and garbage dump. In this sense, the ISA building presents itself to the city as a democratic equipment for public and collective use, while also showing reverence to the natural landscape – the river, with its beautiful dark waters and white sand beaches, in the vastness of the Amazon Rainforest, as far as the eye can see.

Some constructive difficulties of the region were determining factors in the project, due to the city's isolation and limited availability of materials. As a result, we arrive at a simple, synthetic form of architecture. The building is a 16m x 16m cube, with three stories. It was built with traditional techniques of coated and whitewashed masonry. An external layer of wood protects it from the heavy Amazonian rains and gusts of wind, and a great roof of Piassava straw (a well-supplied product of the region and largely employed in the indigenous *maloca* huts) provides it with thermal comfort.

We turned to native handcraft and labor – not only of the region, but also from Colombia and Bahia – in the wood, liana, and straw work of the roof and also for the peripheral structure that covers the central building and holds all the vertical and horizontal systems of circulation, forming marquees, balconies, ladders.

The ISA building seeks to combine and merge all spatial concepts with the rich and varied use class program proposed by the institution's leaders and the indigenous councils. An independent external circulation system – stairs and balconies – gives access to the multipurpose working room; exhibition, projection, and conference areas; library; apartments for researchers and visitors; a communal kitchen; and a large communal room set up with hammocks for meetings and/or rest.

With its balconies, outstretched and welcoming lobby, panoramic terrace on the roof, the building as a whole is a great gathering space for users and visitors to work and have leisure as well. The entire project is rooted in principles of coexistence and in its double relationship with both the city and nature.

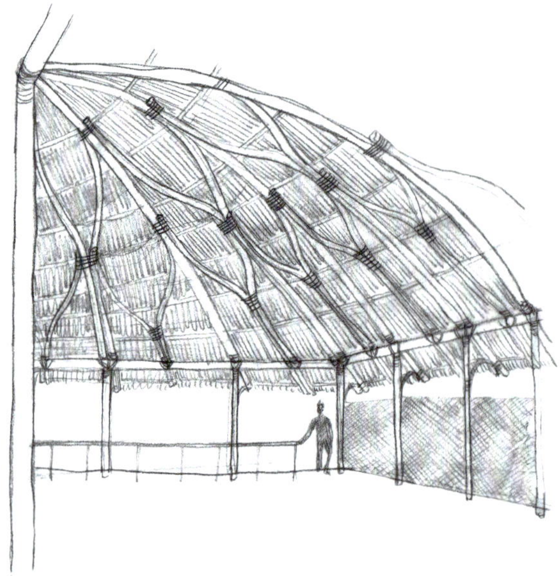

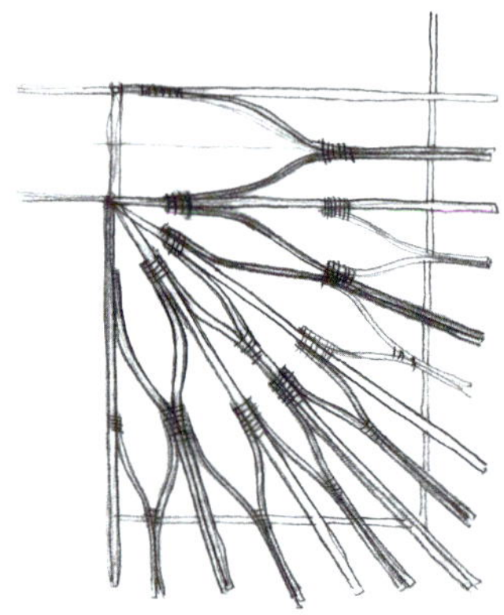

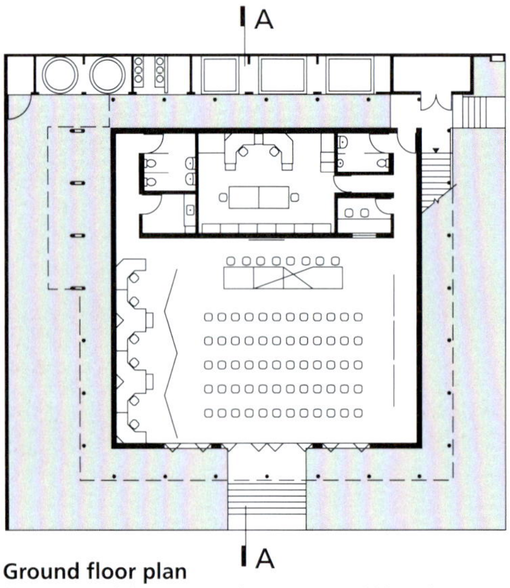

Ground floor plan
(lectures, exhibitions, working area and library)

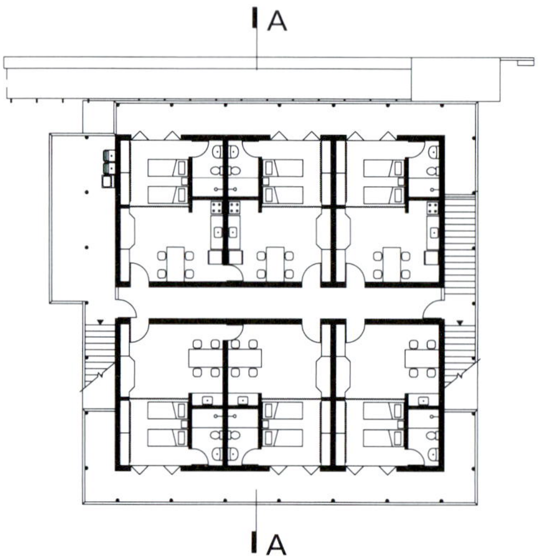

First floor plan
(apartments for researchers and visitors)

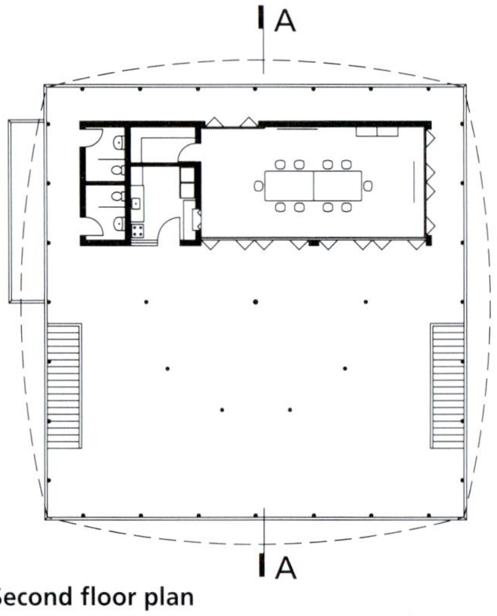

Second floor plan
(living area, collective kitchen and area for meetings)

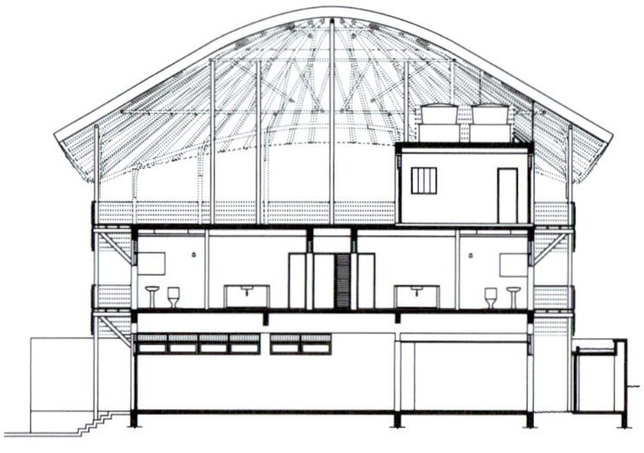

Section AA

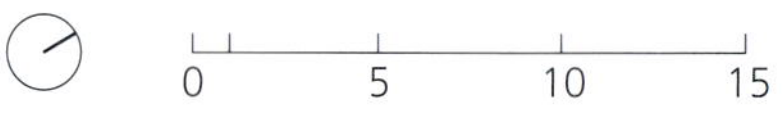

Federation of the Indigenous Organizations of Rio Negro – FOIRN

São Gabriel da Cachoeira, Amazonas, 2003

Also located in the urban center of São Gabriel da Cachoeira, the headquarters of the Federation of the Indigenous Organizations of Rio Negro – FOIRN was designed to bring together about forty organizations that are gathered around the entity. FOIRN was created more than thirty years ago and is dedicated to the strife for demarcation of indigenous territories, the promotion of health and education, and the valuing of the culture of the peoples of the region.

The plans for the building delineate offices, exhibition rooms, and a meeting hall. Besides handling the administrative activities of the entity, the office building serves as logistical support and radio station for the communication between the organizations.

The slope where the center was built is limited by an *igarapé*.[1] On account of the humidity of the lot, it was determined that the floors that are on the street level or above would hold areas for public utilization. The exhibition hall is on the ground floor and the meeting hall is on the floor above that. Below street level are the administrative sections: Offices on the first floor below, storage rooms in the second.

The architectonical design is structured around two masonry lateral towers painted white. They flank the unit, its floors, wood works, and remaining structure. The towers hold service areas and vertical circulation systems, while the central parts of the building house the halls and offices. The contrast is highlighted by the difference in roofing: Slabs in the former and a thatched wood structure in the latter. The ends of the wood work leave spans open to permit constant cross ventilation. In 2004, the building was destroyed by a fire.

Note

1. T.N.: A first, second or third order Amazonian watercourse consisting of a long arm of river or canal.

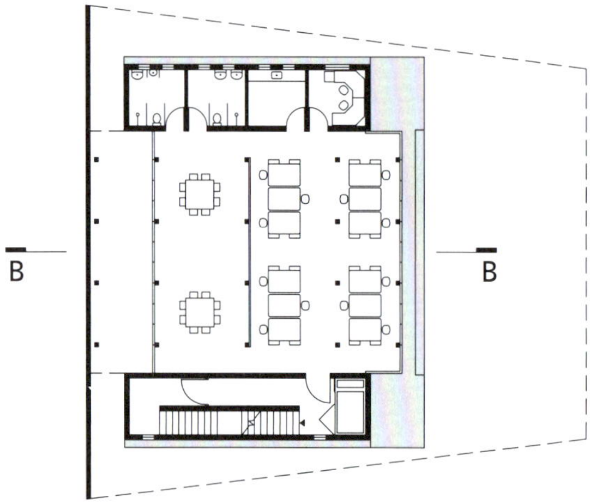

Underground plan
(working area and offices)

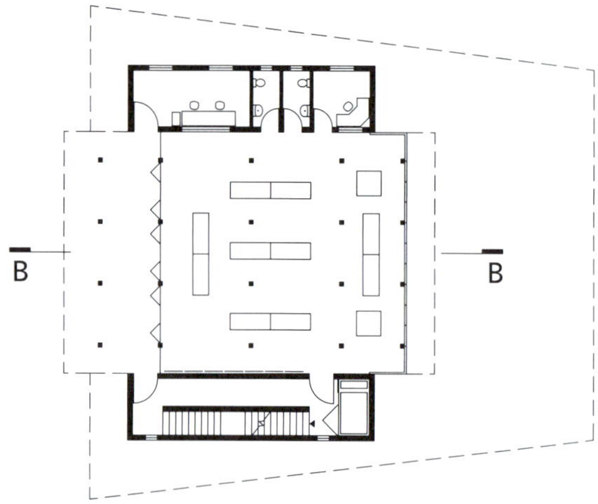

Ground floor plan
(exhibitions and shop)

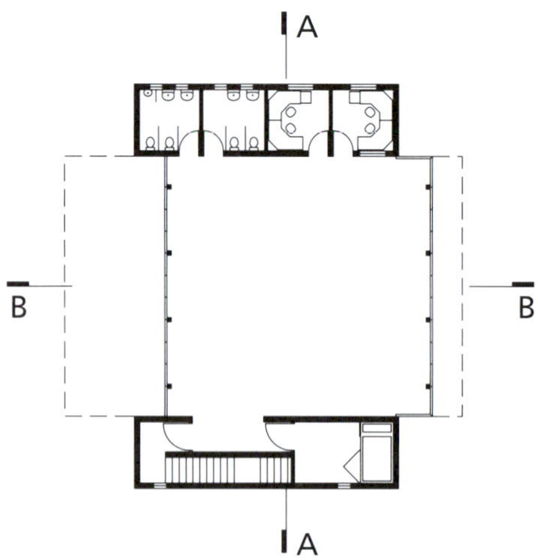

First floor plan
(multipurpose room)

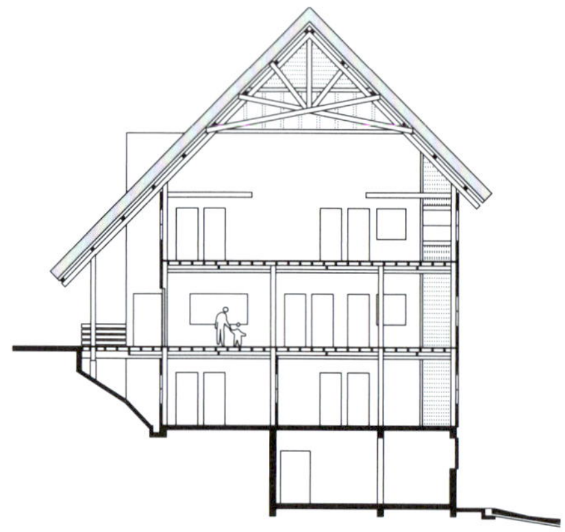

Section AA

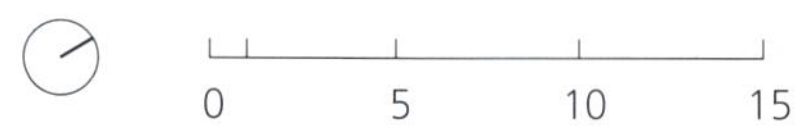

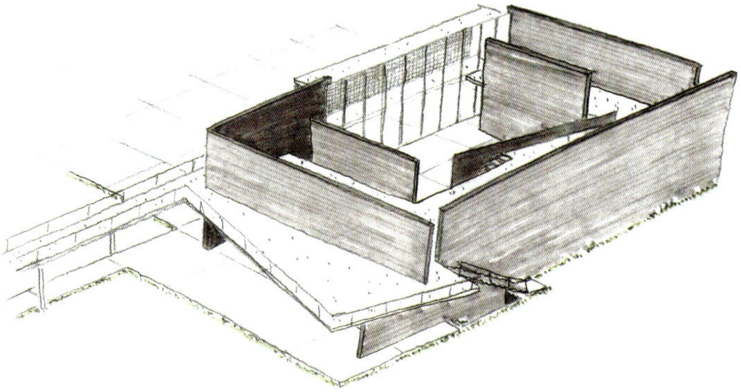

Rodin Bahia Museum

Salvador, Bahia, 2002

In one of these crazy, bold ventures that announce themselves from time to time, Emanoel Araújo and Jacques Villain decided to create a branch of the Paris Rodin Museum. More precisely, they decided to implant it at an early 20th century mansion on Graça Street, in Salvador. The government of Bahia agreed to the project and carried on the brilliant idea. Many people wondered then: "A Rodin Museum in Bahia? But why in Bahia?" The only answer was: "Why not in Bahia?"

Thus, the museum, popularly known as Palace of the Arts, was conceived as the first subsidiary of the Paris Rodin Museum. It inhabits the Comendador Catarino Palace, an eclectic French style building erected in 1912, with resources drawn from the cocoa business. The edifice halls and its beautiful garden would be occupied by the works of the French master Rodin, while temporary expositions would be showcased in a new building, designed and constructed towards that end.

Each building should express its own individual time, value, and character, without imposing on or submitting to the other. That disposition should include the garden, with its ancient mango trees and other tropical vegetation. Both the eclectic and the contemporary architectures should develop a "respectful, warm, tense, challenging, and loving" relationship, a coexistence of adjoining diversity.

The mansion has received delicate and precise interventions, necessary to prepare it for a new life, while maintaining its essential character. To the original staircase, a new flight of steps was added, in order to give access to the attic, a surprising amount of space. It now serves as a small auditorium destined for lectures, seminars, and musical concerts.

The need to create a new and efficient vertical circulation system for the mansion lead us to propose its deployment on the exterior part of the building, precisely at the geometrical center of the entire complex. A unit of exposed concrete fuses with the old building, connects its three main floors, and makes the newly-added annex known to visitors. It provides the ensemble with ladders and an elevator.

The principles that guided our proposal for the insertion of this new unit were: Not to interfere considerably with the centenary trees of the garden; not to compete with the dominant presence of the historical building; and, above all, to add meaningfully to what was previously there, giving form to an articulated and fluid set.

A concrete slab, constructed as walkway and marquee, sets forth from the old mansion penetrating and embracing the newer building, which, in turn, is implanted in a clearing between the large trees at the back portion of the lot. It maintains at a respectful distance, even as it stablishes a relationship of scale and dialogue with the palace. The dialogue is stated in its vertical and horizontal alignments, given that it has a total constructed area equivalent to that of the mansion.

From the ground floor or the walkway, it is possible to access the new building through several entrances. Its spaces are built with associations of great surfaces of exposed concrete, glass, and wooden trusses. The core of this building is its central, double-height hall with controlled zenith lighting. The walkway outside and the inside mezzanines offer different angles to observe what is in display there.

The treatment given to the garden values its paths by using modulated Portuguese pavement across the entire terrain. Along these paths the works of Rodin are spread, amidst the rich tropical vegetation, lections shaded under the mango trees, school children having their snacks, simple contemplation, nothingness to be done... As the primary inspiration for the entire project, this garden – which houses a coffee shop, a restaurant, and a gift shop – has the greatest appeal for acquaintanceship. Since today's museums take on the role of meeting grounds, by means of art and culture, this is a mandatory quality to be displayed: A communal area for inhabitants of Bahia and for all who pass through there, Brazilians and world citizens.

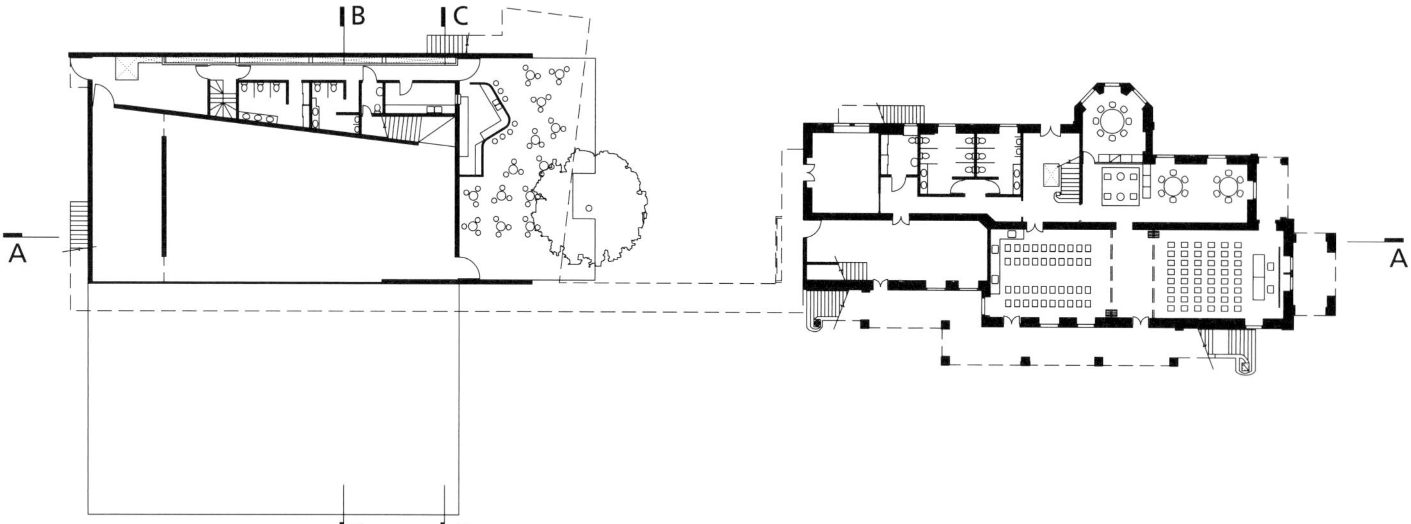

Ground floor plan

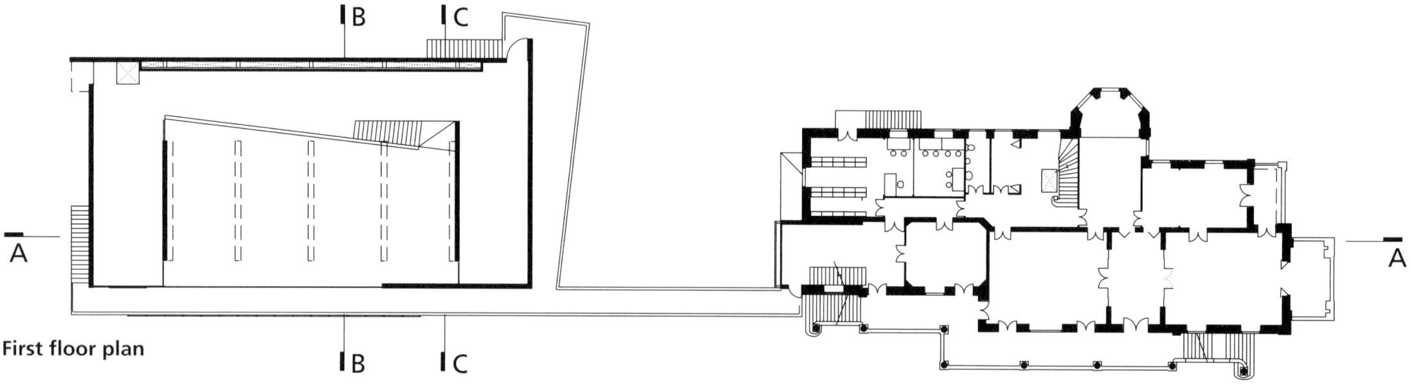

First floor plan

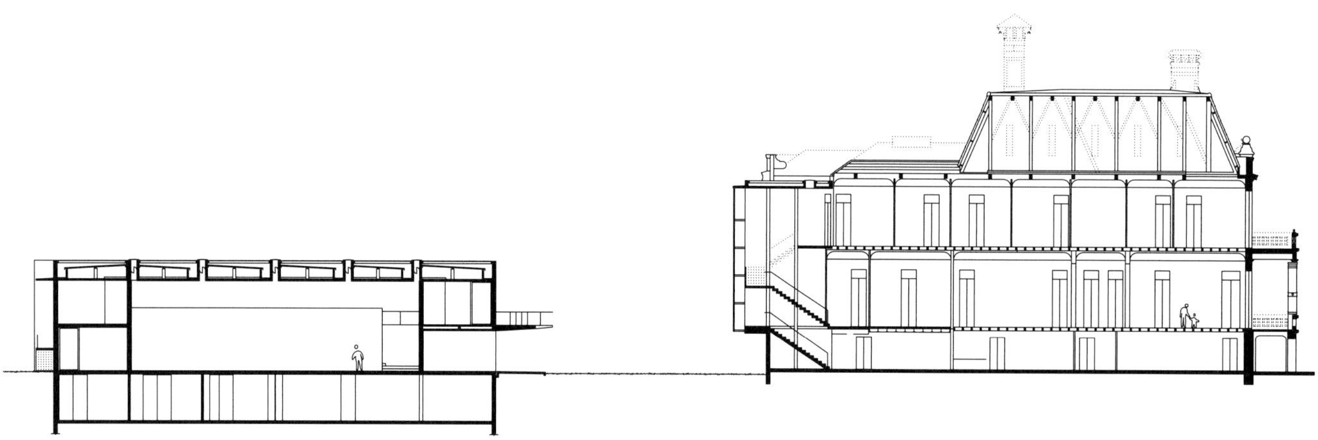

Section AA

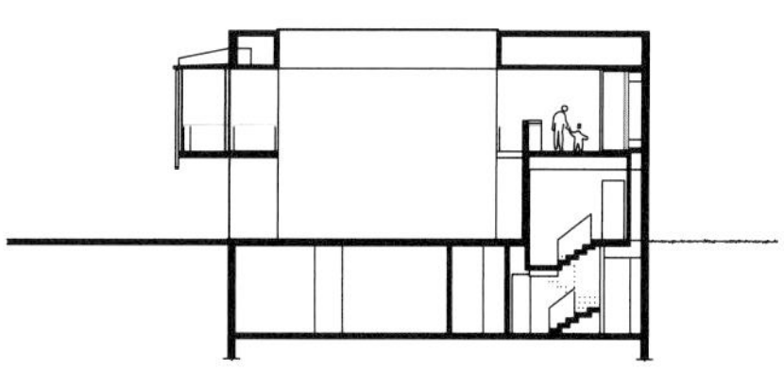

Section BB

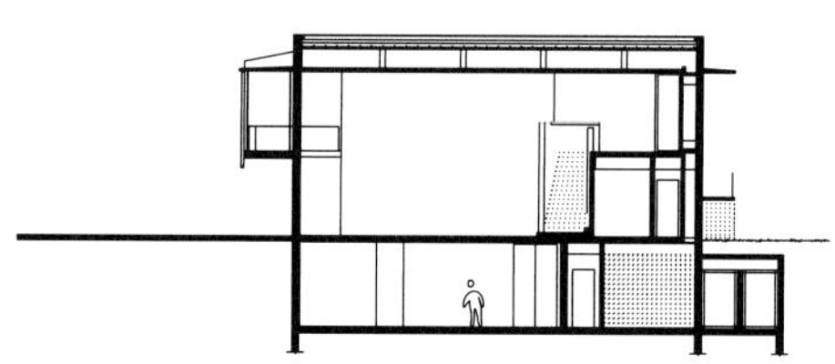

Section CC

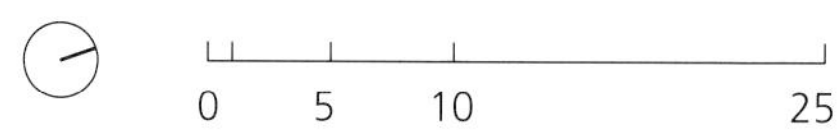

Girassol Pavilion

São Paulo, 2004

A metal structure supports a discreet building, accommodating the uneven terrain of Vila Madalena. It is not a house, it is not a club, it is not a meeting hall, it is not a gym, it is not a studio. It's a little bit of all of those things together and, when the project started, it was even named the Pavilion of Everything.

Two large inverted metal beams, in the style of Mies van der Rohe at the Crown Hall, give support to a flat cover for a secondary structure (also in metal), throwing its weight onto the ground over four pillars. On the two lateral edges of the grounds, two large walls are a part of the structure, dividing the load and serving as end points. The pillars serve as landmarks for the large doors that open to the front and the back of the lot, large entrances – like airplane hangars – designed to create full cross ventilation and integrate indoor and outdoor spaces.

A concrete retaining wall slices the terrain and gives support to the frontal section of the metallic structure. In the design, it was projected that a large kitchen, a sauna, a heated pool, a studio, and several places to rest or even to reside in would surround a covered plaza. Right at the entrance, an intimate garden, with plenty of vegetation and fish tanks, welcomes in the guests. On the back of the lot, connected to the large plaza and the pool deck, a retaining staircase connects the buildings and a small football field. Multiple spaces, pavilion of everything.

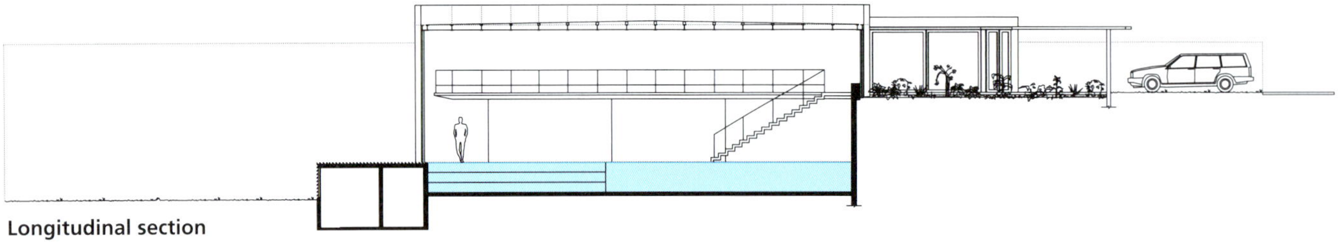

Longitudinal section

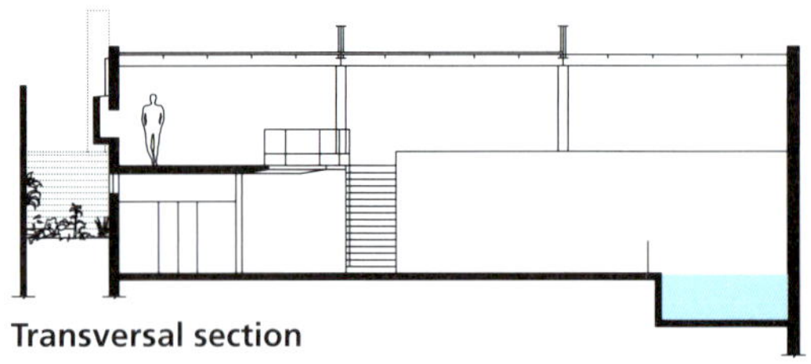

Transversal section

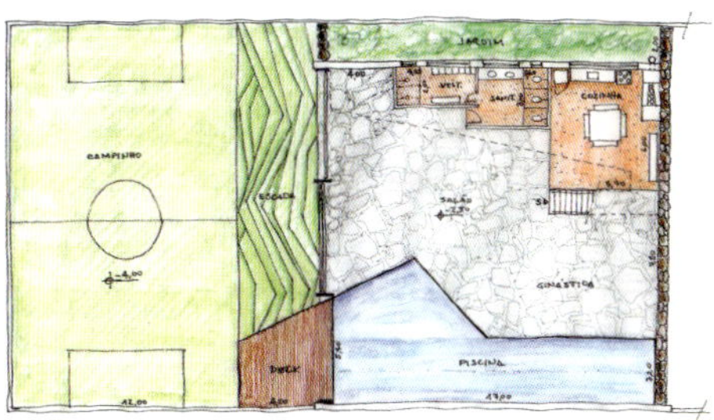
JARDIM
VEST.
SANIT.
COZINHA
CAMPINHO
ESCADA
SALÃO
GINÁSTICA
DECK
PISCINA

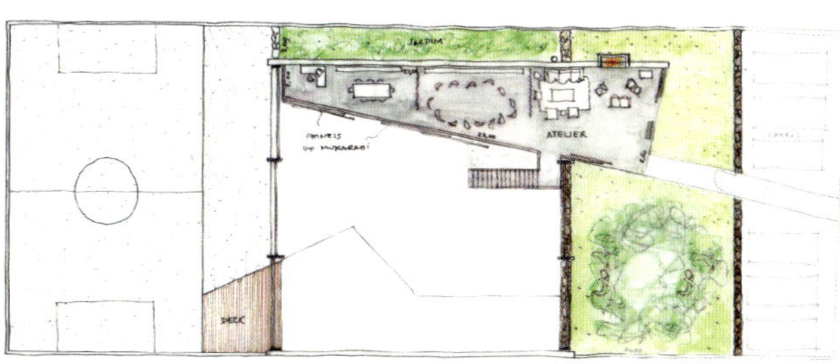
JARDIM
ATELIER
DECK

Bread Museum – Colognese Mill

with Anselmo Turazzi

Ilópolis, Rio Grande do Sul, 2005

One must view culture as something that goes from tradition to creation. We have to preserve the best of what we have created and built in our history, otherwise we risk being trapped in a deformed present. On the other hand, we must also invest on novelty because it constitutes fundamental affirmation and transformation of our communities and society as a whole. This permanent dialectic of tradition and creation, added to our critical openness to assimilate languages and information produced in all corners of the world, is a defining trace of Brazilian culture. It was within this perspective that Italian immigrants built the Colognese Mill. It was also in the same spirit that we have restored it to create the Bread Museum, an ensemble that includes the museum facility, a baking workshop, and the mill itself.

Towards the end of the 19th century and in the beginning of the 20th century, Brazil received a large quantity of immigrants coming from several countries, such as Germany, Japan, Italy, Lebanon, Ukraine, and Poland. It constituted an attempt by the Brazilian government to whiten a predominantly colored society, which had just undergone centuries of slavery, by receiving immigrant workers who fled their native lands to escape poverty and hunger.

Most of the Italian immigrants were from the impoverished Veneto region. They made residence, for the most part, in São Paulo and in the Southern parts of the country. As new colonizers, these immigrants braved the lands they received from the government. The lands were, largely, in mountainous regions of difficult access, since the more levelled and fertile grounds had already been taken by other immigrants who arrived first, like the Germans. It was the conquering of America all over again; the dreams of a new life, a new era. From the exchanges between Italians and Brazilians, a mixed culture was born with original characteristics.

One of the most powerful testimonies of these epic times is the construction of the colonial mills, which, to this day, can be found in the mountainous regions of Southern Brazil. These artefacts, originally employed to help stablish the communities around the production of flour, are a result of the immigrants' knowledge and ingenuity, much like they are a result of their encountering of new regions and materials – basically araucaria, the Brazilian pine tree. The remnants of these mills, found here and there in the lush landscape of the mountain range, are beautiful and irreplaceable documents of their great combination of technique and aesthetics.

However, despite their historical relevance, these mills were doomed to fade away due to the typical sort of abandonment and forgetfulness of our times. In 2003, at a friendly get-together, the idea of creating a cultural-tourist route in the region came up – the Route of the Mills, as it would be called. Later, a campaign to raise funds to restore the Colognese Mill, in the valley of the Taquari River, began. Its restoration would serve as a primary model for the ensuing work.

In order not to fall into a project of nostalgia, we decided to add to this mill – which was supposed to be restored and go back into normal production of corn flour polenta – the Bread Museum and the Confectioner School, newer needs for contemporary employments. And, so, the architectural project of the ensemble was born.

Two new units in concrete and glass pose a dialogue with the old wooden mill, in a contemporary – and quite Brazilian – language. A hundred years set them apart, but an idea unites them; and that idea is precisely the celebration of the woodwork. Everything there is araucaria: The mill; all its apparatus; the new terrace and walkway that recall the houses of the immigrants; the brise-soleil sliding panels; the capitals on the pillars, reminiscent of the fantastic internal structure of the mills; and even the reinforced concrete, designed – as if it was made in photographical reprints – with patterns of wood boards.

Over time, all of these elements sort of meshed in their appearance by the grayish tone of the aging wood: Mimesis at a distance and the truth of the materials when seen up close.

In this small ensemble, all is museum and museology, including the architecture, the garden, the objects, and their meaning. The main artifact of the museum is the mill itself: In the yard, a collection of millstones of granite and basalt with several shades and levels of hardness, intended for different types of milling work, be it corn or wheat; in the surroundings, a small water canal fed by a spring under the mill gives the lot its boundaries. This is a reference and homage to Carlos Scarpa, the great architect, also from the Veneto region, who taught us so many lessons regarding the dialogue of ancient and contemporary architectures.

We believe that, in this project, architecture serves its noble role of renewing culture, by allowing the reencounter of a local community with its historical background, now set up in new basis of dreams and utopia: Architecture of roots and antennas.

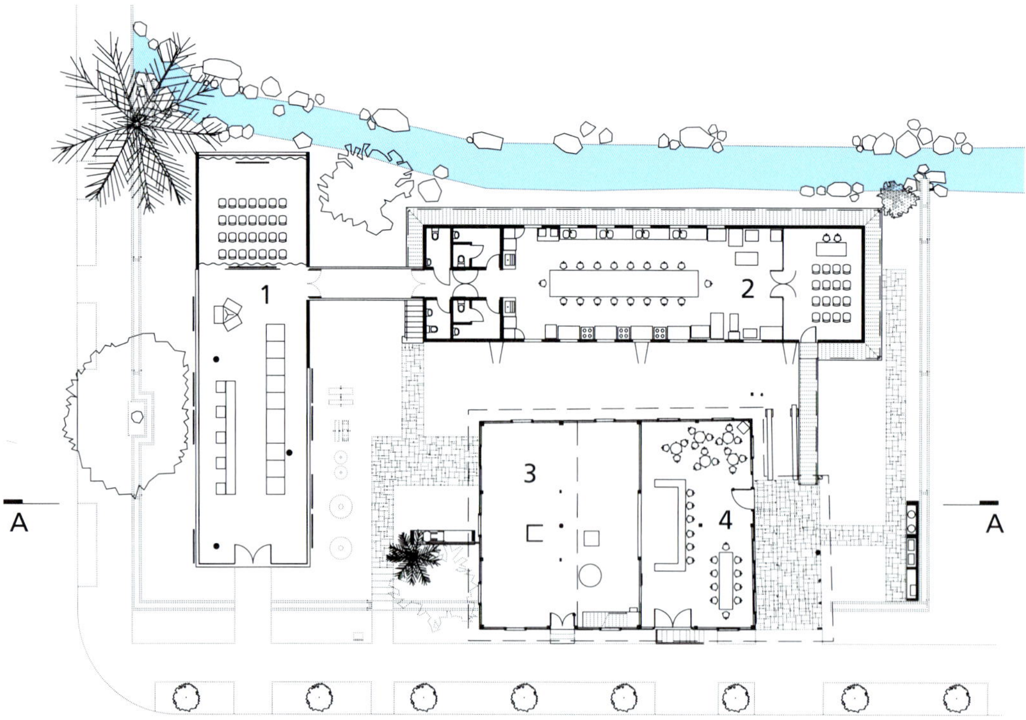

CAPTION
1. Bread Museum
2. Bakery school
3. Mill
4. Bodega

Site plan

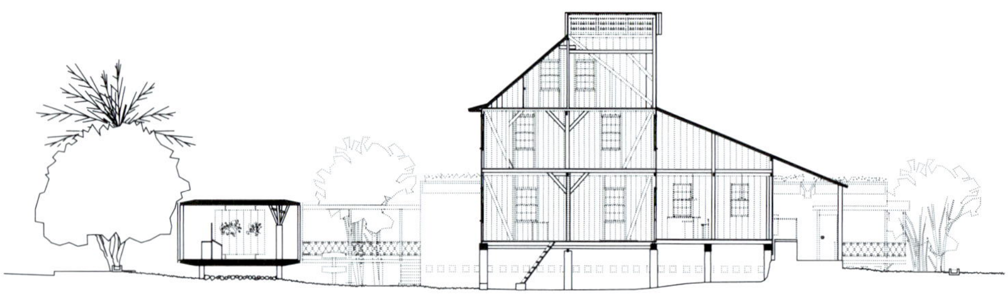

Section AA

Northeast elevation

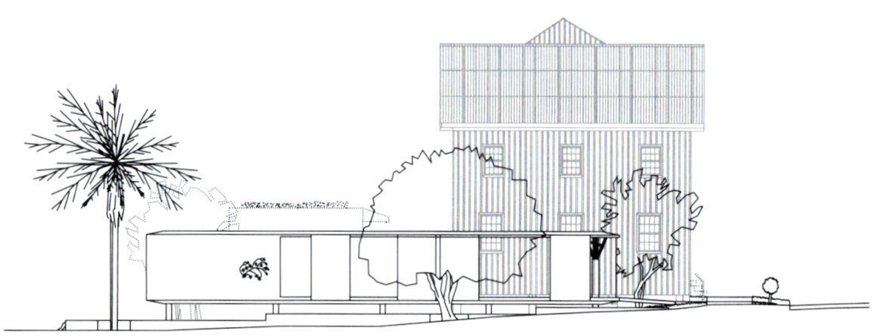

Southeast elevation

Villa Isabella

Finland, 2005

It is impossible to think about modern Brazilian architecture without considering the strong Finnish influence it received, by means of the genius work of Alvar Aalto. In our academic years, we would take apart his designs, eager to understand his arduous logic and the fascination it instilled. It was like trying to figure out an enigma inlaid in something we thoroughly enjoyed, but which bothered us somehow because we didn't fully grasp it; it is so with most great works of art.

When we were invited to participate in a contest between four Brazilian architects to design Villa Isabella, the competition brief was clear and explicit in the fact that the clients required a house with Brazilian elements or, at least as far as possible, a house executed in Brazilian fashion for a Brazilian way-of-living. We even came to believe that such things actually existed. Well, either way, the challenge was posed.

We immediately delved into self-analysis, dissecting of our architectural know-how in search of our roots or, better put, our referential matrices. And, much to our astonishment, we came upon several structures, spatial concepts, constructive rationales, appropriations of materials, and relationships with the natural and urban environment that were sprung from the Finnish experience with architecture. More precisely, these came from Aalto's work. Brazil and Finland, "faraway, so close!", via architecture.

We might say that the Villa Isabella project is marked by a desire to both appear and disappear, to show oneself clearly and forcefully in the landscape, across the territory, and, on the other hand, to imitate the forest, to design a camouflage, to be almost invisible. It seems contradictory, but in architecture it is possible.

The house presents itself as a strong element in the landscape, without assaulting it. There is a measured integration with nature, calculated, and variable according to each season: Under different circumstances – especially given the severity of Finnish seasons – lights, materials, colors, and constructive elements provide different experiences.

Due to the aggressive weather and dominant cold present throughout the majority of the year, life takes place indoors. This finding led us to abandon the idea of a more compact space in favor of a more sprawled out house, in which the displacements from one ambience to another were valued, as if they constituted a stroll through a minuscule village. Hallways in glass, floors in white stone from Goiás, rough stone walls from Lapland (which, to this day, keep their little bits of moss alive) enhance this sensation and allow these strolls to turn into small expeditions to the outdoors without leaving the inside of the house.

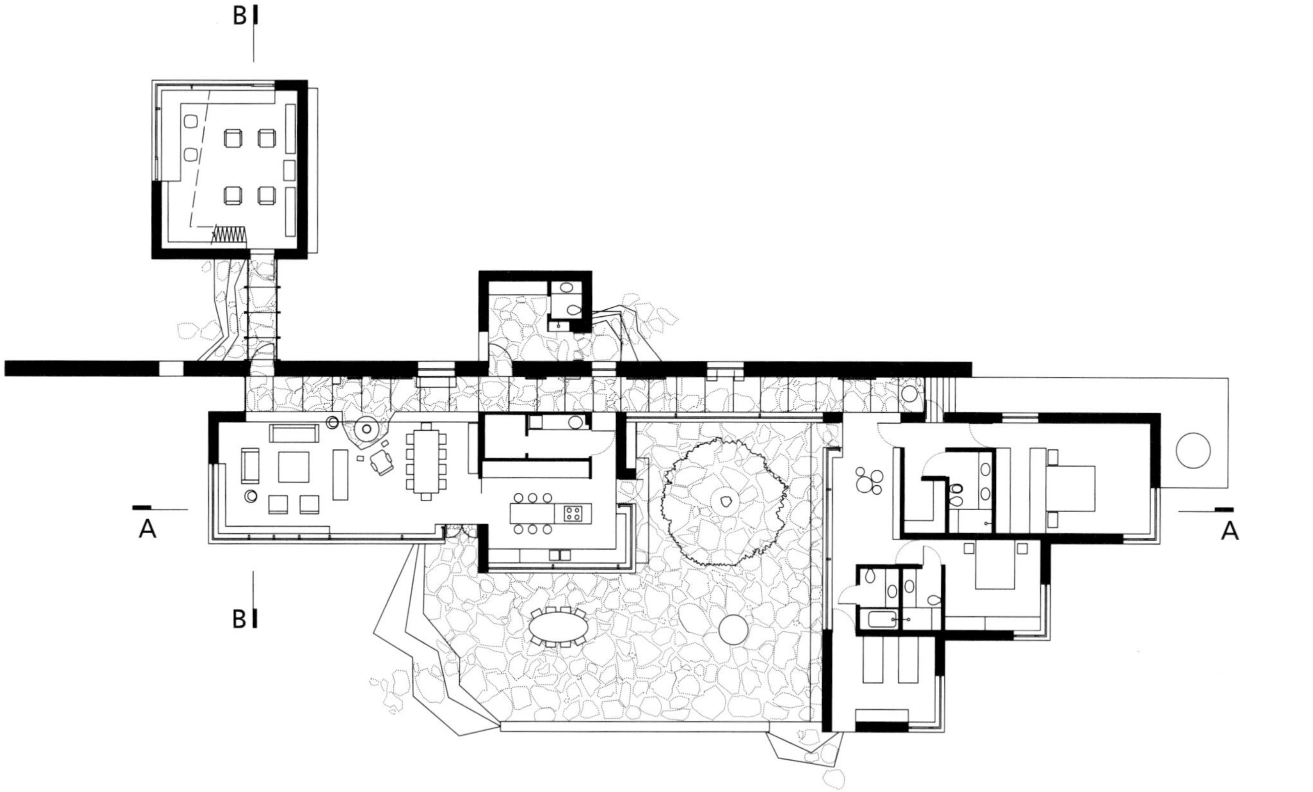

Ground floor plan

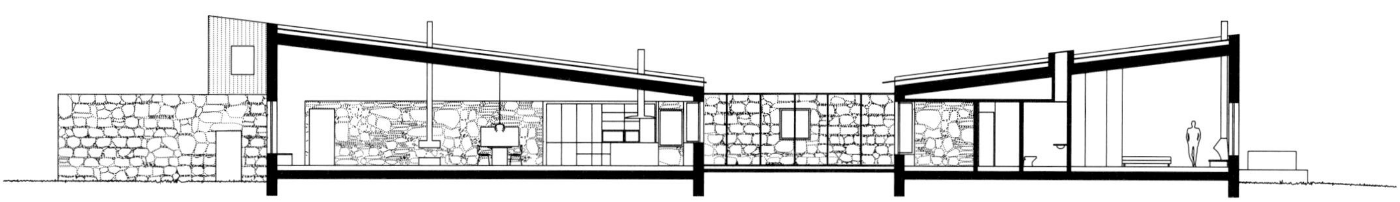

Section AA

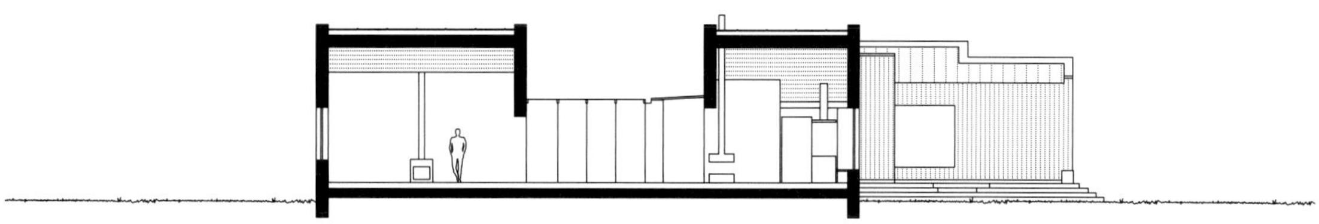

Section BB

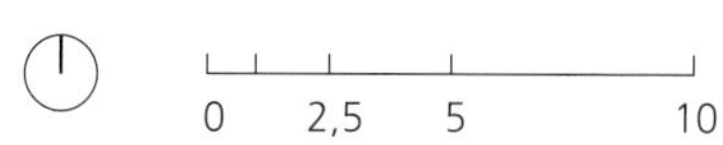

Villa Carolina

Finland, 2017

Ten years after Villa Isabella was finished, we were asked to design a neighboring house. This time, the project was a bit smaller, set between the woods and the sea. Along with the house, there was also to be a sauna with guest apartments.

We attempted to employ stone and woodwork as much as we could for this project. The design projected two units with tilted green roofs, resembling the Finnish turf roofs. The two buildings are connected by an elongated veranda to the South, which gives the ensemble a sense of unity, but also independency of usage – house and sauna.

The Southern façades, built in glass and woodwork in both units, are open to sun and sea, with an unimpeded view of an extensive horizon. In contrast, the Northern façades are near-sighted, with walls of stone and restrained openings, small and precise as arrow slits watching over the deep woods.

The almost flat cover of the veranda contrasts with the tilted roofs of the main buildings and will permit the sunlight to enter through the upper parts of the cuboids by the Southern façade. We will employ pillars of solid stone with capitals in the veranda to support its wooden roof structure.

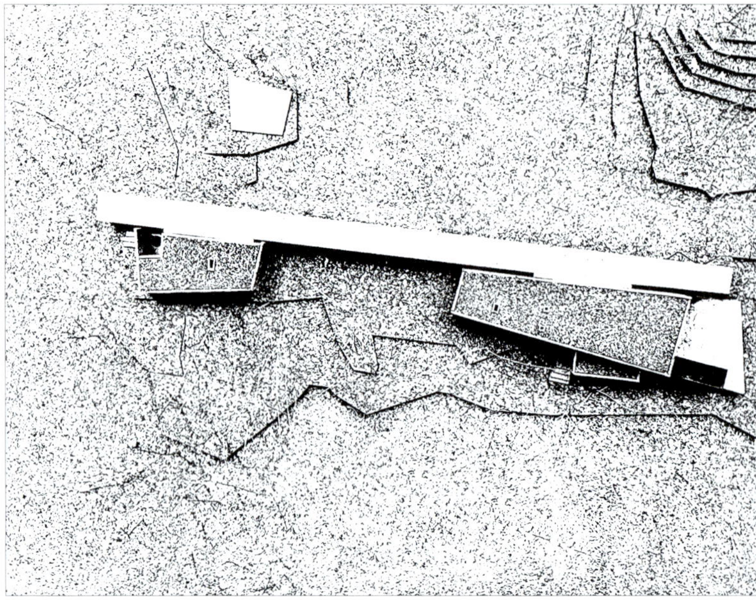

INSTANT SPAN

Praça das Artes

with Marcos Cartum

São Paulo, 2006

There are architectural projects that impose themselves with sovereignty in large open spaces, accommodate pleasant situations, and are made visible from a distance. On the other hand, there are projects that accommodate adverse situations, minimal spaces, scraps of land compressed by pre-existing buildings, leftovers of urban areas. These are projects in which the parameters of development are dictated by the difficulties encountered. The case of Praça das Artes fits well with the latter.

Our project begins from within and outward, from the bowels, and takes shape in them. It presents itself to the city as denouncement of a bankrupt urban model which no longer functions; it is no longer applicable to the scale of our metropolis. Houses and small buildings with backyards and ample lots are no longer justified, as they end up giving place to useless hollows. Thus, we have tried to understand that which was obsolete, useless; what had expired of this ancient city planning. The new plan was to make that our raw material in the project. Out of these leftovers or, better yet, out of this bagasse the city had crushed, we built Praça das Artes.

Because of this inception, as a denouncement, the hollows at the ground level were not occupied, not even by columns. Instead, we created a great public passageway out in the open – a place for gatherings, the plaza that names the complex. The new buildings are supported by structures on the edges of the lots, as a result of a form of architecture molded by adversity and restriction, but also, an architecture that does not require scorched earth to serve as pedestal.

The aspects that brought us to this conceptual decision were, precisely, the nature of the place and the understanding of its spaces as products of social-political factors that have been in play for decades – if not centuries – in the development of the city. Everything matters, once you begin to realize that a place is not only a physical thing, but an arena of tension, conflicts of interests, underutilization, and even abandonment.

If, on the one hand, the project should respond to the demand of a brief that includes various new types of use related to the musical and performance arts, it should also respond, in a clear and transformative fashion, to a pre-existing situation of physical and spatial nature, which encompasses intense life and a strongly present community. Further still: It should regenerate degraded spaces, create new grounds for shared living, derived from urban geography, the history of the place, and the contemporary values of public life. In this case, we can say that to design is to capture and invent the place at the same time, in the same gesture.

Beginning at the center of the block, the new building unfurls in three directions – Anhangabaú Valley, São João Avenue and Conselheiro Crispiniano Street. As an octopus, it extends its tentacles and occupies spaces. The main element to establish dialogue with the remaining buildings of the block and the surrounding area is a set of pigmented, exposed concrete edifications, with a total area of 28,500 square meters, suspended over the urban walkways.

The old Dramatic and Musical Conservatory of São Paulo, an important historical and architectural landmark of the city that for decades had been unused was incorporated to the complex as a space for recitals and exhibits. Once restored, this edifice was integrated to an ensemble of new buildings which hold the facilities of the schools of music and dance, as well as other installations of the Municipal Theater – the orchestra, the city ballet and choir, the documentation center, restaurants, parking lots, and other communal areas.

Besides supplying the long-lasting demand for a working space for the Municipal Theater, this new cultural complex plays a strategic role in the requalification of the central areas of the city, by giving priority to pedestrians. It stablishes the public aspect of its rich and complex use class program, by focusing on professional and educational activities related to music and dance, in order to foster urban life and shared living.

PRAÇA
ARTES

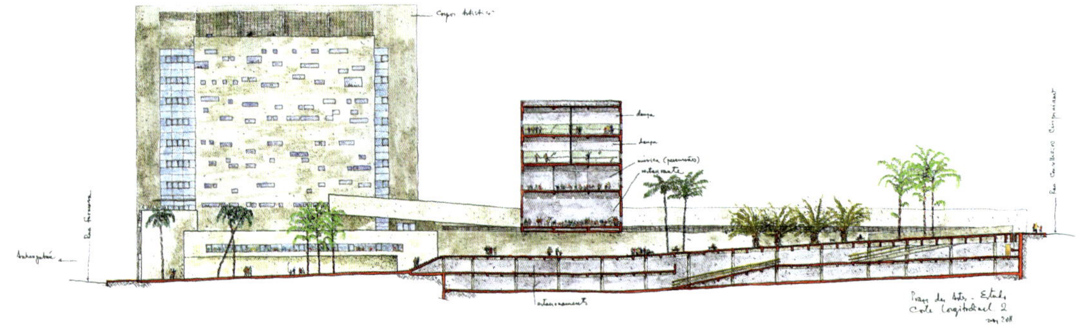

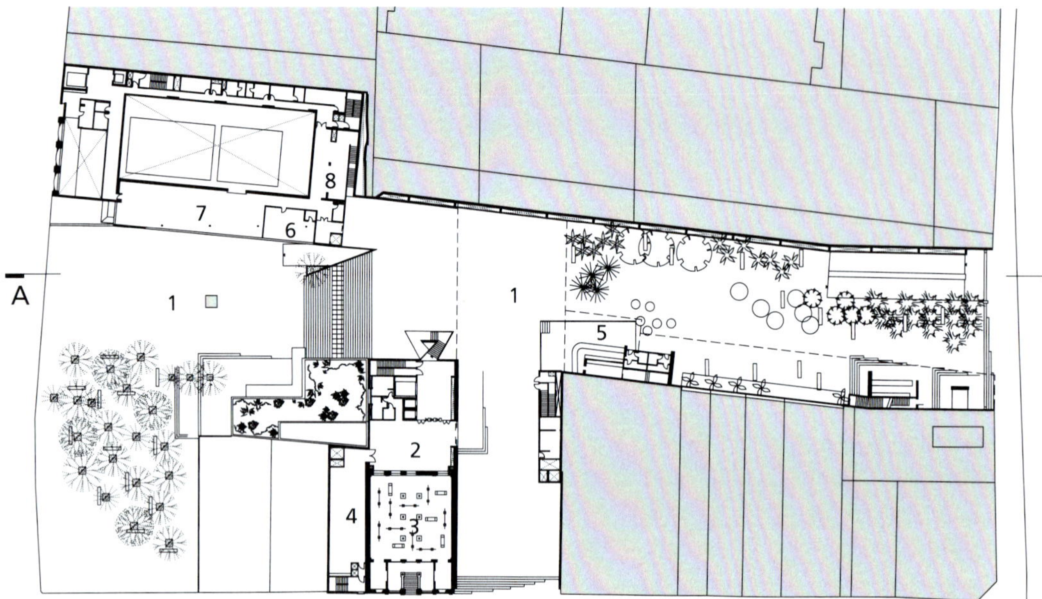

Plans levels 735.45/738.38

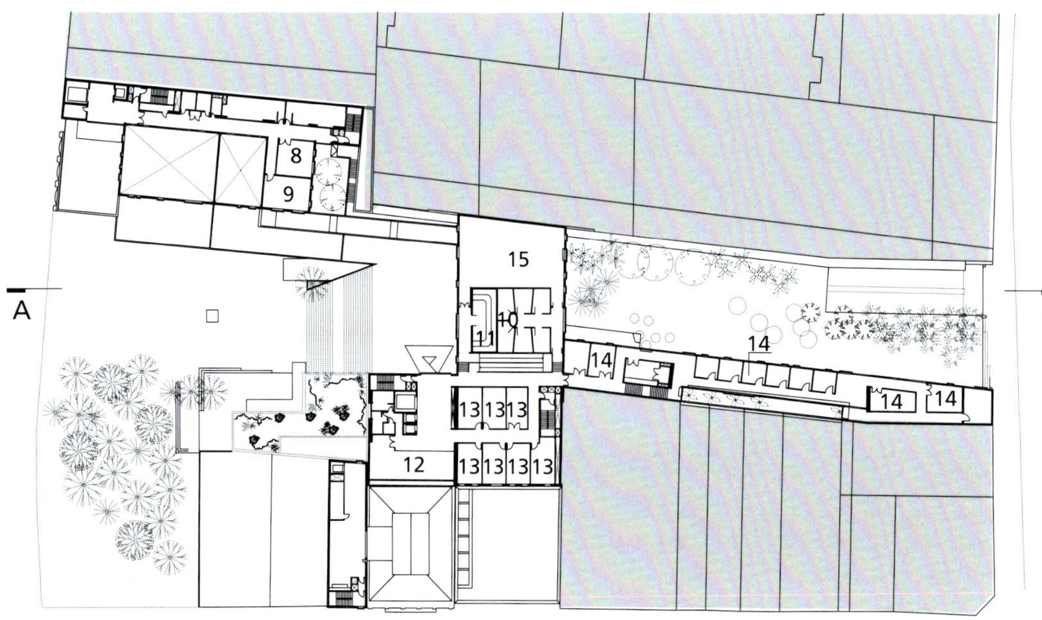

Plans levels 749.97/751.14

CAPTION

1. Central plaza
2. Museum's foyer
3. Museum
4. Museum's support
5. Diner
6. Maestro's room
7. Municipal Theater artistic direction
8. Archive
9. Quartet
10. Percussion
11. Choral's room
12. Instrument's restoration and keeping
13. Theory's room
14. Intrument study room
15. Orchestra rehearsal room

Future restaurant and living room, tapestry of Edmar de Almeida and Triângulo Mineiro's tapestry makers

Top, concert room with Urucum fixture, design and execution by Rodrigo Moreira and Madeeeeira Marcenaria Serralheria; bottom, exhibition room

Former Dramatic and Musical Conservatory changed into exhibition and concert room

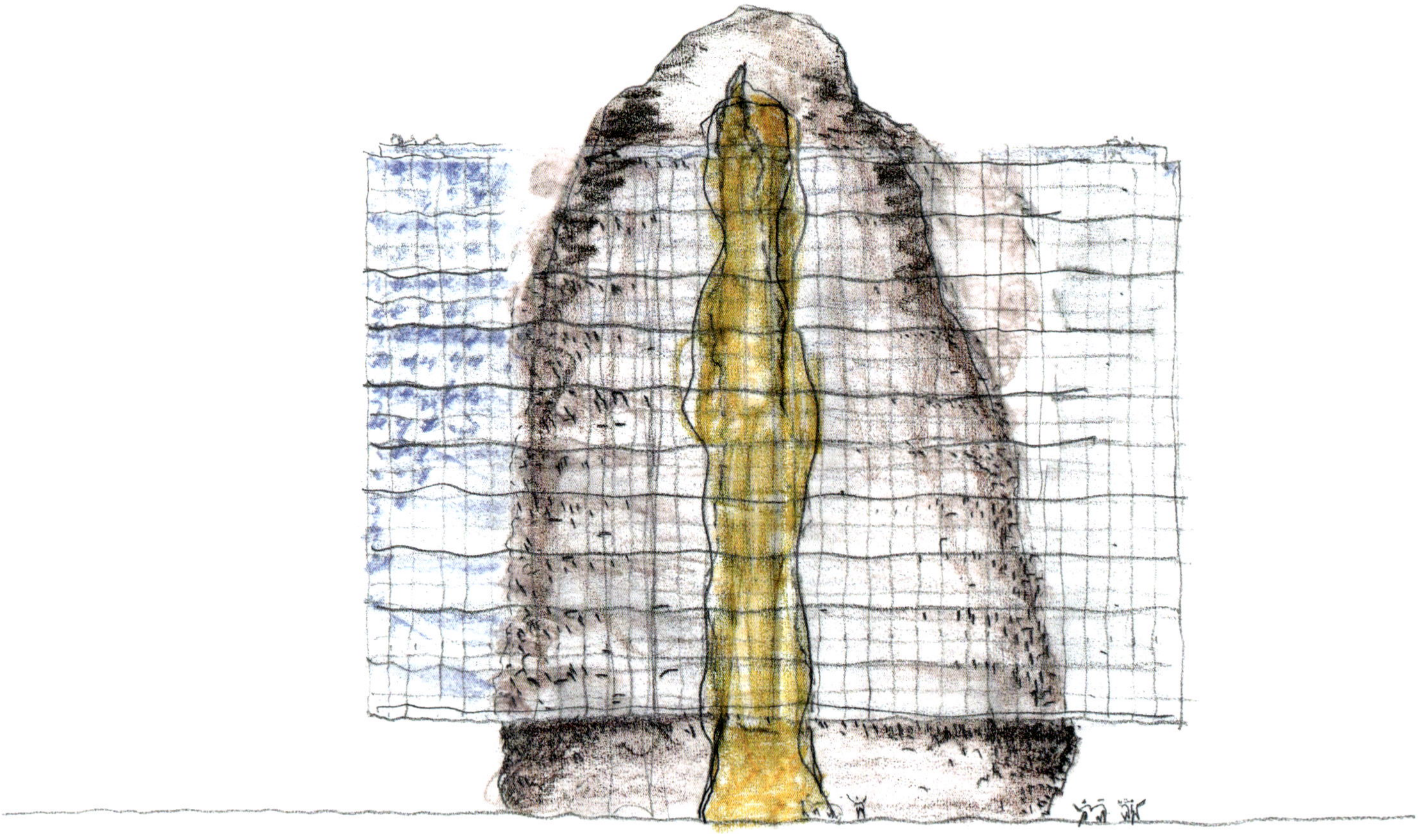

Prague National Library

Prague, Czech Republic, 2006

The building of the new library is a natural unpolished stone shrouded by the pure, human forms of geometry. A glass cube suspended by a monolithic, uneven core of concrete – the stone – that holds a treasure of gems inside. A large vertical gap facing the North side opens to the city and reveals the interior of this treasure vault as a magical cave: The habitat of the books.

The double walls of this large volume of concrete, two layers interlocked by horizontal and vertical septa, form a structural core that anchors the slabs in internal and external overhangs. This creates three very distinct spatial configurations. First, on the outside (within the glass cube), there are reading areas, research areas, and administrative offices, with views of the urban landscape. Second, in the space between the two layers of the structural core, there are special rooms for storing rare books. Here, also, the entire building infrastructure lies on a vertical axis. Finally, inside the core stone, built around a great central hollow, the rows of books are protected from sunlight and distributed in semicircular shelves in a sequence of mezzanines across the eight double floors.

The outer surface of the structural core will be executed with pigmented and sandblasted concrete, giving its surface an appearance of roughness and irregularity. The inner layer will be built in concrete with triangular shapes of different dimensions. The triangles will combine with their vertices to result in a rich, multifaceted surface all in white.

The entire ground floor area will be open and public. Doors in the form of holes in the structural nucleus will give access to the inside of the building, the elevators, and the stairwells. The great hall, located in the first basement, will be a generous space destined for gathering visitors. It will also hold a coffee shop, a bookstore, and exhibition areas. On the roof (the convergence of the stone core and the glass casing), we will add a restaurant, encircled by a great belvedere terrace. The Prague Library could become a new landmark in the city's landscape.

SKRIVANEK

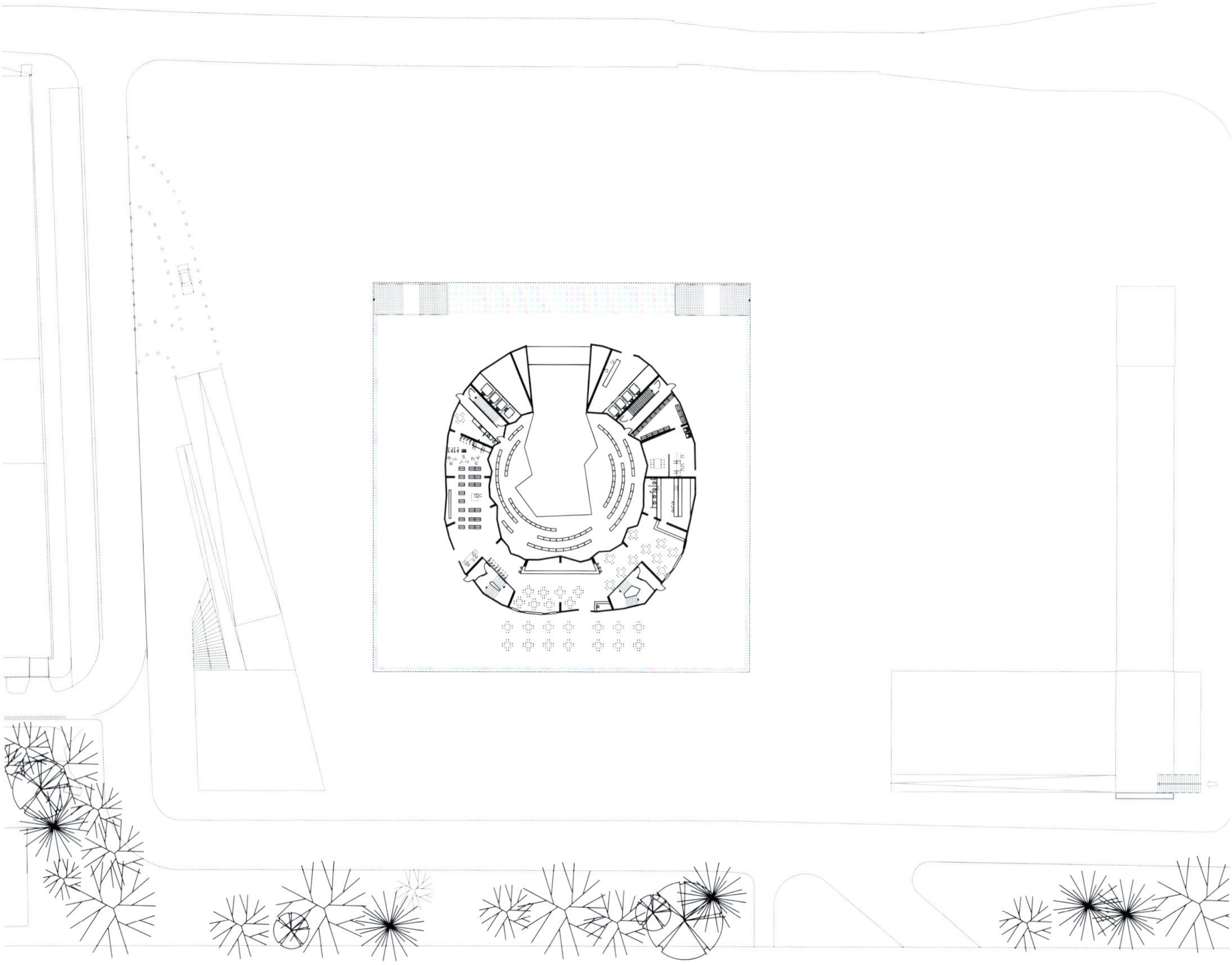

Site plan

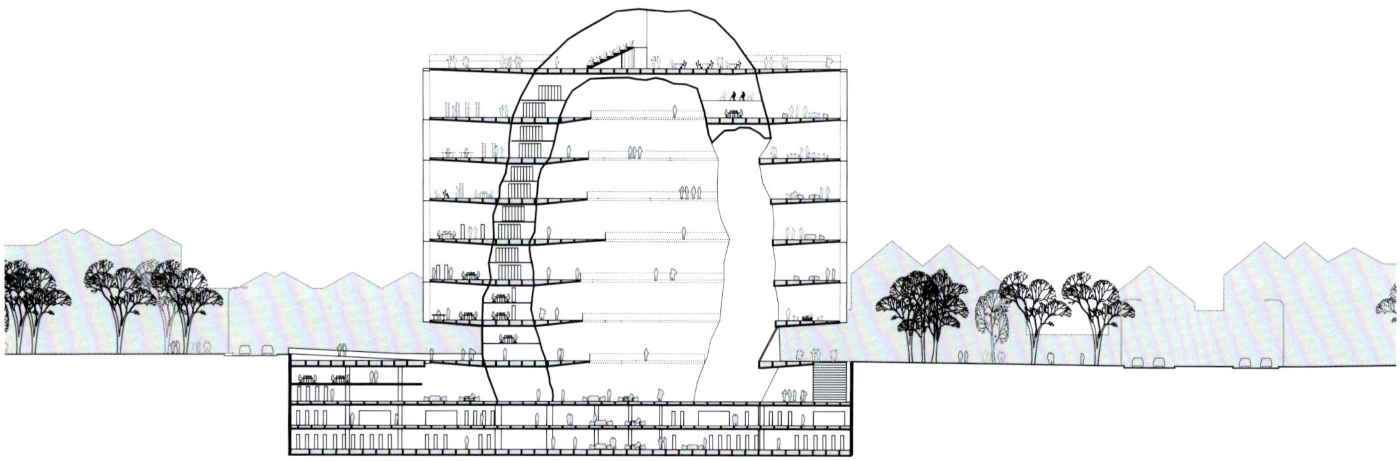

Transversal section

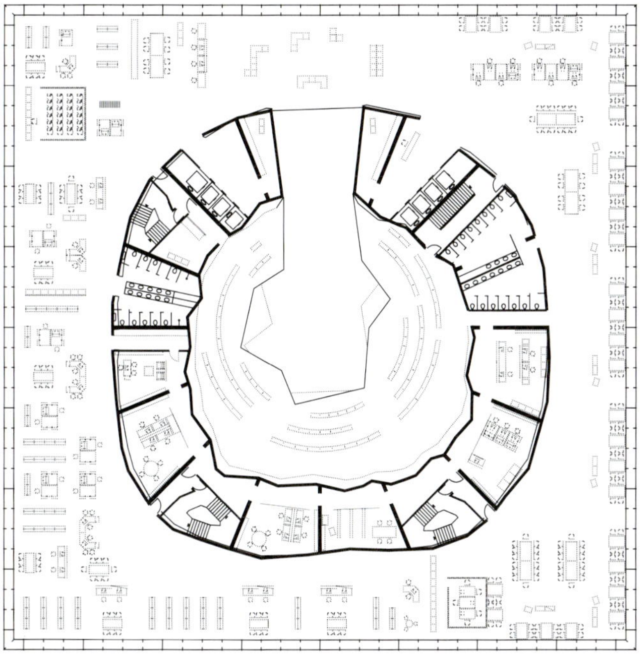

First floor plan

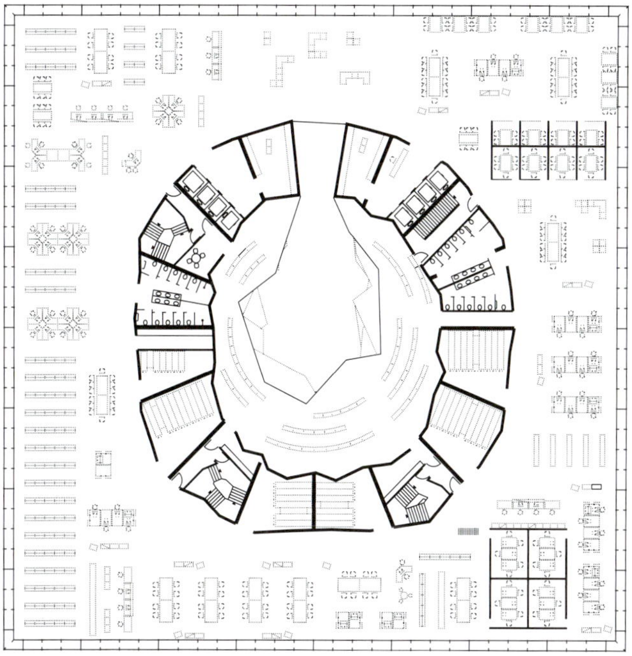

Fourth floor plan

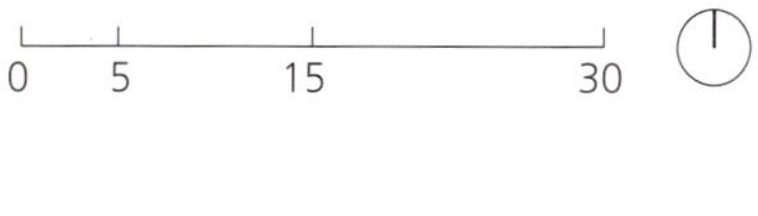

São Bartolomeu

Salvador, Bahia, 2008

The São Bartolomeu project has the purpose of conducting re-urbanization actions to give an entire community, currently living in a precarious and unhealthy situation, decent housing conditions. Due to their occupation of a mangrove area, the area has a high risk of flood, and the community is deprived of public services and facilities for collective use.

Located near the mouth of the Cobre River in Enseada do Cabrito, the entire area received urbanization interventions that placed the area's houses and facilities above the 2,5m high-water mark, for the safety of the residents and to permit the ensuing recovery of the mangrove swamp, one of the last remnants of the biome in the city of Salvador. 374 buildings were demolished and 360 new homes were constructed in two-story buildings. A daycare and a commercial center were also built, as was the São Bartolomeu Reference Center, which functions as entryway and shelter for regulars and visitors of the São Bartolomeu Park, an environmental protection area and a sort of sanctuary of *candomblé* in Bahia.

The project eliminated all constructions below the 2,5 meters high-water mark and performed necessary maintenance in the rest of the 262 buildings that were already on higher ground. Further, it modified the existing structure of occupation, with the purpose of regenerating the urban fabric through a new design for streetways, accesses, passageways, ladders, ramps, vegetation, public lighting etc. Besides liberating the flood areas for swamp rejuvenation, the new two-story apartment homes provide greater density to the ensemble.

The São Bartolomeu Reference Center stands out in the landscape with two great roof pitches covering the entire unit, which is built at street level. We used low-cost materials and conventional technology: Concrete block walls, reinforced concrete slabs, ladders, walkways, terraces, a wooden roof structure of eucalyptus, and thermoacoustic metal tiles. In the manner of a large *oca*,[1] the Reference Center will hold the activities of a multipurpose community center, a citizenship education program, and studies of Afro-Bahian traditions, especially *candomblé*.

The daycare, set on higher grounds, occupies the slope of the hill. With a view of the sea and flanked by vegetation, it was built with the same materials and in shapes identical to the Reference Center.

Note

1. T.N.: Typical Brazilian indigenous housing.

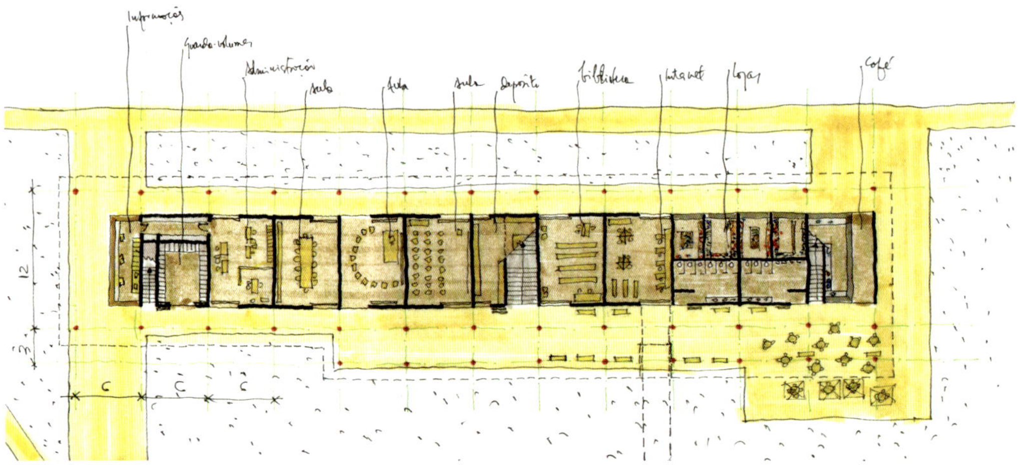

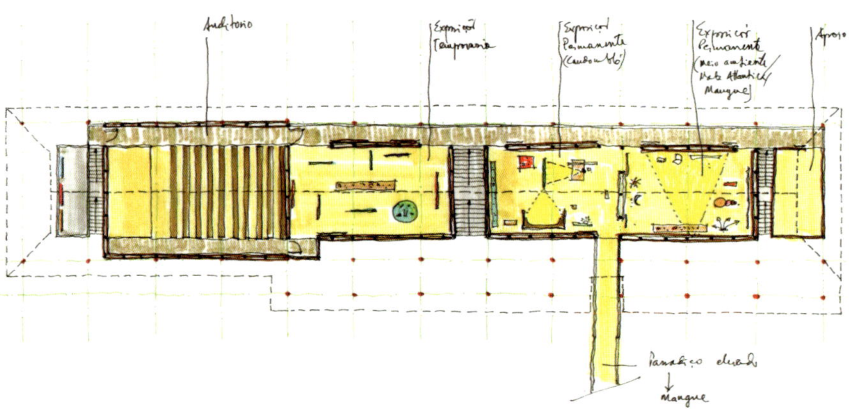

São Bartolomeu Reference Center, plans, perspective and view of the building

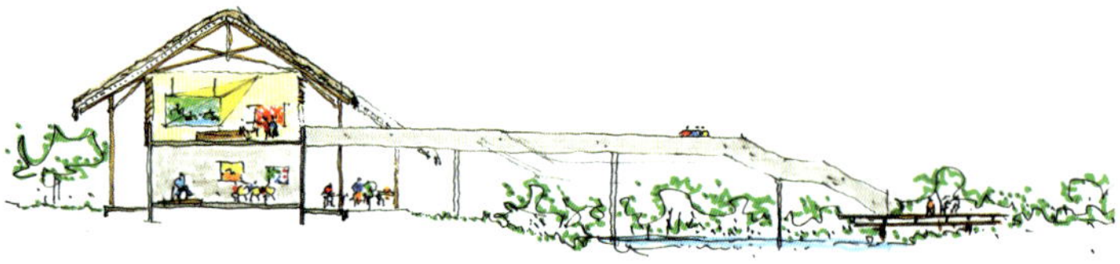

Top, Reference Center, perspective and sections; bottom, Daycare

Residences ensemble, view, perspective and model

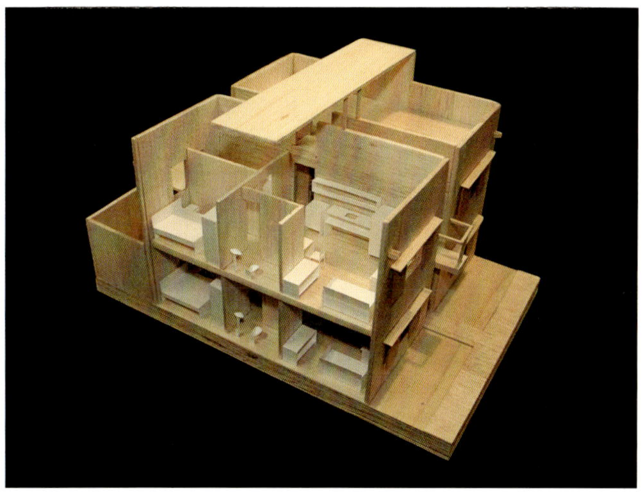

Igatu Museum

Igatu, Bahia, 2008

From the bowels of the overturned stones in the village of Igatu, its Reference and Memory Center will be born, at the entrance of the city's historical park. In the Museum, the history of the place will be restored and kept, from the rise and fall of the diamond panning activity to the decay and abandonment of the place, the gamble and chance of many adventurers.

It will constitute more than a museum. It will be a living center on which the local traces and customs of the people who lived there and who still do serve as themes. Among these traces of local culture are their oral history, the organization of daily life, the dialogue posed by the exuberant surrounding nature, the local cuisine, the hand and stage crafts, and the creations that point towards the future. It will be, above all else, a place to gather residents, visitors, and tourists, in a sharing experience of distinct time lines and frames, past and future; of objects, as shards of memory along the gravel roads; sharing of life amid the water and the stone, between the native rock and the built stonework – the concrete.

The place chosen for the Igatu Reference and Memory Center, right at the entrance of the park, is a kind of basin, embedded in the hillside of the old power plant, now abandoned.

In a contemporary language, one might say that the new ensemble of buildings (which will house exhibits, gatherings, coffeehouse, and auditorium) seeks to create tension and harmony with the natural landscape, as if on a musical piece. It seeks, in its integrity and in every detail of it, to pose a dialogue between the human and the natural order.

Thus, on arrival, a long concrete bridge will lead us to the other side of the basin. At the end of this crossing, we shall be greeted by a circular concrete column, which will converse with other four squared pillars, carved out of a single solid stone, with capitals of stone as well, all of them supporting the lightest of slabs, a real tent to shelter the visitor from the sun and rain. It will also constitute a unique belvedere, with the loveliest view of the Paraguassu Valley.

These columns will be carved from the pink stone of Igatu, a material that will also be used in the composition of the concrete and, so, transformed into *molded stone*.

Still regarding this dialogue, the bridge will cross a water garden of *nymphaea* (water lilies), which will be above the main section of the building, that is, the showroom and the gathering areas. The visitor will be lead to the rock garden, with its boulders, orchids, cacti, and bromeliads. On one side, the geometrical water garden, built and controlled; on the other, the natural garden, unimpeded and rugged.

Concrete and glass, molded stone and ground rock; opacity for the introspection of exhibits and transparency for the surrounding landscape; within and without, taking turns and mixing together; separation and fusion. These are the guiding principles of the architecture of this small ensemble indented in the rocks and undergrowth, principles that seek to fuse content and containment in a genuine and original experience of spatial perception. All senses are in alert and lulled by the magical silence of Xique-Xique de Igatu.

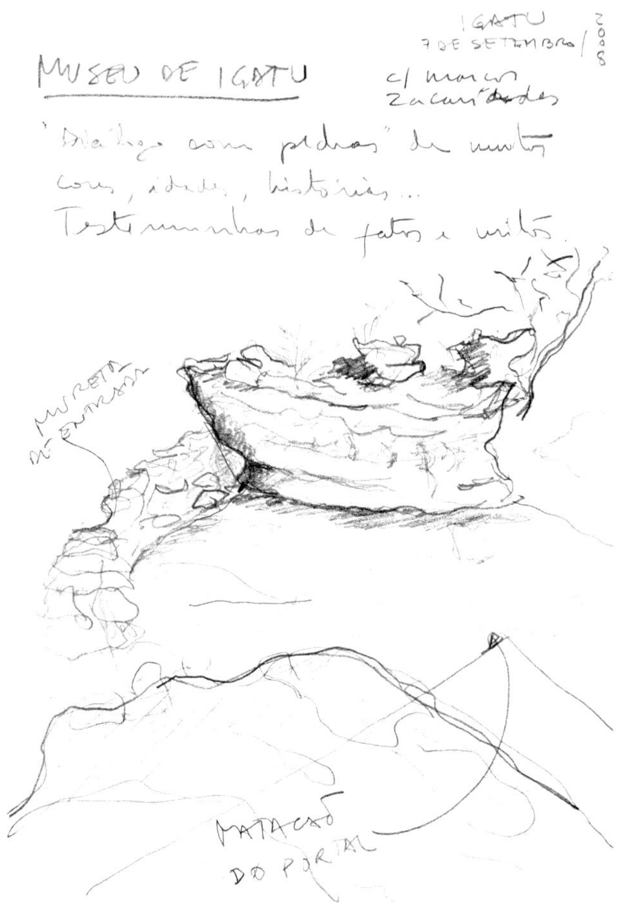

godó de carne com banana
bamburrar cachoeira garimpo
pedra rosa galinha caipira bromélia **água**
chapada **picado de palma** orquídea vento
cachaça caco cerâmico limão-cravo
mato vidro bateia **cascalho** concreto
batata da serra matacão história
jardim rupestre rio Xique-Xique barro
ruína diamante feijão gruna

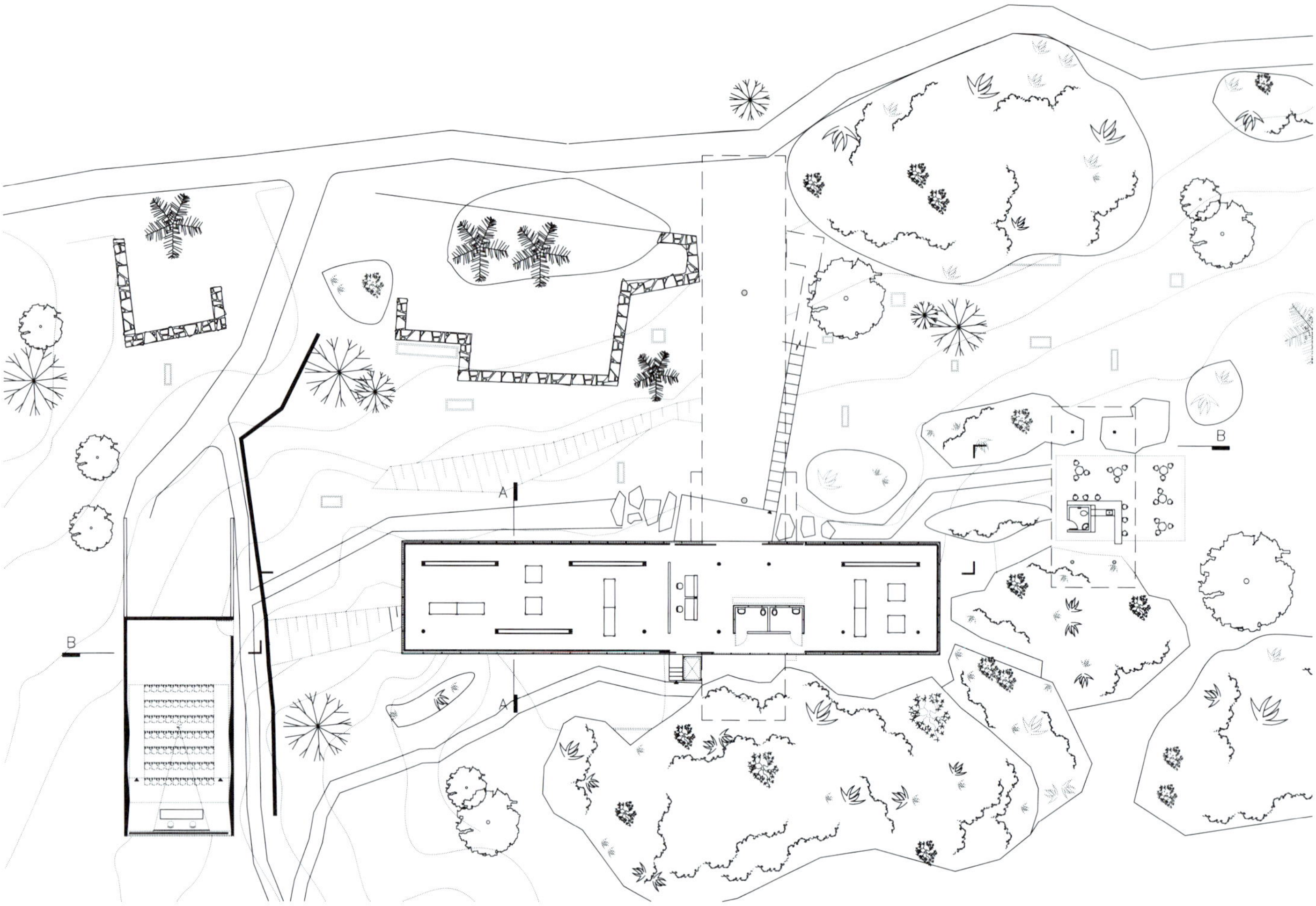

Ground floor plan

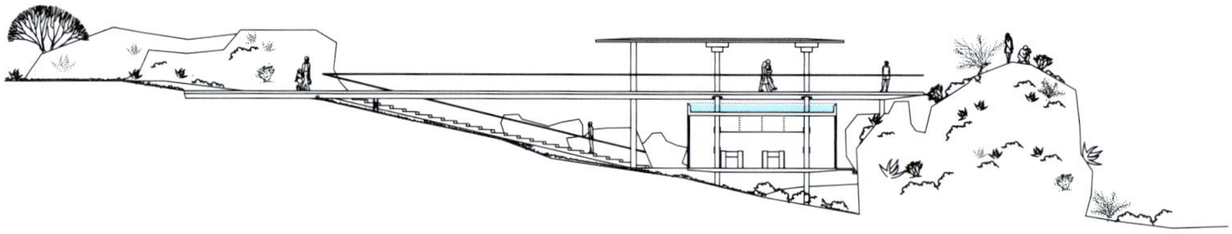
Section AA

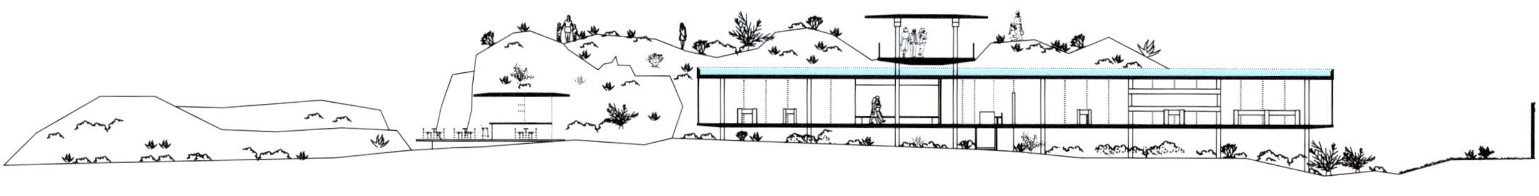
Section BB

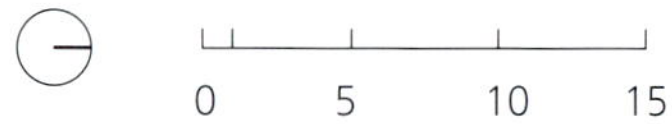

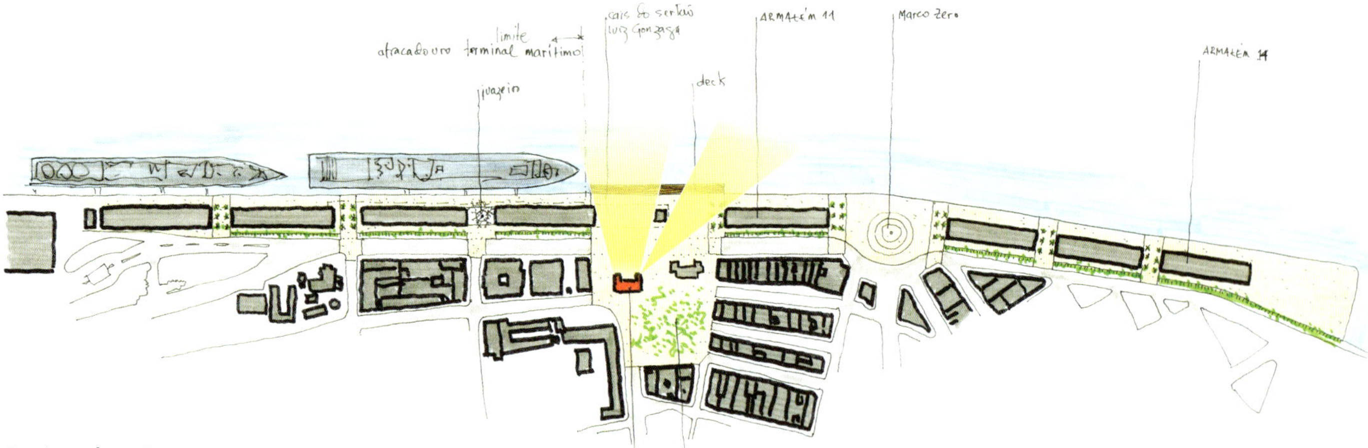

Cais do Sertão

Recife, Pernambuco, 2009

In 2009, the Federal Government decided to build a museum in honor of Luiz Gonzaga. It would display the life and trajectory of this artist, along with his massive body of work, which turned him into one of the most solid pillars of Brazilian Culture. Gonzaga, sometimes called Mestre Lua, inhabits the spirit and the imagination of all Brazilians, even if many of us do not have the clarity to identify his influence.

Anthropologist Antonio Risério, who wrote the foundational text of the museum, appointed our firm, and we were commissioned to design the project by the Ministry of Culture. We assembled a multidisciplinary team so we could, from the get-go, think architecture and content as a unity. We wanted to think about the spaces and the sensations to be created in the visitor, about the information to be conveyed, and in the experiences to be shared in the museum. For its construction, the government of the state of Pernambuco assigned the location at a warehouse in the old Recife harbor and a large adjoining area. It was an area by the seaside, in the historic island where the city was born, near ground zero.

As we delved into the work of Gonzaga, we came upon the obvious: Nobody sang of *sertão*[1] better than him. There is not a single aspect of life in *sertão* that has been left out of his almost seven hundred songs, true gems of Brazilian music. We decided that the museum should, as it sang Luiz Gonzaga, sing about sertão as well and, conversely, tell the story of the genius creator who sang sertão. As it was no longer a museum in sole honor of the musician, it should bring the sertão to the seaside, a move that would open our eyes to a fantastic universe of possibilities, at once, rich and poor, tragic and festive, violent and poetic, a universe inhabited by the great population of this vast territory called *sertão*.

And so, Cais do Sertão Luiz Gonzaga was born. In consonance with the urban planning guidelines of the state of Pernambuco and of the city of Recife to keep the old warehouses of the port intact, giving them new use classes, we began to develop the project, with the appropriation of one of those warehouses (2.500 square meters) and the creation of a new building (5.000 square meters) connected to it. We attempted to preserve the elongated structure of the port buildings to house the entire program of the museum.

The functions of a museum per se were installed in the old warehouse, inaugurated in 2014, with a long-term exhibit in honor of Luiz Gonzaga and the *sertanejo* world. The new building, inaugurated in 2018, holds an auditorium with three hundred seats, showrooms for temporary exhibits and courses, collection storage, library, and a traditional *sertanejo* restaurant on the roof garden. From there, one can see the old Recife town, on one side, and the sea and the great reef, on the other.

We employed ocher yellow pigmented concrete in this new building, a reference to the desiccated soil of *sertão*. We designed a great gap of approximately 65 meters, with a structure of prestressed concrete, right in front of the Malakoff Tower, to create a large covered plaza, a shelter from the hard sun and many raining spells of the city. This covered plaza functions as an urban veranda, allowing for a great number of usages.

However, the most important architectural element of the project is the giant *cobogó*,[2] created especially for this project. It is fitting to use such designs in Recife, the city where *cobogó* was created. The device softens the distinction of inner and outer spaces: A filter of light for the inside and a sweet and smooth façade for the outside. The giant *cobogó* is formed by 2.100 pieces of 1m x 1m, weighting 140 kilos each, with a pattern that references the deciduous trees of caatinga or the desiccation cracks on the ground, so common in *sertão*. Other interpretations are, of course, possible. Either way, it constitutes a white lace over the yellowed concrete.

If we had to summarize in a nutshell what Cais do Sertão Luiz Gonzaga is, we would say that it constitutes the dialogue between technique and poetics, high-tech and low-tech. It is the encounter of a rich and rigorous content with the possibility of free interpretation and enjoyment. It is, at last, a place for aesthetic fruition: *Sertão* by the seaside.

Note

1. T.N.: Very generally explained, the term refers to harsh, dry regions, away from urban centers and large cultivated lands.
2. T.N.: Hollow element, usually made of cement, which completes walls to allow greater ventilation and brightness inside buildings

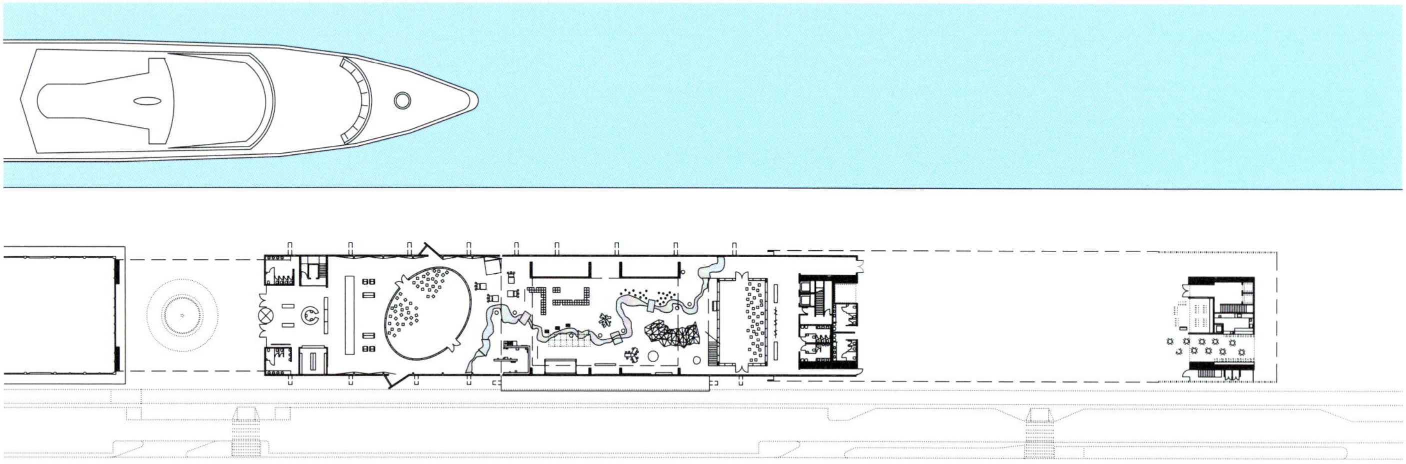

Ground floor plan
(plaza, reception and exhibition)

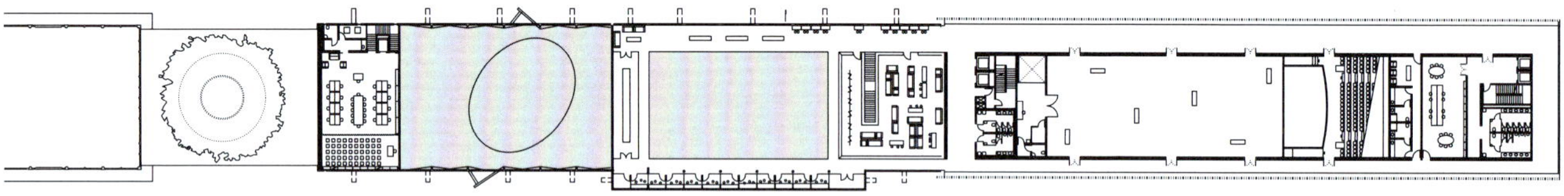

First floor plan
(administration, exhibition and auditorium)

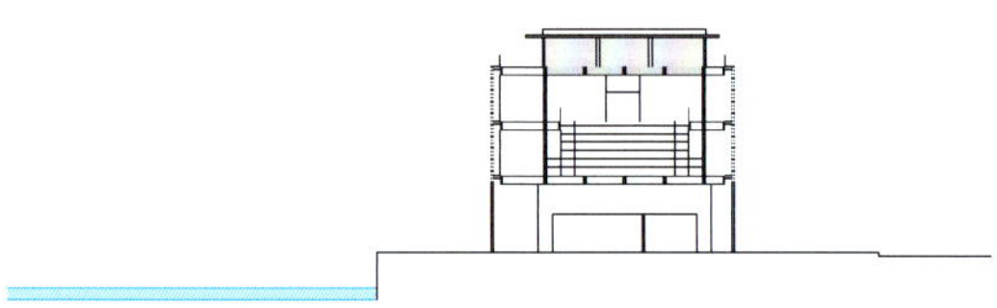

Transversal section

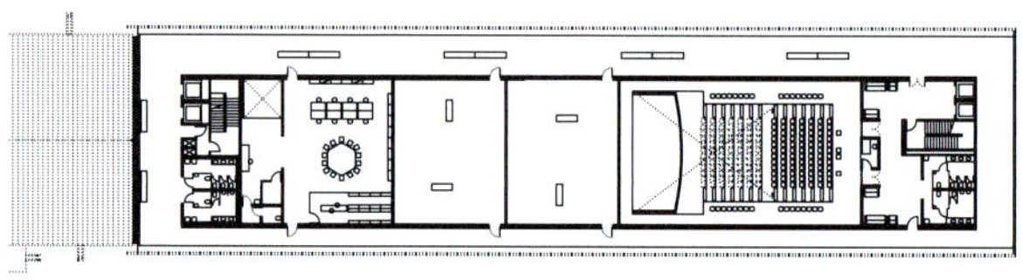

Second floor plan
(auditorium, library and technical reserve)

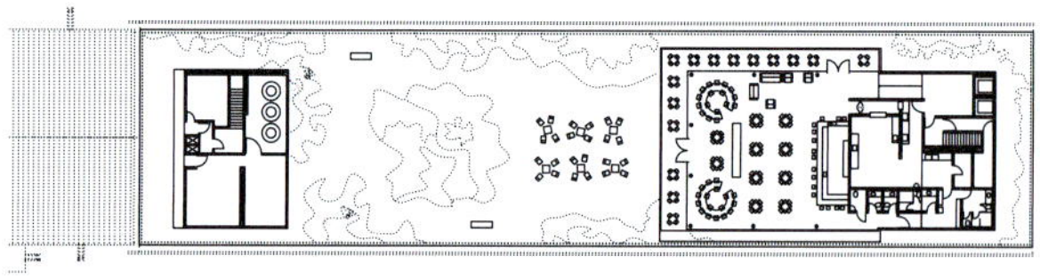

Third floor plan
(rooftop, restaurant)

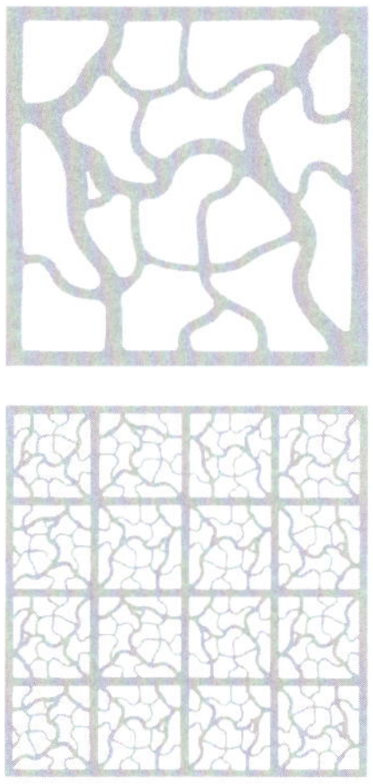

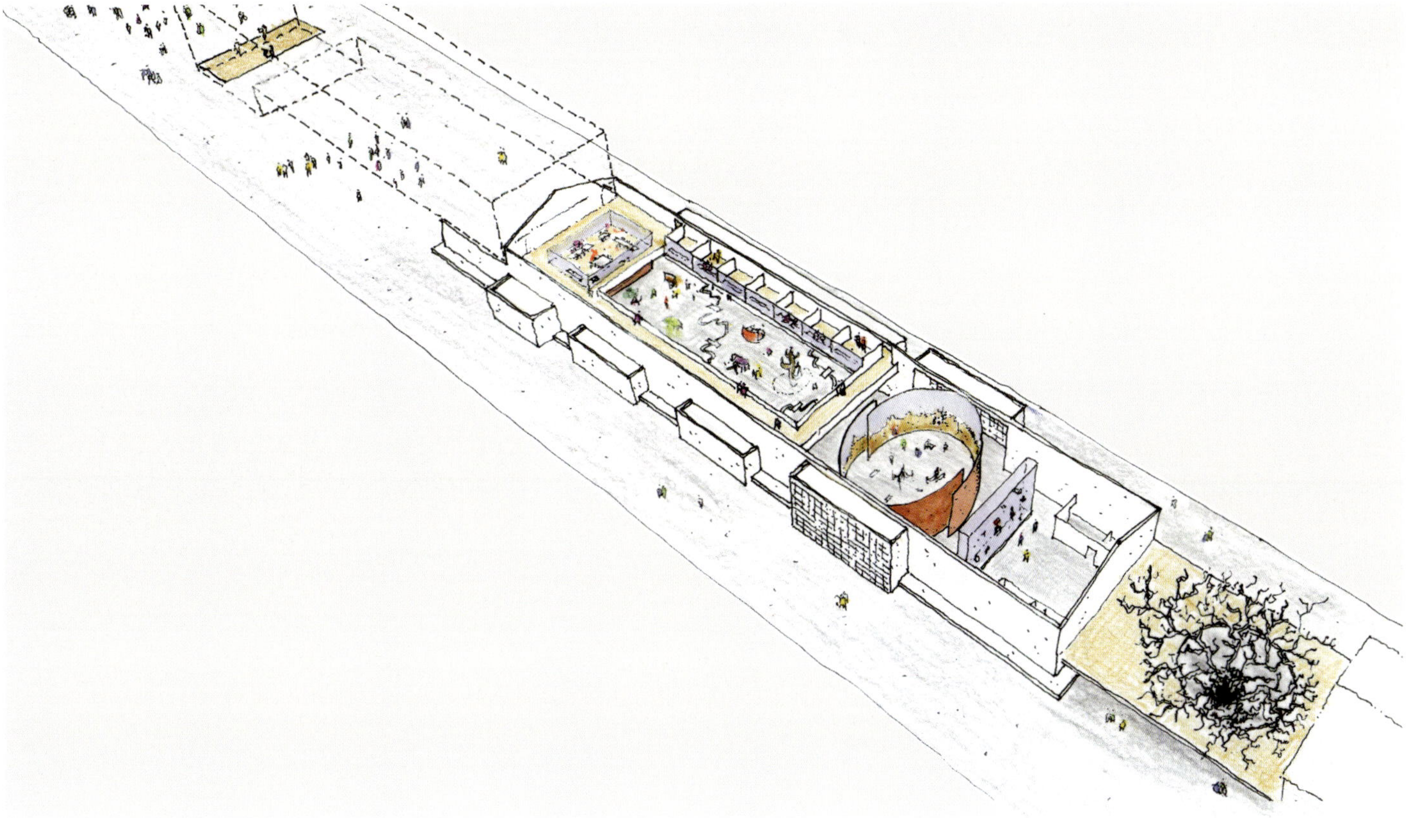

Auditorium, acoustic coating with traditional white lace

SERTÃO

Museum installations at the interior

VI
VER
O
CU
P

Museum of Image and Sound of Rio de Janeiro – MIS RJ

Rio de Janeiro, 2009

The new building of the Museum of Image and Sound – MIS will stand out in the landscape of Rio de Janeiro, by occupying a privileged spot in the postcard scenery of Copacabana. It was designed to display pronounced and hard-hitting architecture, always in dialogue with its surrounding; to be attractive and accessible to all.

As a way of integrating to an already settled landscape, the MIS building should respect the prevailing structural height of buildings across the seafront. As a democratic museum, it will open its doors to the boardwalk in a frank and honest way, inviting everyone to share on a new and exciting experience inside.

The museum will be a seven-story building in white self-cleaning concrete. A large rift (or gap) will tear its façade from top to bottom, posing a dialogue with the beach, the sky, the hills, the Atlantic Ocean. This will be its front, an intriguing image that should invite the passerby to come unravel its content: As in the caverns, the fascination of the unknown and the search for wonderment and new experiences – the eternal attraction to what is inside and cannot be seen.

Once inside the building, the visitor will not only get to know the contents displayed in the museum, but he/she will also enjoy the winding view of the gap, with several possible frames of the landscape outside, as it varies also in rain, sun, and moonshine... This tour will have its climax on the gazebo terrace, where visitors will uncover all of Copacabana, surrounded by the magnificent natural vistas of Rio de Janeiro.

When accessing the ground floor, one shall be facing a large hole, or rather a sequence of holes piercing all the slabs; holes of various dimensions, free and anomalous forms, which will enact the internal visual communication between all floors and allow an immediate understanding of the inner workings of the museum.

The building will have an extremely rational and simple structural system: Ribbed slabs supported by thick peripheral walls. The lateral setback of the ground floor will be used as a forward esplanade for the bar/café and also as a public passageway from Atlântica Avenue to Aires de Saldanha Street. Therefore, if the building is integrated to the Copacabana landscape, on the one hand, by leveling its building height; on the other hand, it reinforces the fluidity of pedestrian circulation, with accessibility, kindness, and urban comfort.

Over the passageway, as if it were a floating object, a shining steel sphere will house the multiple projection auditorium. It will constitute a new urban sculpture, another intriguing image in the waterfront of Copacabana, and also a mirror to one of the most beautiful landscapes of this marvelous city.

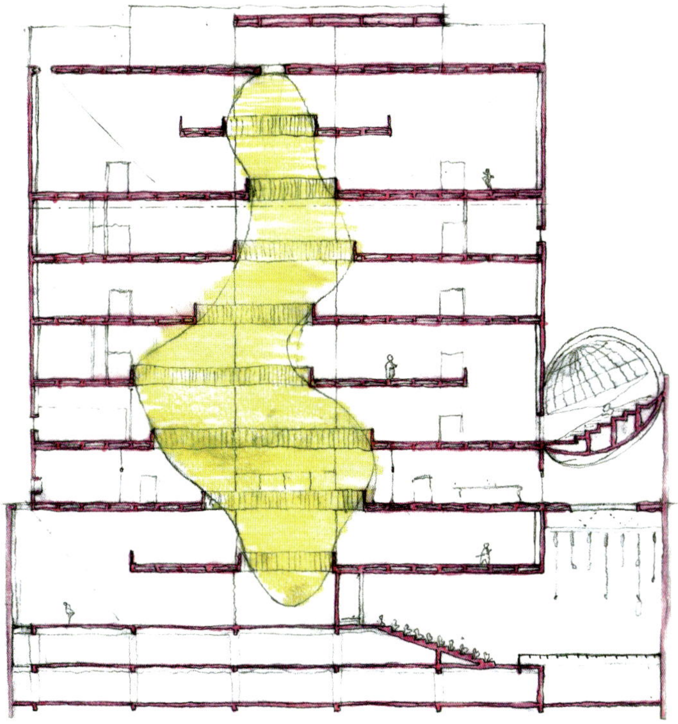

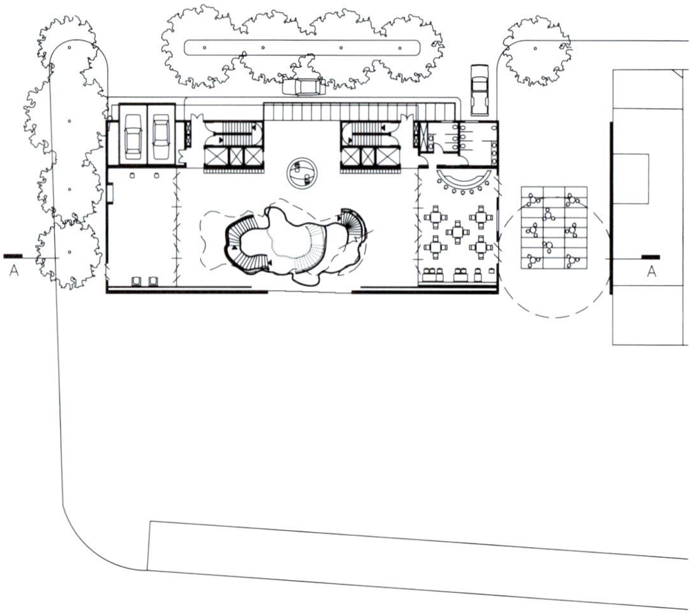

Ground floor plan

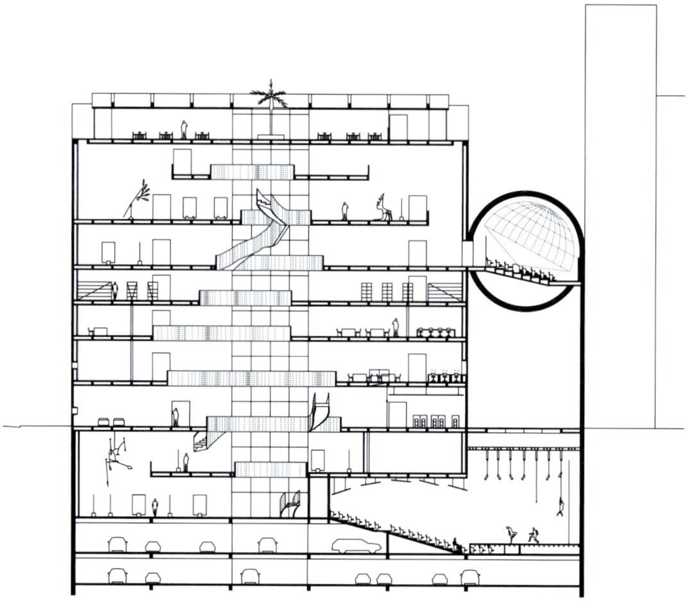

Section AA

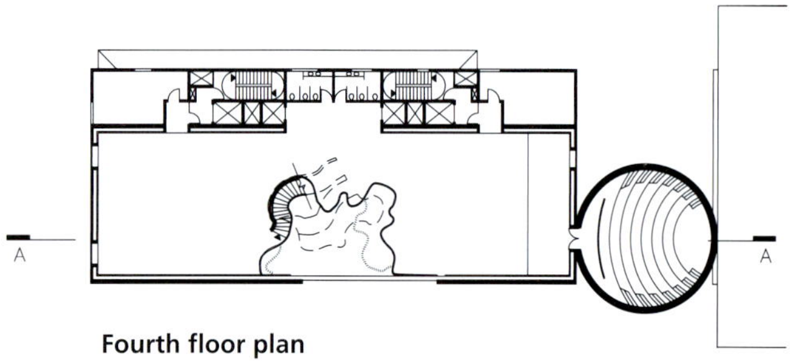

Fourth floor plan

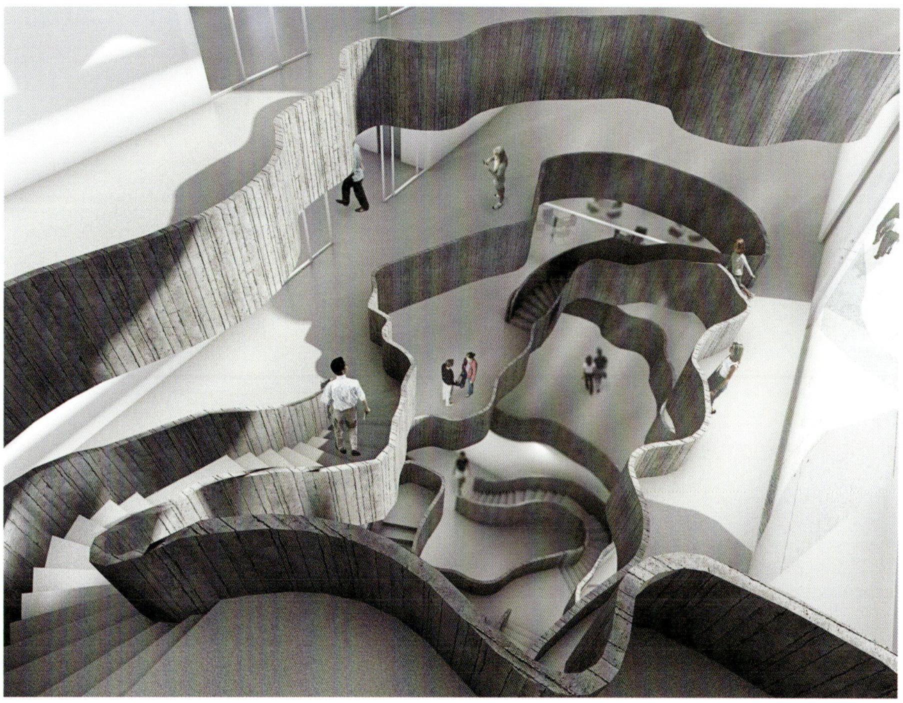

Central Mill Theater

Piracicaba, São Paulo, 2009

Few Brazilian cities have a healthy and respectful relationship with their rivers: Piracicaba is one of them. The Piracicaba River slithers across the center of town with multiple free, public areas on its margins. These spaces work as recesses and they allow for the possibility of developing an exemplary intervention to affect lives and the general urban comfort. All of this is, partly, due to historical or contingent factors. Such is the case of the Central Mill, an old sugar and alcohol industry building located near the banks of the river. It was deactivated in the 1970s and received the title of municipal and state historical heritage. Later, it was expropriated by the government and it became a part of the local inhabitants' life as an important culture and leisure center.

The Central Mill sits on the right banks of the Piracicaba River, very close to the urban center of town. Its buildings of red exposed brick offer an impressive view for passersby walking along the other side of the river. The running waters, after a series of rafters, return to a calmer nature and mirror the lights coming from the mill: A singular scenery of urban landscape.

The ensemble maintains the integrity it had when it was deactivated, resisting the great changes that came about its surroundings. However, the mill was not constructed as it is now. During its lifetime, it was subjected to several additions, renovations, demolitions, at various times. In the process, beautiful things were lost and others were incorporated to give form to what perhaps constitutes its best feature: The citadel.

The Central Mill ensemble is one of the largest and most important architectural evidences of the means of production of sugar and alcohol that were at work from mid-19th century until mid-20th century. Very little of its machinery was left, but the numberless and varied structures are there. And the most important aspect of this legacy is precisely the relation it is stablished among these various structures, which help us unravel the logic of production and its transformation throughout the hundred-year life span of the mill, an artefact of industrial urbanism. The entire structure of the mill is composed of industrial warehouses and several other buildings in varied scales, almost all of them in exposed brick – a universal language of industry in the 19th century.

In 2002, together with a group of collaborators from Piracicaba, we developed a master plan for the entire area of the Central Mill. This plan was intended to set the course and guide future interventions that were made there. In one of the oldest and most beautiful of all the warehouses, we designed the Erotides de Campos Theater (Teatro do Engenho Central). The theater is constituted by an architectural gesture that starts from the interior of the building and transforms its hollows into several devices: A public hall, acoustically equipped rooms, audience, stage, galleries, a bar/restaurant, rehearsal rooms, dressing rooms, and technical support rooms. That is, everything that a contemporary theater requires to function to its fullest.

The theater features an expanded stage with the possibility of opening a second view for the audience, since the arena also opens out onto the central plaza – the heart of the entire ensemble. It constitutes an important promotion and support device, especially for outdoor celebrations and events. The result is a contemporary multipurpose venue that is also invested in the history of the place. Yes, the old warehouse served as storage for giant casks and an alcohol distillery. This memory is impressed in the industrial dimensions of its roof height, in the great central gap, and in the materials employed in the construction – brick, clay roof tiles, beams of steel and concrete. All of it makes a great impression on the visitor and leads us to reflect upon these human artifacts built long ago. In this case, an ancient working site of arduous labor, the suffering of many, but a testimony of human toil that was transformed into a factory of entertainment, creation, celebration, and coexistence, without erasing its early life.

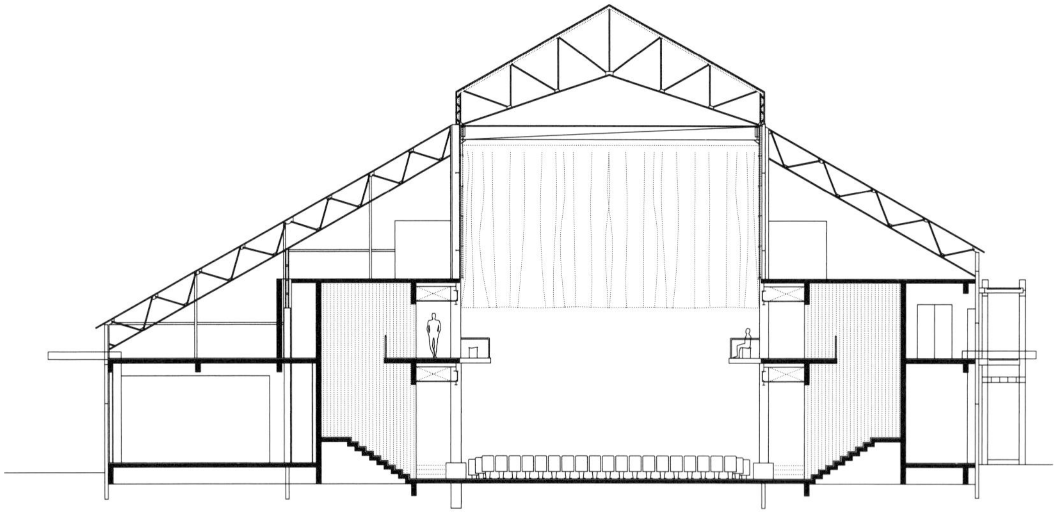

Section AA

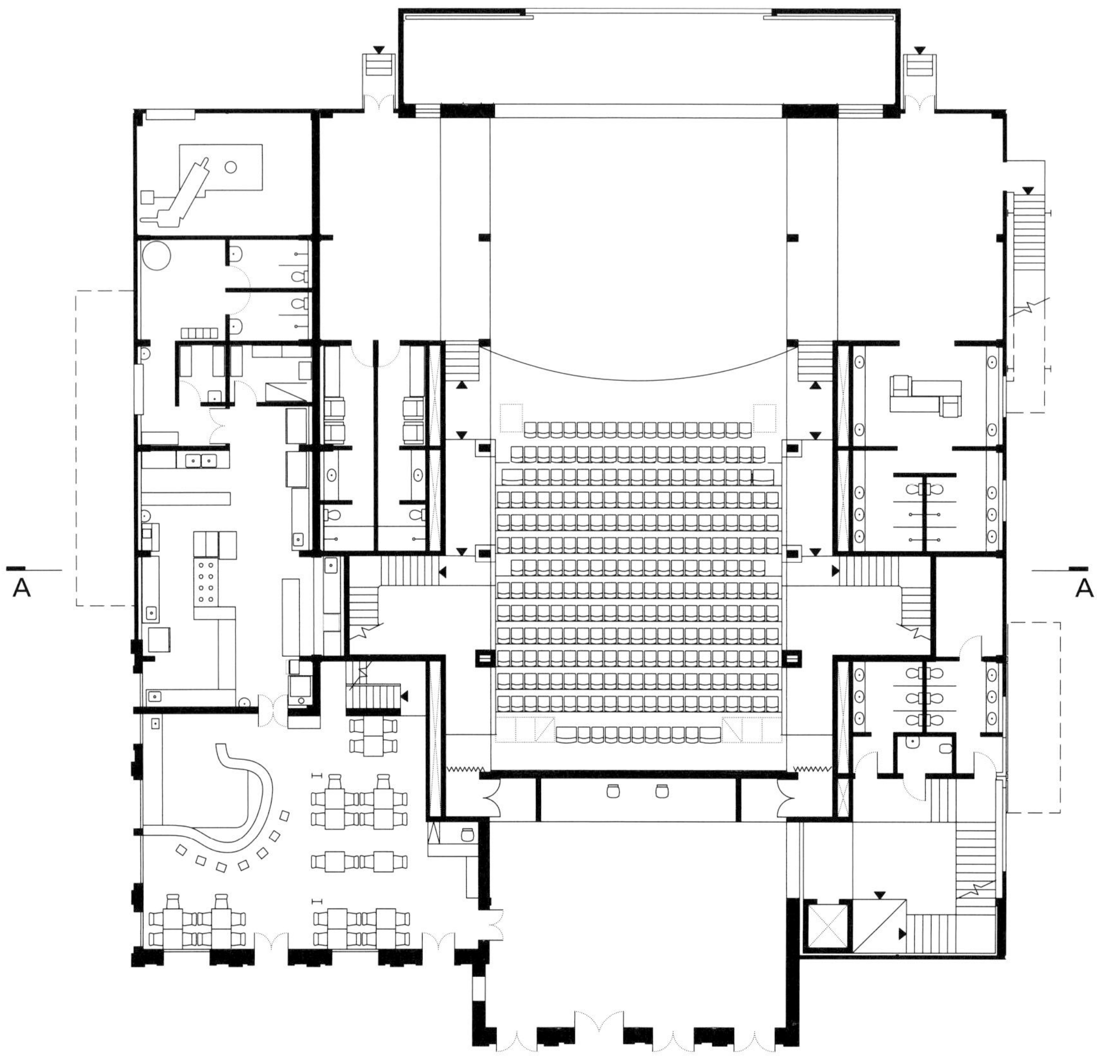

Ground floor plan

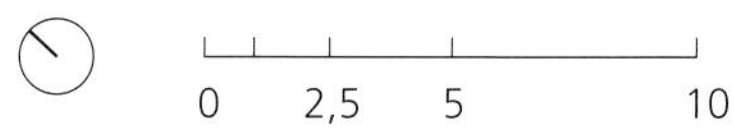

Cidade Baixa

with Roberto Pinho, Maurício Chagas, Alexandre Prisco, Nivaldo Andrade, Sergio Ekerman, and Marcio Targa

Salvador, Bahia, 2009

We can assert, with a good degree of certainty, that, from the 1960s until now, our great cities have grown uncontrollably and deteriorated much, whether it was in the functions of public areas or in the necessary comforts of gregarious life. Ultimately, we have regressed in urbanity.

As a paradox, the cities never stopped symbolizing the hope of a better life, with work, education, and future for the youth. They have taken in wave after wave of migrants from the fields and smaller communities.

Yet, reality hits hard: This uncontrolled growth is a symptom of a perversity ingrained in the relations of power and land property. This swelling, allied with ignorance and vested interests in the management of urban space, has transformed the city; it went from a heavenly promise to a hellish reality of violence and tragedy.

We have a large debt to be paid if we still believe in the possibility of a life in full citizenship. The tecno-burocratic master plans designed in the last few decades have been ignored by an absolute lack of political sensibility and an unwillingness to listen, to see, and to propose interventions derived from the observed reality and the necessities of each of the locales in our plural society.

Each city must point to different solutions to its urban problems, based on its own history, physical and human geography, characteristics, and originalities. There is no ready-made plan. However, Salvador, in all its exuberance and acquired know-how, has a lot to teach us. And we should begin from these teachings, from this lesson on how to build cities, in order to deal with any of the current urban problems.

When we were invited to elaborate a master plan for the entire Cidade Baixa (or lower city, in free translation) in Salvador – from Solar do Unhão to Ribeira, encompassing all the Itapagipe Peninsula –, we presented an ambitious project that goes from the water's edge to the top of the frontispiece ridges. The project was presented in a public session, as part of a wider set of operations by the City Hall.

More than an isolated project, it is a city plan that could be summed up in a few major points: Opening the waterfront of the city to the population; creating qualified public spaces with the goal of achieving universal accessibility – both in the physical and in the socioeconomic sense – and urban comfort; restoring the hillside landscape and urbanity, nurturing a stronger image of the city, especially in the frontispiece; designing an efficient system of public transportation that will articulate all the sectors of the Cidade Baixa and stablish new connections to the Cidade Alta (or upper city, in free translation); providing a surplus in housing, with the restoration and occupation of degraded or underused buildings and areas; creating a network of large cultural, sporting, and leisure venues for the population, the so-called social citadels.

It is a viable project. The engine that drives it is the notion of what Salvador has been for the past centuries, up until the 1850s, paired with the design to take this urban and architectural wisdom from our forebears as a mirror and a challenge in our new interventions. This should encourage us to propose new ideas and make decisions.

We believe that an integrated effort of public and private initiatives, along with our civil society, will be able to alter the path of a city that has been mistreated and abused for decades of negligence and abandonment. To paraphrase Antonio Risério, in his brilliant essay about Dorival Caymmi, may the City of Bahia be once more a "utopia of a place."

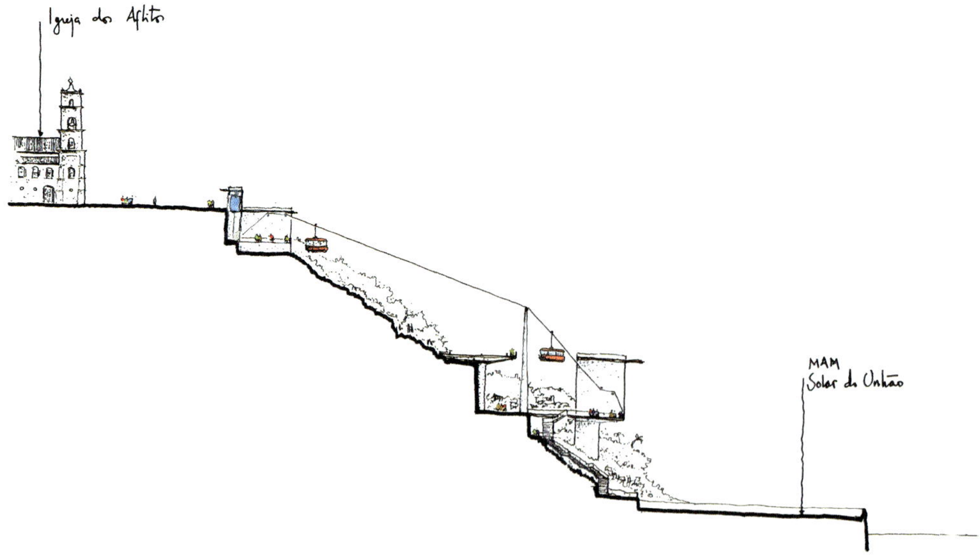
Igreja dos Aflitos
MAM
Solar do Unhão

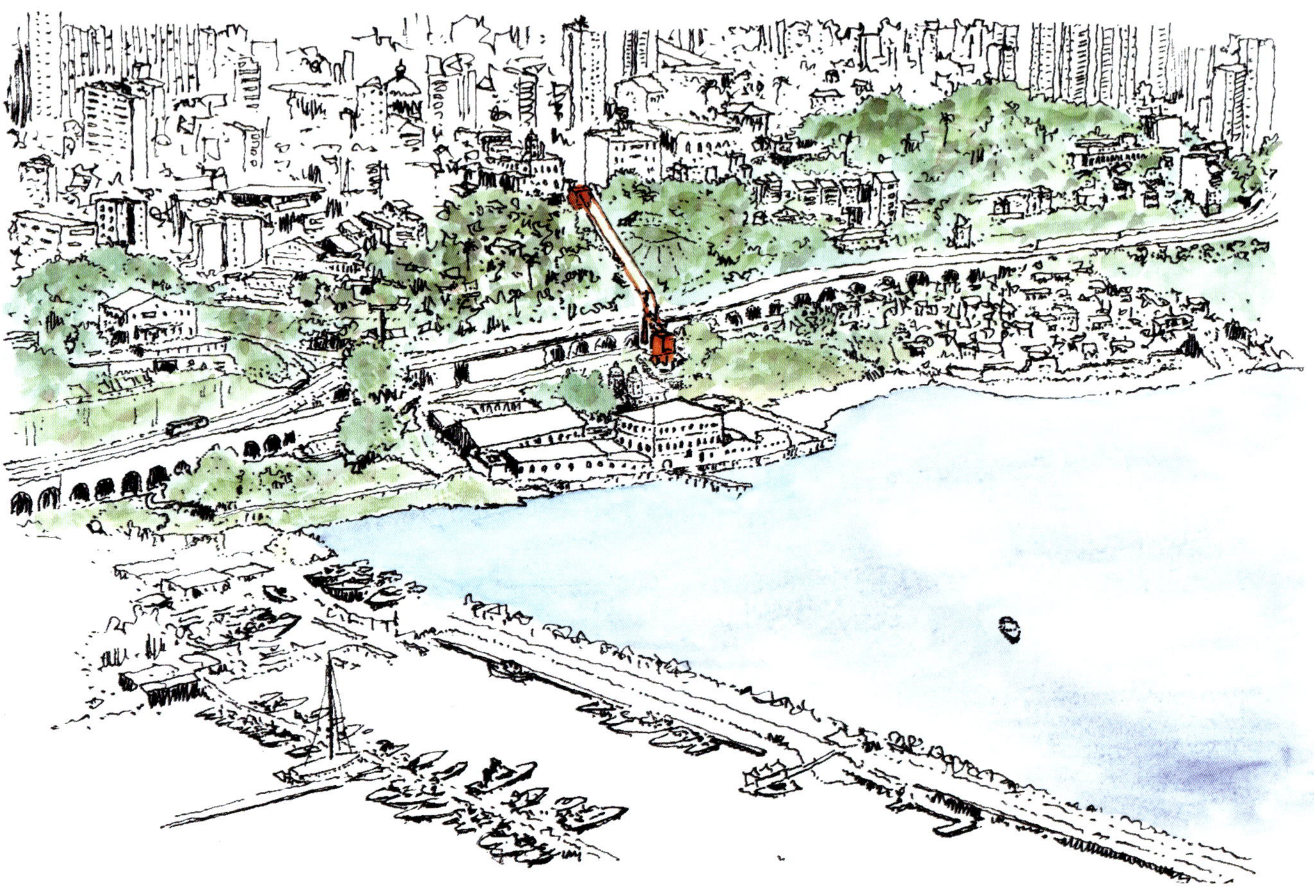

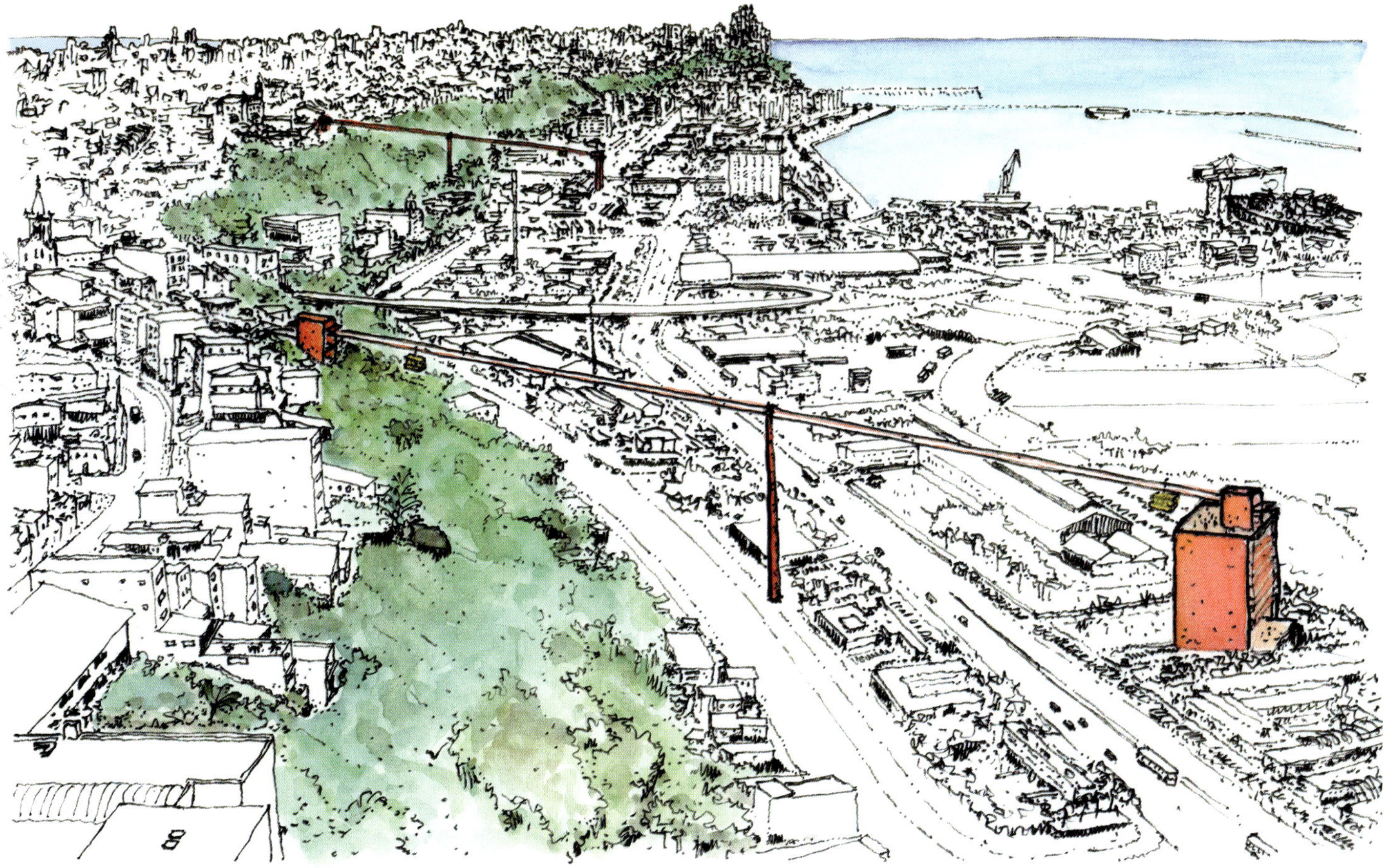

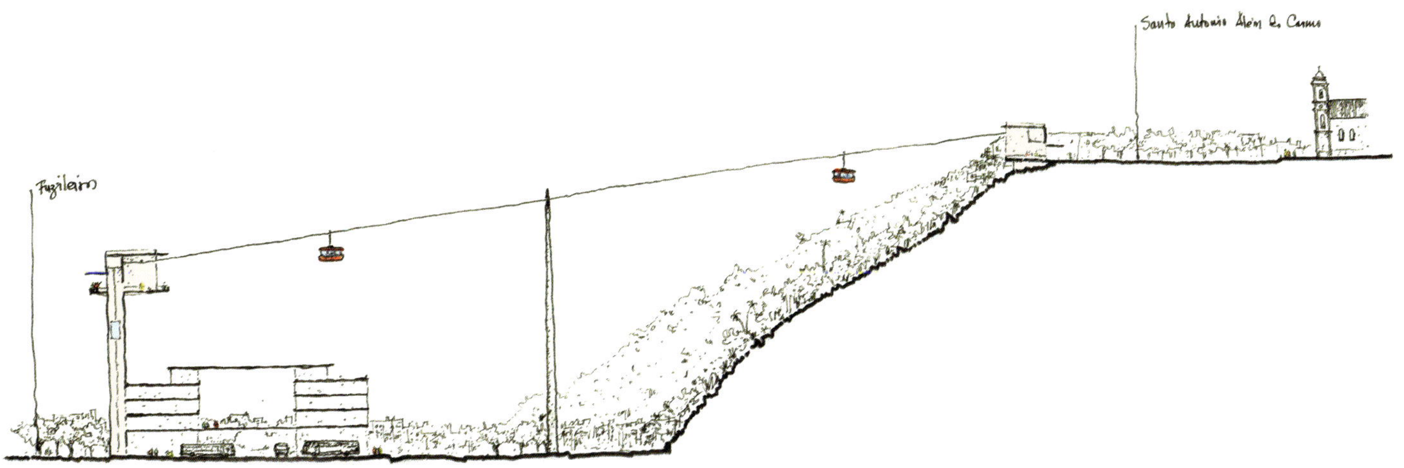
Santo Antonio Além do Carmo
Fuzileiro

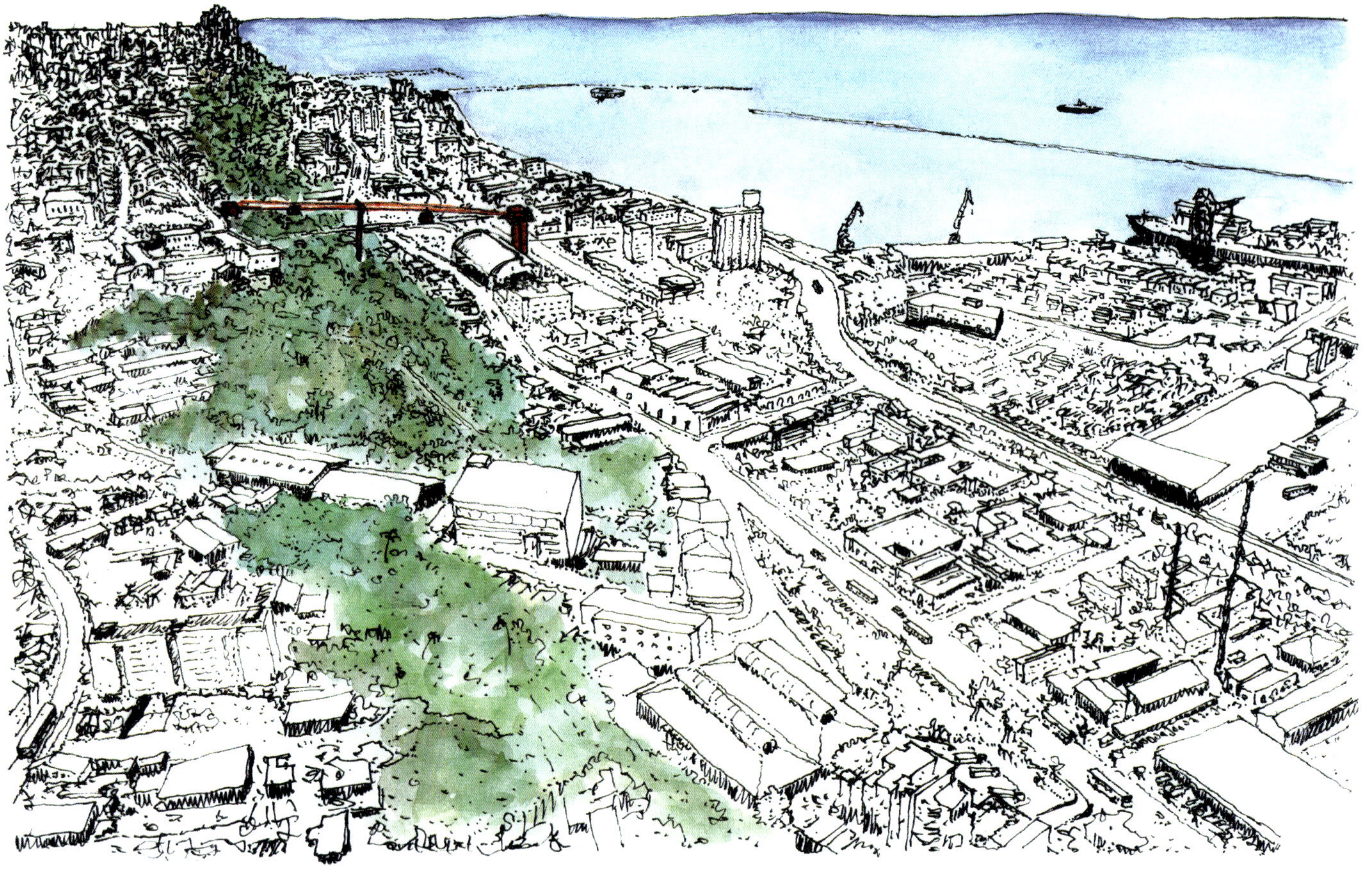

Lapa House

São Paulo, 2009

Set four meters above the street level, in sloping ground, the house was developed in a "U" format around a central squared patio, the epicenter – or core – of all daily activities in the house.

The main floor holds the shared living environments – living room, dining room, kitchen, and studio. These rooms are connected by the patio, but also by a single, long red wall, which defines each room's usage and holds other openings, passageways, reentries, and supporting surfaces, as well, for objects and works of art.

The exposed concrete of the slab, developed from the entrance marquee on the main gate all the way to the studio on the back of the lot, has a unifying presence across all the space. The floor of hydraulic tiles also reinforces this unity.

The upper floor is composed of the bedrooms and a leisure area that extends into the roof garden, with a generous view of the surrounding area.

The system of construction was quite simple: A typical concrete structure and insulation with common whitewashed bricks. Frames of wood and glass, at times fixed, at times with sliding doors, allow ample spaces, giving continuity and integrating the indoor and outdoor sections

803

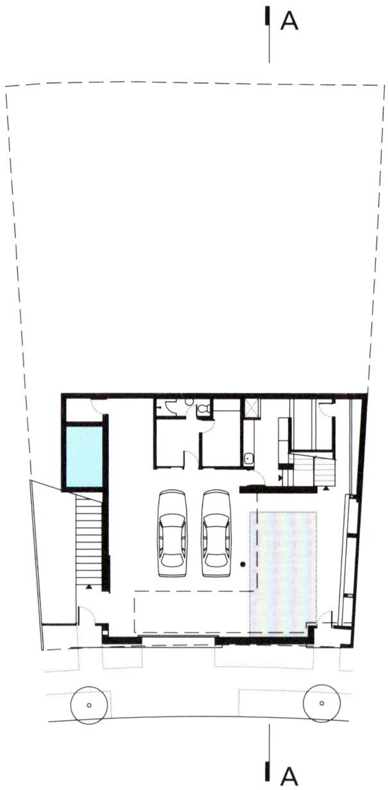

Ground floor plan

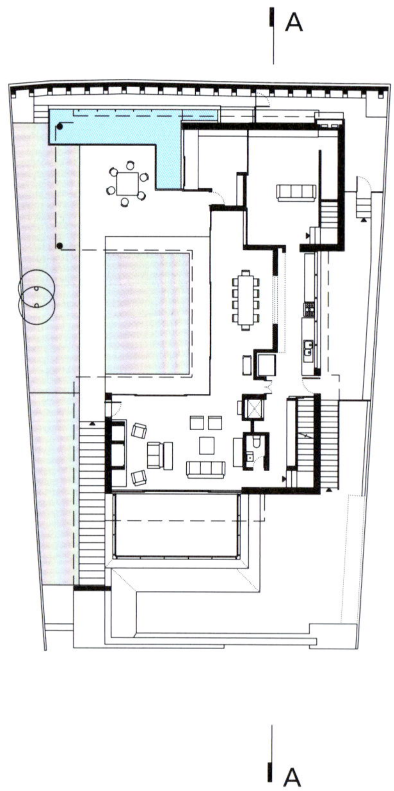

First floor plan

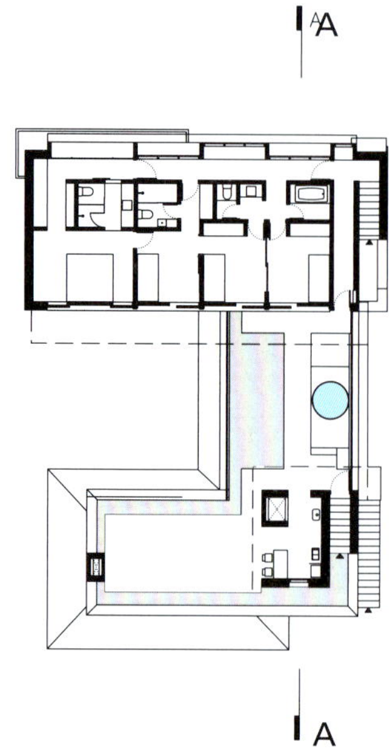

Second floor plan

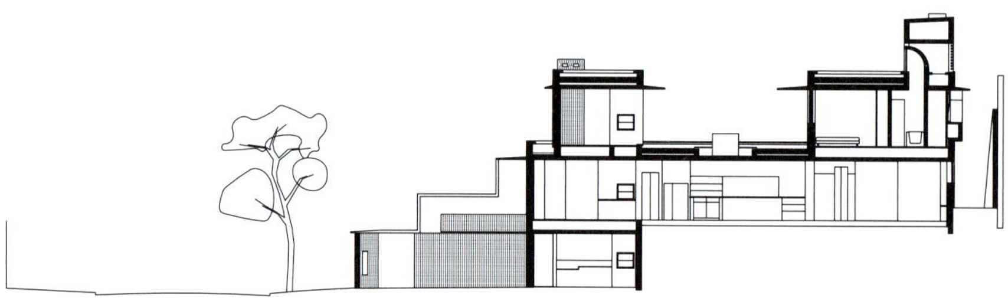

Section AA

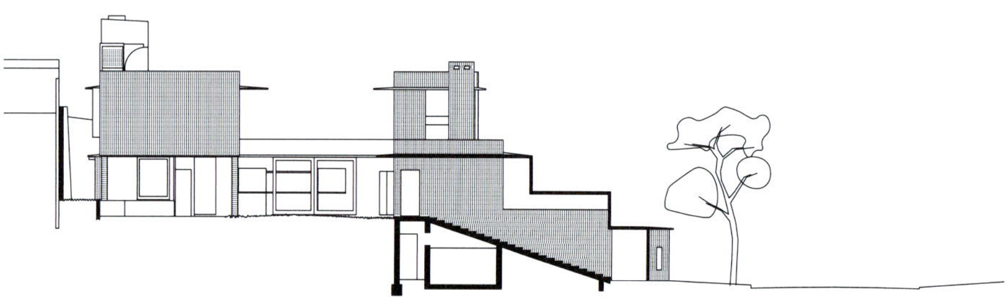

Section BB

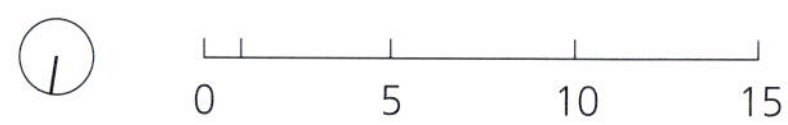

Pampa Museum

Jaguarão, Rio Grande do Sul, 2009

The central theme of the Pampa Museum is the singularity of the physical and human landscape of what is called, in the greater frame of Brazilian culture, the pampa region. It is a museum in which the visitor can experience the specificity and richness of local nature, culture, and history, as well as its importance for the formation of our country.

The museum organizes a vast pool of information gathered around a few main axes. The first of them is the singularity of the natural landscape of the pampa ecosystem. Secondly, the ancient records of the occupation of this land, successively inhabited by different peoples and cultures since pre-historic times. The third aspect is the unique genetic and symbolic crossbreeding that took place in the pampas, a singular mixture of Indigenous, Iberian, and African peoples that resulted in the gaúcho. The specific cultural production that this crossbreeding generated is also part of this axis. Finally, the fourth axis relates to the frontier wars and the formation of a local identity resulting from them.

The space destined for the museum is an old military building dating back to 1883. In a neoclassic style, it was strategically built at Cerro da Pólvora (or gunpowder hill, in free translation). The building, which today is recognized as national historical heritage, was abandoned in the late 1970s and entered into slow decay, until the works of restoration and rehabilitation began and the implantation of the Center of Interpretation of the Pampas (official name of the museum) was under way.

By the quality of the architecture and the loftiness of its grounds, the edifice is a strong landmark in the landscape of Jaguarão. From there, one has a vantage point to peer into neighboring Uruguay. The building is almost a forward sentry, keeping the borders of the pampas. Known as the old infirmary of Jaguarão, the ensemble received its name due to the part it played in the Paraguayan War. In the hardline years of military dictatorship, it also served as a political prison.

The old infirmary building was restored, but it maintained the external aspect of a ruin. The project seeks, precisely, to value this image of abandonment in order to capture the symbolic force that has resonated in the imagination of the community of Jaguarão for nearly forty years.

A contemporary structure of concrete and glass, internal and discreet, within the ensemble, completes the demands of the museum brief with additional areas. Other parts of the old building that had been destroyed were rebuilt in cement, like the walls that define the perfect quadrature of the ensemble or the corner edge of the main structure. These are the new scars time has left, among many others. They amalgamate to tell a story through stone masonry.

The old windows, long gone in time, were not rebuilt. In their stead, corten steel or glass covers were fixated, reinforcing the concept of open gaps in the façade. With the same goal of accentuating the idea of abandonment, the roofs were replaced by flat slabs that gave room to an undergrowth garden to develop with vegetation carried by the wind and the birds. The project is completed by an underground auditorium dug in the basalt rock. The underlying mystery that permeates the history of the place spills over into its new architectural gestures.

Once the work is finalized, we shall gaze at the solemn, *ghostly* outlook of abandonment the landscape outside displays, inviting and intriguing the visitor to discover the contents within. Inside, the finishing touches and comforts of a contemporary museum provide a travel across the pampas, its natural wonders, and its folklore, with the most modern exhibition technologies.

All of these elements and concepts utilized in the restoration of the historic building will promote the transformation and suitability of the ensemble to its new life. A document of the past, ridden with glory, grief, suffering, human stories, and history, will now serve as a tool for the future to be built, primed in coexistence.

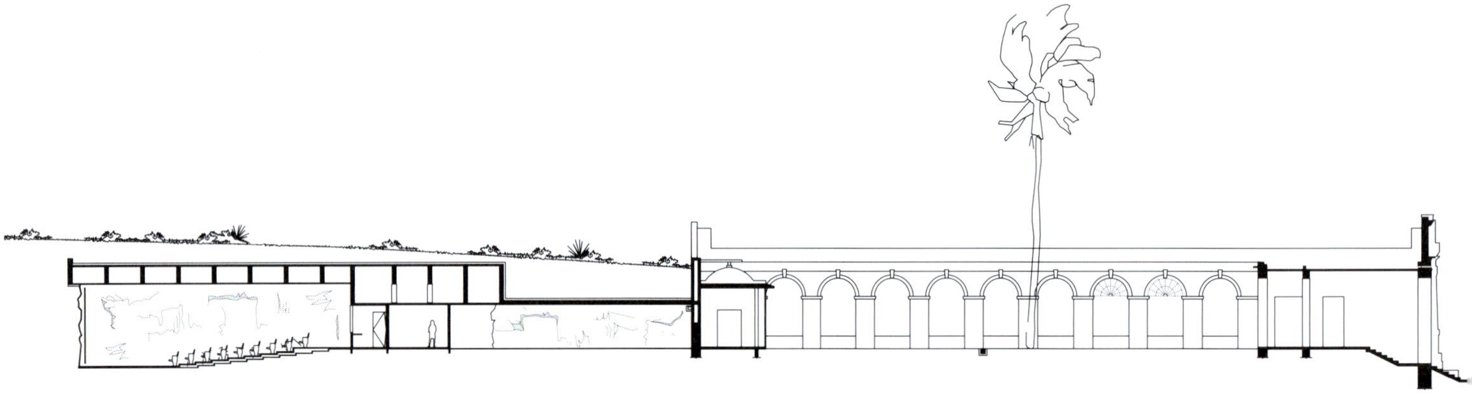

Longitudinal section

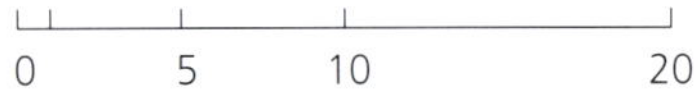

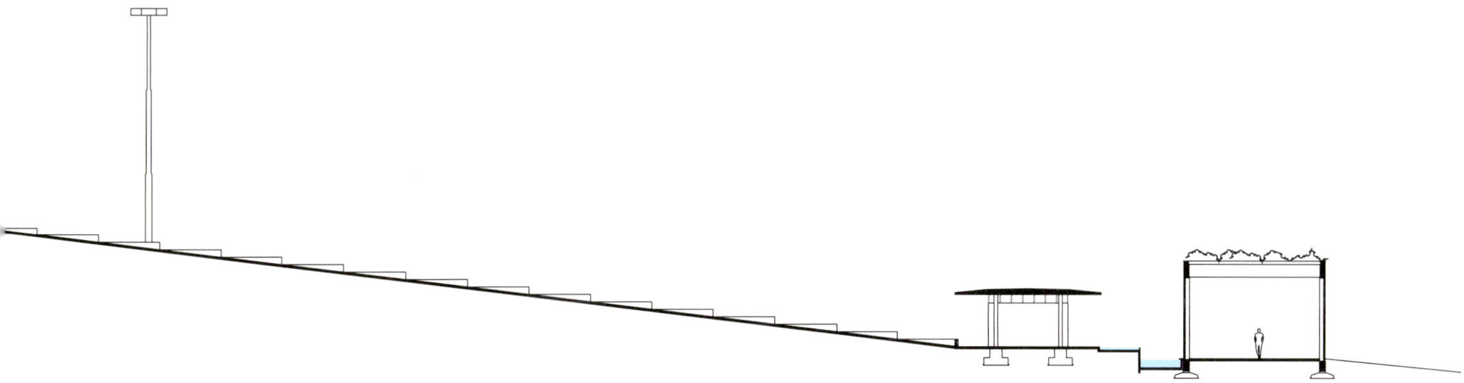

Study for the use of Danúbio Gonçalves' engravings at museum's entrance wall

cabo de relho trotear coxilhas milonga
pelego charque **fronteira** butiá encilha
mate bate-coxa guaipeca minuano
capim-mimoso povoado charrua bagual
chinoca farrapos macela crioulo **trova**
folguedo anu-preto guaiaca querência
história **fortificações** pilcha guaraxaim
pandorga gaudério mondongo piá chiru
meia-lã califórnias farinha de cachorro
cevador tropeiro **guarda do cerrito**
morocha poncho zorillho caturrita cuia
cerro da pólvora **estância** maturrango
ruína quer-quero arroio soga tachã

Auditorium excavated into the rock, study and construction

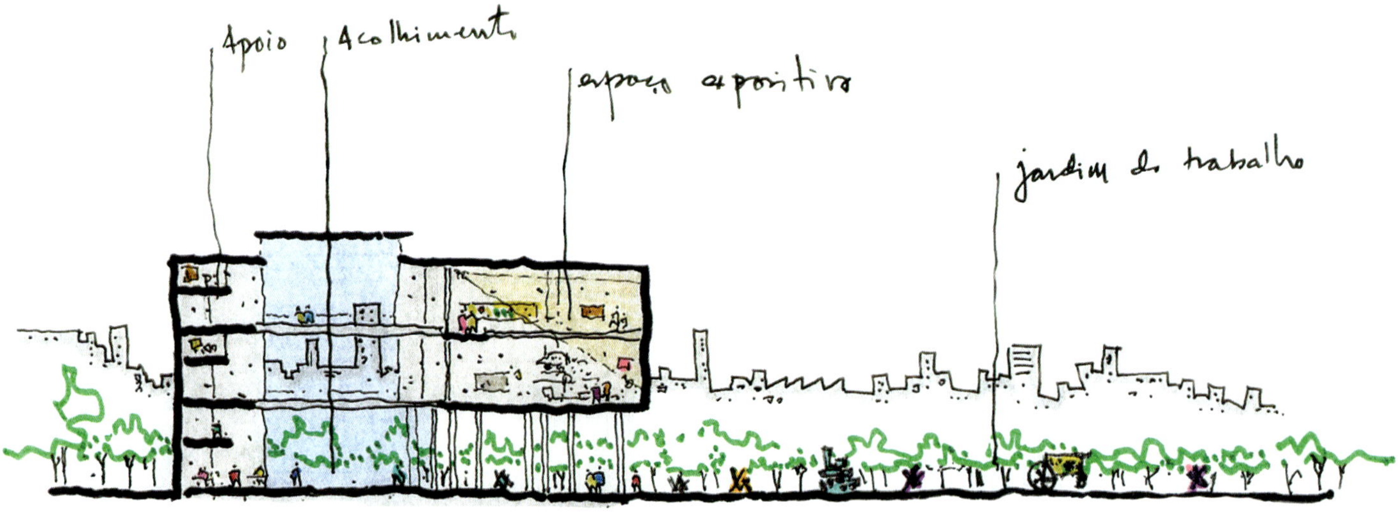

Work and Workers Museum

São Bernardo do Campo, São Paulo, 2010

The Work and Workers Museum was conceived as part of a larger urban planning project for the new downtown area of São Bernardo do Campo. The center of the city displays a modern architectural complex, with large public spaces. The problem we found there was that its design became compromised with accelerated and unplanned development, resulting in a decline of its spatial quality as centrality. The new plan defines new urban references, with the creation of a central park that redefines the road systems of the area, clearing the ground level for pedestrian circulation. The park also stablishes a continuous green space that connects several public facilities. It is there that the Work and Workers Museum inserts itself, in a 10 thousand square meter terrain, originally occupied by the Municipal Market, right next to the City Hall.

The museum is set up along this park, amid a garden with trees, bushes, and vines entangled with big machines and unused industrial artifacts – objects that relate to the origins and experience of labor along history, especially tied to industrialization. The garden will stage a definite confrontation between human and natural, with the vegetation surrounding and enveloping the machinery.

This public garden of labor enters the raised body of the museum to reveal its great central welcoming area. This is an area/streetway that gives access to the building, crosses it lengthwise, and organizes the terrain and the edifice, inserting them into the very fabric of the city.

On one side, we have the unit that holds support and administrative functions, the technical collection, a small auditorium, an engine room, and the vertical circulation systems. On the other side, we have the raised unit that holds the exhibits.

The units are connected by walkways that cut across the vertical gap of the *streetway* below. This welcoming site, enlarged in its center by the folding of the structural walls of concrete and protected by large glass panels in its periphery, displays the movement and life of the museum to all. On the ground level, the store and the coffee shop are a part of the main communal area – among visitors and passersby, between museum and city.

The Work and Workers Museum will deal with the history of labor in an ample and universal manner, from the prehistoric era to contemporary times, posing a permanent dialogue with other museums across the globe.

On the other hand, it will also deal with local and national specificities. São Bernardo do Campo and the ABC region are probably the best representatives of our country's modern industrial development. Since the 1950s, when several industries were set up in the region (among them: Automotive, auto parts, appliance, chemical, and plastic industries), the city has entered the national folklore as automotive capital, a symbol of industrial progress and a new age of development. The region is also nationally and internationally known for its history of strong labor unions and social strife.

In this sense, the museum intends to be a center of articulation of the memory and history of the workers, presenting the diversity of their experiences in both working and living environments, their multiple forms of sociability and collective action. With the aim of being traversed by gender, ethnic, and generational relations, the narrative seeks to stablish a permanent dialogue with various sets of practices, delineated across the region, the country, and the world.

The Work and Workers Museum intends to constitute a vibrant living space, for leisure and education, welcoming visitors from the region and from all over the country.

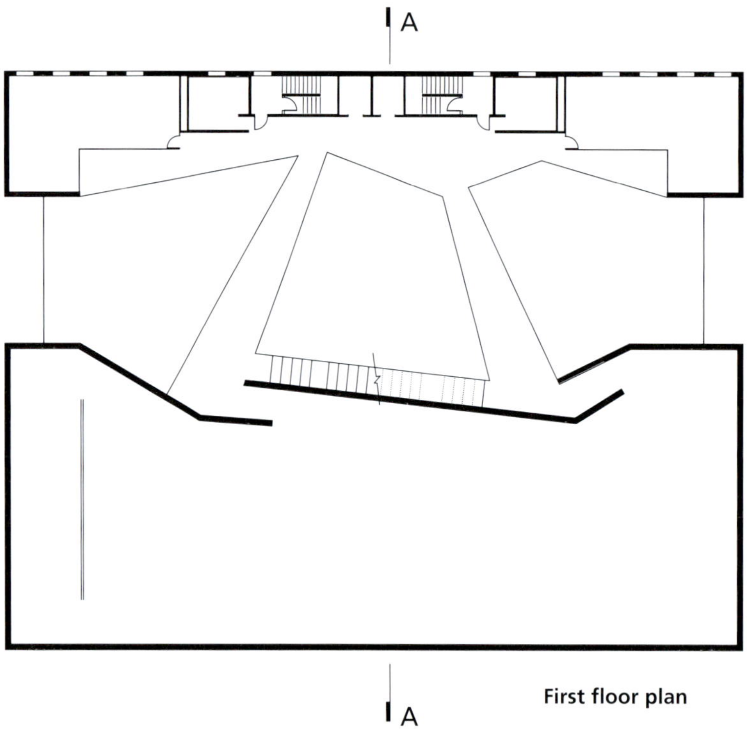

First floor plan

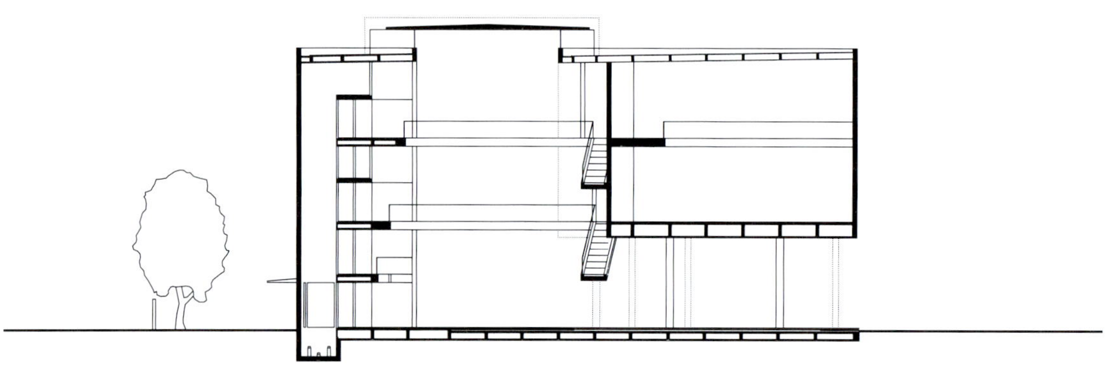

Section AA

Building in the final stage of construction

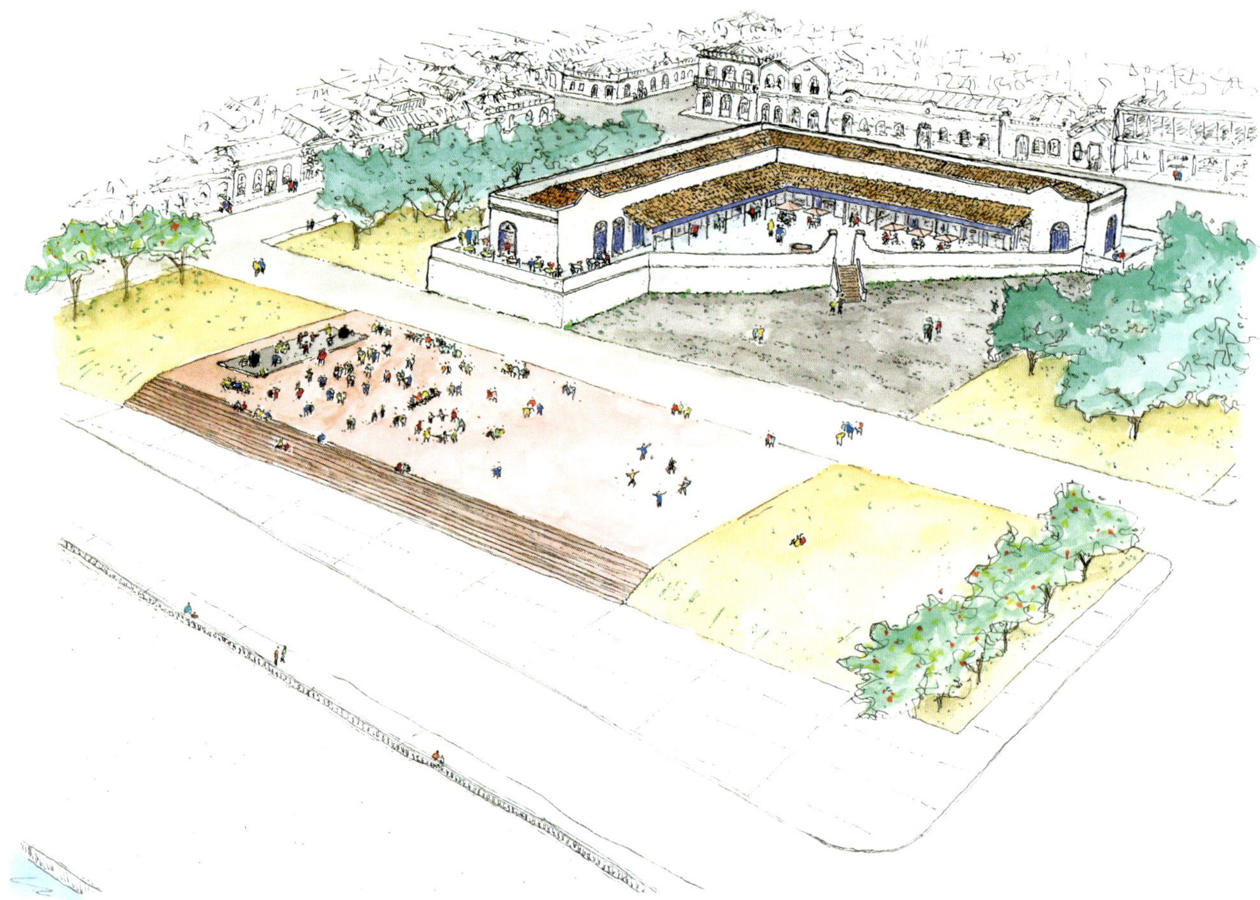

Jaguarão Market

Jaguarão, Rio Grande do Sul, 2010

Marketplaces are mirrors for the city and portraits of entire civilizations, as ultimate meeting grounds they are ripe for the practices of citizenship and urbanity. We see, we learn, and we feel the culture of a city within its markets. In them, we can understand human gatherings and their values a little better: What they eat, what they drink, what they wear, how they communicate, how they relate to one another, how they deal with their problems. Markets are at the unequivocal center of urban life, a climax of human coexistence.

The restoration and reopening of the Municipal Market of Jaguarão is another important landmark in the history of the city. Recognized as estate heritage by the Estate Historic and Artistic Heritage Institute – IPHAE and as a national monument by the National Historic and Artistic Heritage Institute – IPHAN, the building is a testimony of urban settlement in a frontier territory.

Aside from the preservation of its original constructive qualities, the Market is an example of wisdom when it comes to the choice of terrain in an urbanistic setup. It is strategically situated at the center of town, in a gentle slope near the Jaguarão River, exactly where the settlement first came to be, over two hundred years ago. Built between the years 1864 and 1867, it has always served as an important supply and shopping center for the population, but in the last few decades it had gone into decay.

A few basic guidelines directed our project, aimed at the urban requalification of the entire precinct, all the way from the river banks to the marketplace. With the demolition of the buildings that obstructed the direct view and access to the river, we were able to delineate a new plaza to be built between the market and the riverbed, a place that will be able to receive small concerts, kermises, fairs, and thematic events. It will also provide a beautiful view of the waters, of the Barão de Mauá Bridge, and of the Uruguayan hillside on the other margin. It constitutes a leisure and walking area, like the *malecones*, present in so many Hispanic cities.

In the marketplace, the interventions were subtle and delicate, seeking to maintain and value the original characteristics – colors and materials – without harming the functionality of the new use class related to gastronomy and shared living between regulars and visitors.

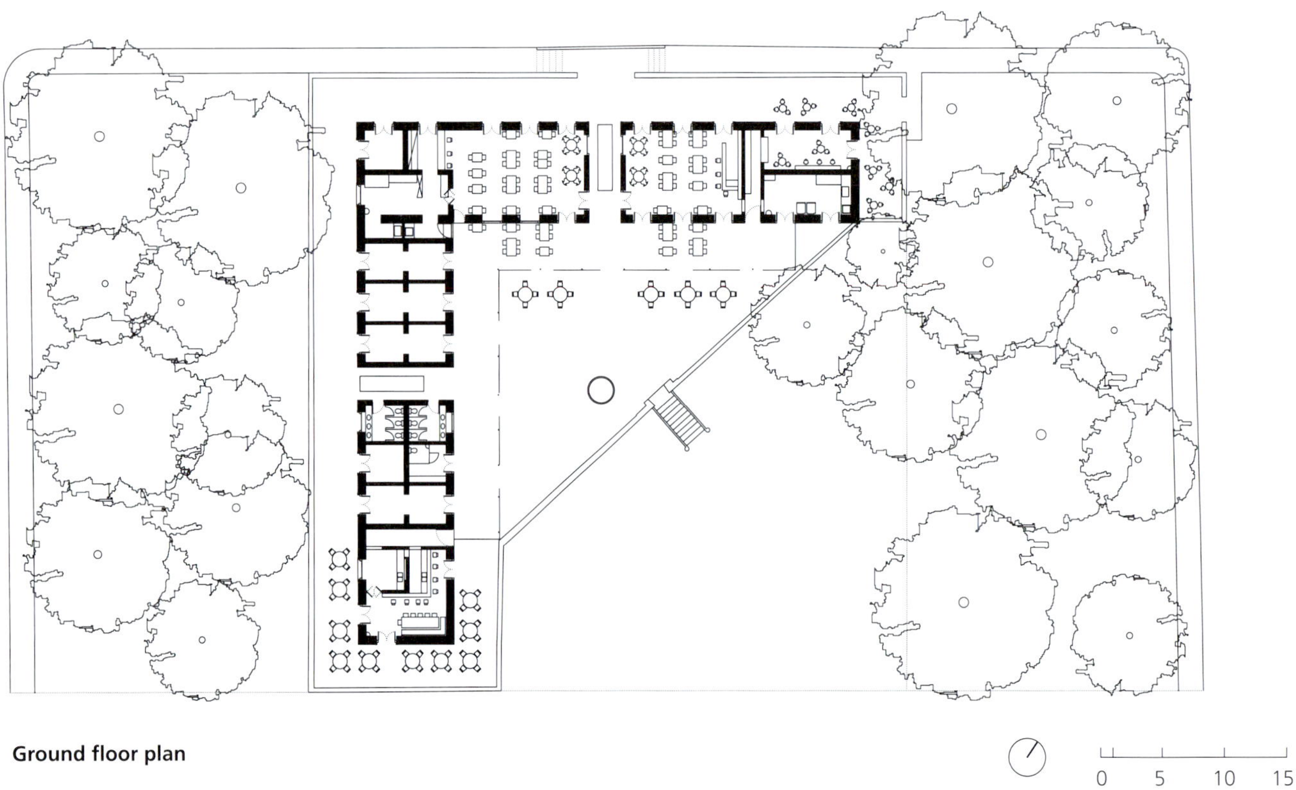

Ground floor plan

Dom Viçoso House

Dom Viçoso, Minas Gerais, 2010

Placed in a typical landscape of the Minas Gerais section of the Mantiqueira Mountain Range, the Dom Viçoso House is implanted on the edge of a small plateau, amidst an ocean of hills. A highlight of the design is the emphasis on the enjoyment of the open view of the valley below, seen from the northern façade of the building. On the opposite façade, we have the proximity of the mountain that limits the gaze, but adds an introspective quality to the house.

The careful perusal of the landscape is what guided the decision-making process here: On one side, an expanse, as far as the eye can see; on the other, a convent-like regathering that gives shape and scale to the body.

The house is designed in two units, volumetrically differentiated and functionally demarcated: Living room, dining room, and kitchen in a single shared environment of the first unit and three bedrooms in the second unit. These two cuboids are aligned and arranged along the longitudinal axis. They are joined by a small glass hallway (or tunnel) that, at the same time, connects and divides the social environments from the private areas.

Walls of cyclopean concrete made out of local stones define the foundations, the base floor, and the leveling of the terrain for the house and the surrounding structures: Terrace, working areas, and the coffee processing yard.

The building is dominated by whitewashed walls, allowing them to become bright spots in the exuberant green landscape. In the house itself, the dominant white contrasts with the red color of the windows and the toilet and utility room facilities. The porches are distributed along the body of the main units. They are covered by concrete slabs, which are supported by wooden pillars. As the slabs of the porches are built at a lower level than the roof, they allow the entrance of light inside the house, by a glass slit designed above them. The roof, also made of concrete slabs, provides insulation, holding water and much ground for a natural garden to flourish with vegetation carried over by the wind and the local birds.

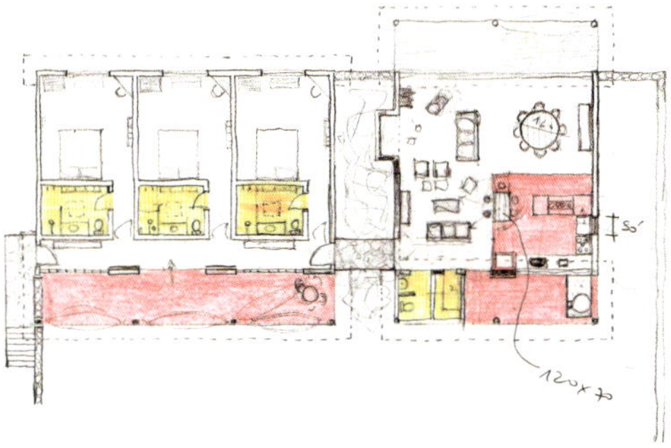

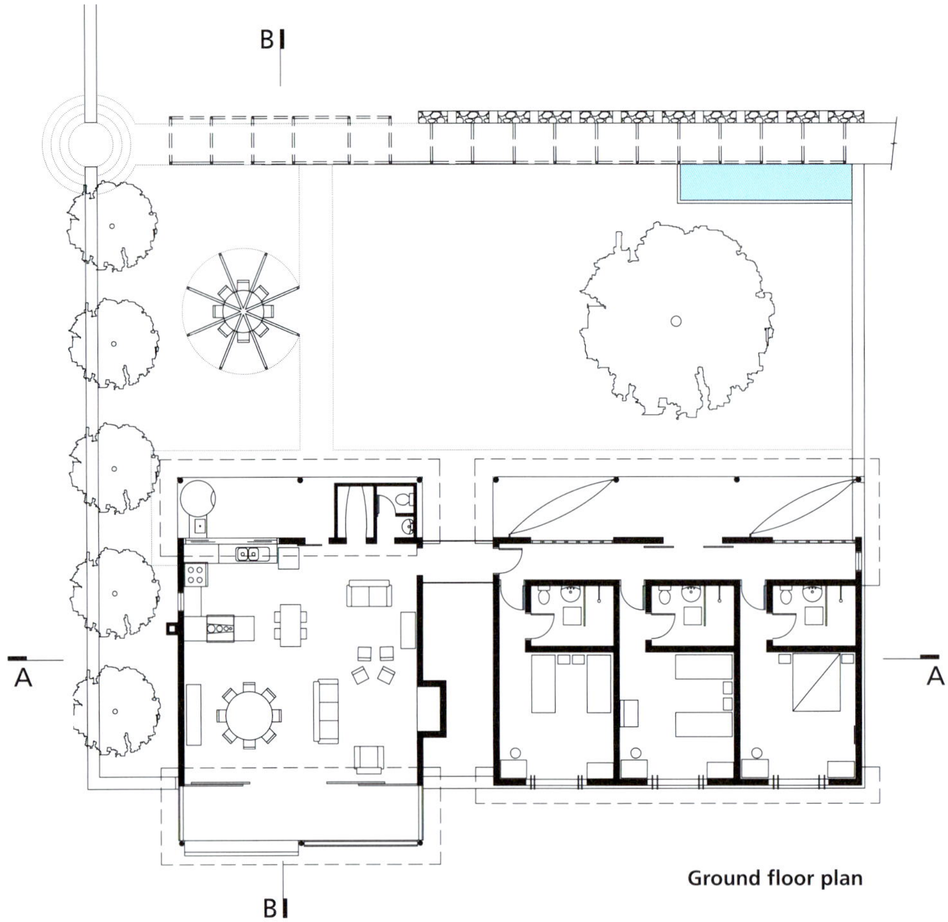

Ground floor plan

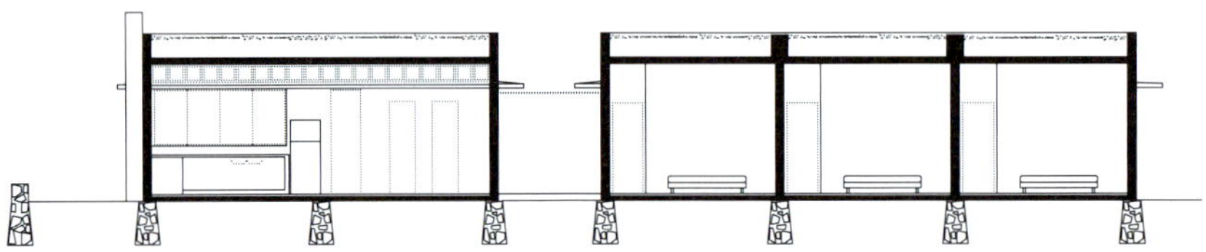

Section AA

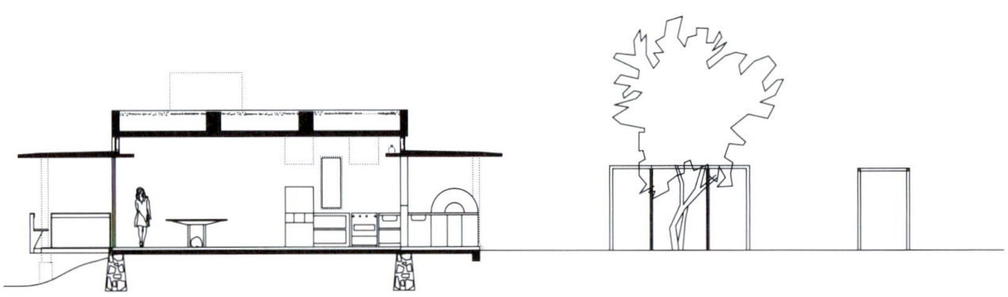

Section BB

Dom Viçoso Chapel

Dom Viçoso, Minas Gerais, 2019

Set up on the top of the hill, between the coffee plantation and the woods, the Boa Vista Farmhouse Chapel springs from the desire to create a symbolic venue comparable to so many others that are traditional all across rural Brazil.
A small cyclopean concrete hexagon made of local stones receives a round cover slab – circumscribed to this hexagon – in a way that sunlight enters through the edges, illuminating its interior.
Internally, five niches will receive religious figures, following the example of Ghezo Royal Palace, in Abomey, Benin. The central niche, open to the woods, will harbor Oxóssi's arc.
We created an ecumenical space, introspective, bare, and solemn, all at once. A room of silence, designed on a buttress of the Mantiqueira Mountain Range. It is silence within silence.

Zoomorphic figure at Ghezo Royal Palace's wall niches, in Abomey, Benin; the other photos, Holy Spirit at the ceiling, Edmar de Almeida's paiting; empty niches that will receive belief figures; niche open to the forest, that will house Oxossi's arc

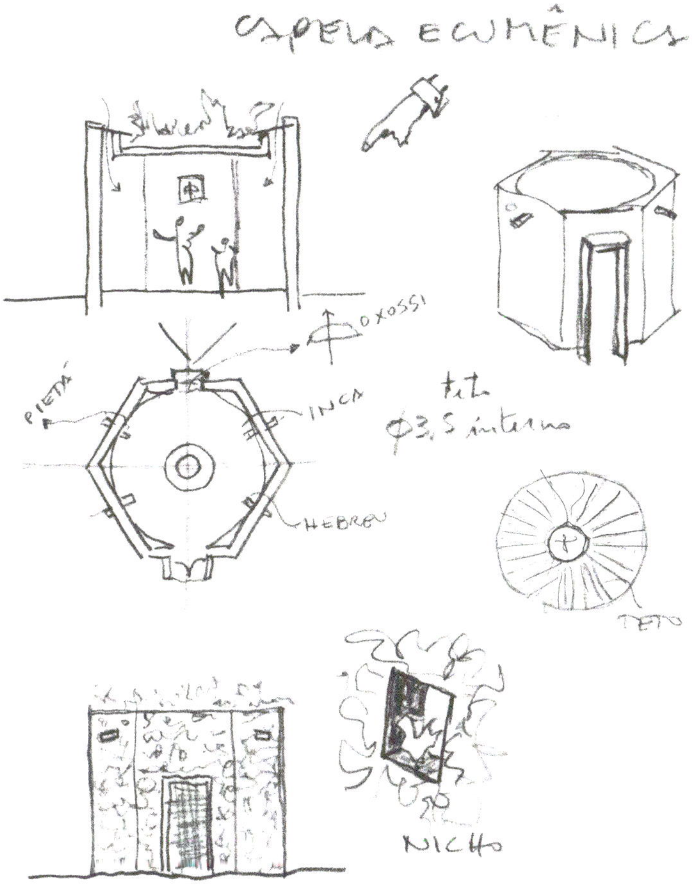

Pepiguari House

São Paulo, 2011

This house reworks the rationale behind one of our firm's first projects, the Cambuí House (Cambuí MG, 1979) – perhaps it was our very first project. The Pepiguari House is a compact building that occupies its lot from side to side without any lateral setback, preserving a separation only to its front, as it is mandatory, and in the backyard. The main hall functions as a sort of covered streetway between these two recesses.

The main characteristic of this design is the rational organization of space, primarily structured by a concrete wall which slices the unit all across the front yard and the main living section, defining the internal areas of the ground floor. This wall also provides support for the upper levels. The first floor is composed of three bedrooms and a small studio, while the roof displays a garden and an exposed water tank. The latter is visible from afar, resembling the bridge on a ship.

On the back of the lot, a building isolated from the main unit holds a library and an office. As its façade to the main house is glazed, it permits a clear view of the backyard, with its old and, yet, terribly fertile tangerine tree on the center, conforming a kind of square between the house's two buildings.

Exposed concrete, corten steel, glass, whitewashed walls, and floors of *pau-marfim* timber, these are the basic materials that provide the house with its particular features. Two staircases cling to the steel frontal façade: An internal one, made of concrete, leads to the first floor; the other one, in steel, is external and leads to the garden terrace on the roof. From there, one can enjoy the urban landscape of São Paulo and the horizon outlined by the Cantareira Mountain Range, all the way to the Jaguará Ridge.

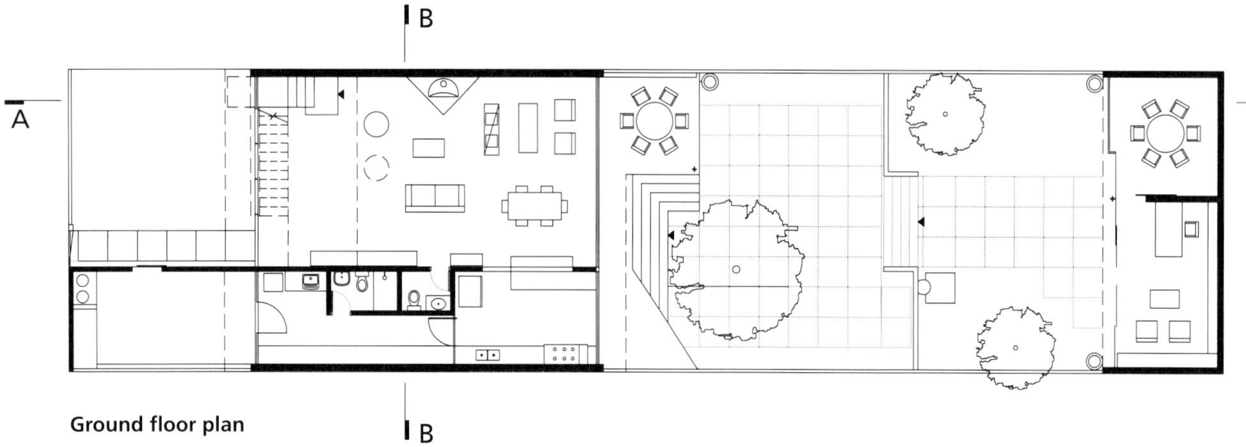

Ground floor plan

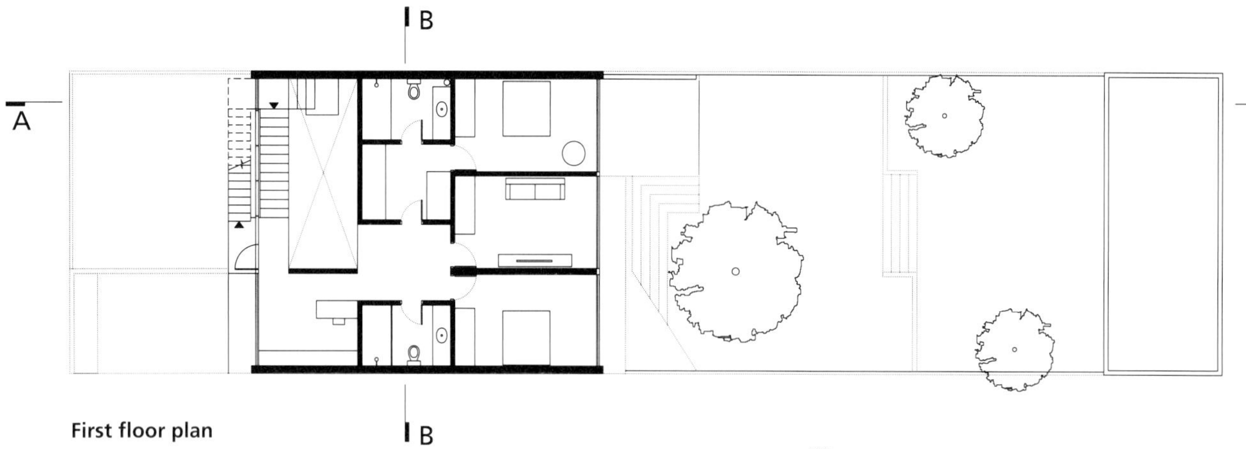

First floor plan

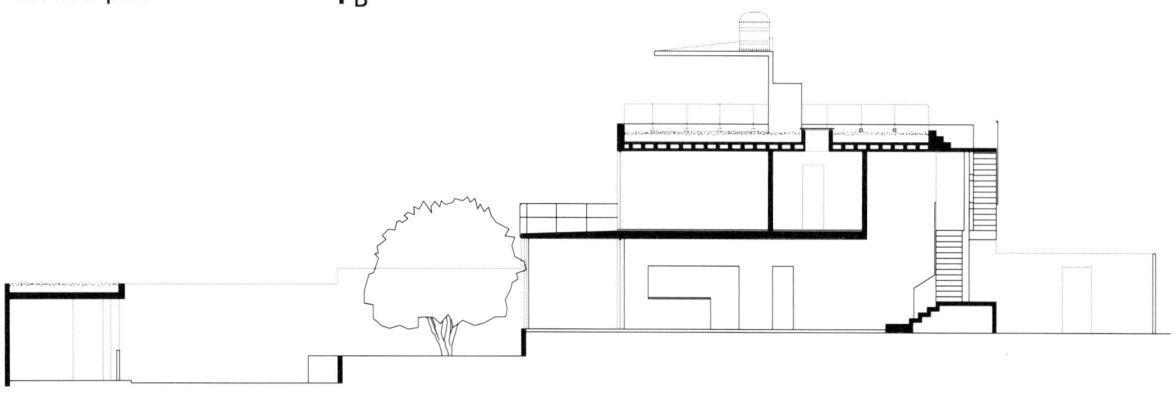

Section AA

Section BB

Democracy Memorial
São Paulo, 2012

The architecture of the Democracy Memorial building should express solidity, transparency, clarity, diversity, and urbanity. It should also be inviting, accessible, gentle.

Our project is derived from a proximity to the place where the edifice will be built, the physical place and the socioenvironmental area – the urban history and geography of the Luz region in São Paulo. As a resultant of the two city-block layout, come forth the plans and the shapes of the two units that will host the entire brief, the entire life of the future Memorial. Hence, the Memorial will reassert the urbanization and the preexisting occupation of the surroundings.

We designed a large complex that Gusmão Street will divide in two. The two blocks will reach one another through walkways and ramps. Due to the triangular shape of the lots, the set resembles a large wedge nailed down on the central area of the city. Thus, its architecture derives from dialogue and reciprocity with the existing place, and not of formal desires or abstract premises based solely on the arbitrary gesture that every architectural design, to a greater or lesser degree, seems to carry.

The architecture of the Democracy Memorial is hard-hitting, affirmative, much like its signification as a memorial should be: An institution whose purpose is to tell the story of the popular strife for democracy in several fronts across Brazil; and its insertion among numerous important monuments of the region – Luz Garden and Station, Sala São Paulo, Pinacoteca Museum and Station will be among its neighboring buildings.

We have opted for the reinforced and prestressed concrete technologies as structural and material basis for the construction. Self-cleaning concrete, specifically, will be greatly employed. Thus, we shall have a great white ensemble that, seen from up close, will reveal a range of colorful aggregates, with stonework, gravel etc.

In one of the most visible façades, the large white wall facing Mauá Street, we designed a concentration of stones brought from all parts of Brazil, like the nucleus of a galaxy that explodes into a myriad dots and colors of varying textures. These stones of different shapes and dimensions will be put into the concrete as the wall rises, and, so, they will be amalgamated forever. As a result, the architecture and its execution will already be incorporated into the theme of the Memorial, symbolically reaffirming the struggle for the construction and establishment of democracy with these stones from all parts of the country.

With the exception of the areas that give access to the basement and to the upper levels, the ground floor will be, basically, a public site. The city enters the building, by its large gateways, and utilizes it as a covered streetway, like the more traditional and democratic examples of urban galleries that highlight the very best of public architecture, designed to serve pedestrians.

The two units of the ensemble, connected by passageways and aerial ramps, will fulfil different tasks and use classes, with exhibition areas, an auditorium, a garden/terrace with a coffee house and a restaurant, research and class rooms, collection storage, and support areas. Universal accessibility and reduction of energy cost during construction and afterwards are fundamental and non-negotiable guidelines of the project.

This will be a home for Brazilian democracy: A forward sentinel, keeper of our achievements and struggles, suffering and glory of our people.

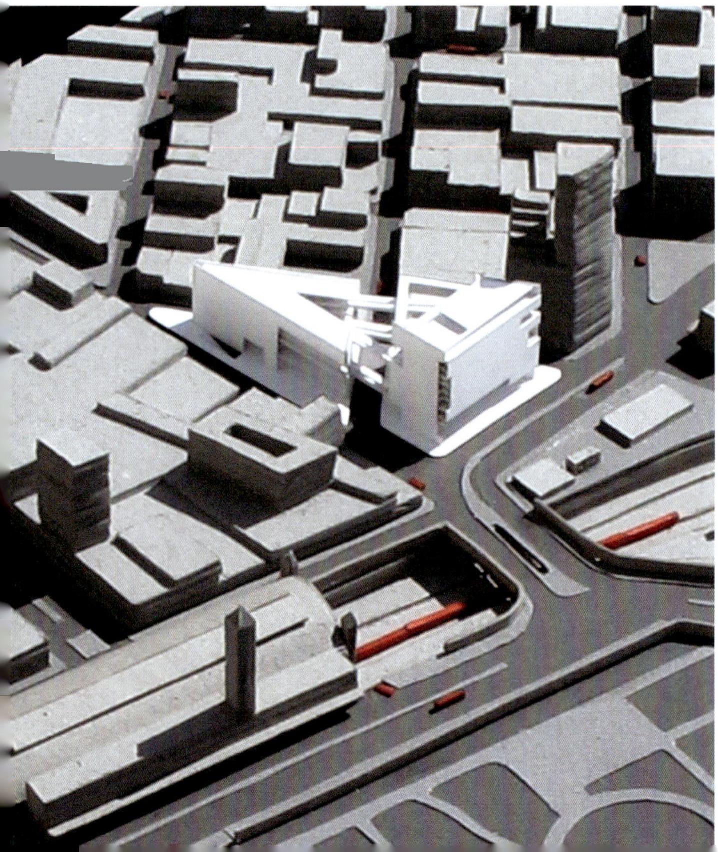

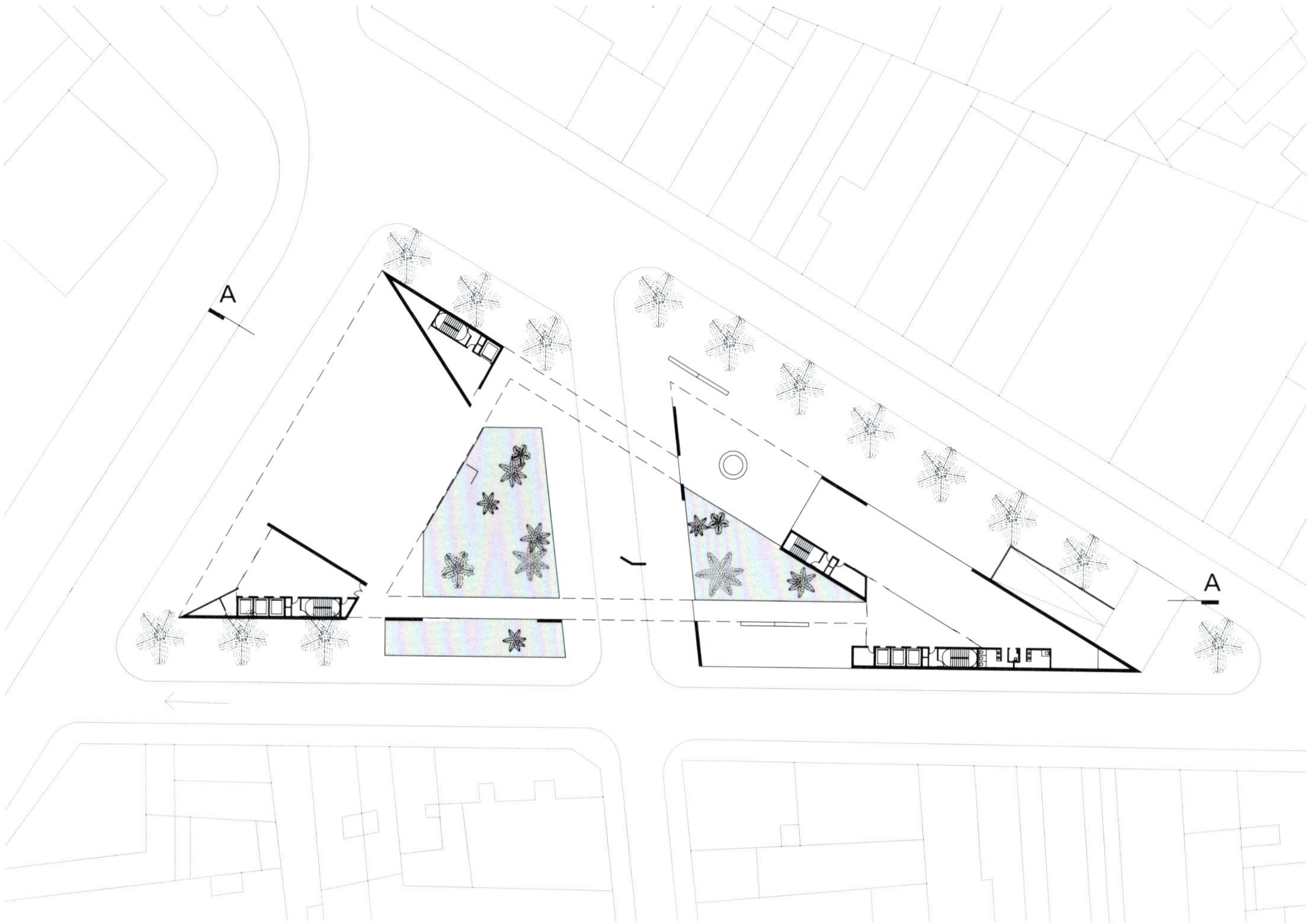

Ground floor plan

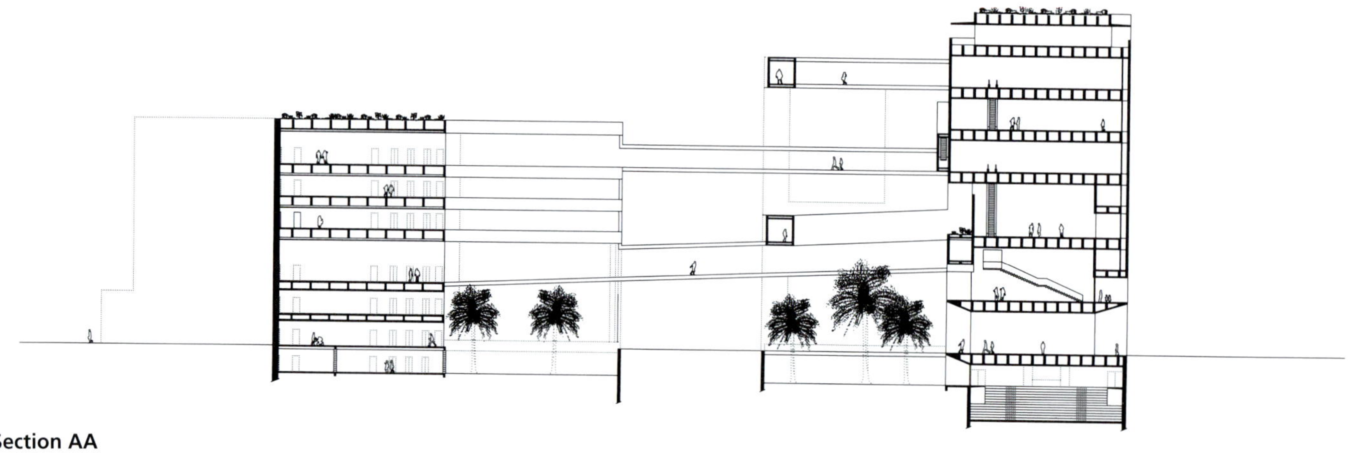

Section AA

International Olympic Committee – IOC

Lausanne, Suíça, 2013

Walls represent, throughout the course of human history, division, of property, or territory. They are defensive barriers. And, yet, there are those walls that, even as they separate, connect. These are porous walls that filter light and frame the landscape. They give shape to passageways, regulate contact, and define neighborhoods. They could be seen as unifying walls that poll together collective interests, physical and symbolic landmarks of human achievements of great social importance, documents of historical and technological achievements. These are the walls of aqueducts, dams, and retaining structures, walls that make up bridges. From one of the most archaic actions of man in the construction of his living space, walls emerge, associating human labor to the stone they found in nature.

A long, high, thick wall of structural concrete, both solemn and festive, will delineate the future head-offices of the International Olympic Committee – IOC. Along its Southwest façade, facing the park and the Geneva Lake, we designed the assembly of a collection of stones of varied sizes, colors, and textures, which will be inlaid on the concrete of the wall, resting there, in union forever. Each stone will represent one of the 204 nations associated to the IOC. Arenite, granite, marble, basalt, or dolomite, these stones should be sent from all corners of the planet by each nation.

Consequently, this same wall will tell the story of the construction of this new head-office building, as a record of collaboration and solidarity amongst the peoples. In its tectonic structure, the architecture of the place will symbolically reaffirm the strife for peace between our nations and the emergence of the olympic spirit.

The setup and positioning of these new buildings are also defined by the presence of the historic Château de Vidy, which occupies the center of the ensemble, framed by the great wall. The old edifice, integrated to the new set, should receive a different use class, appropriate to its spaces and symbolic imagery. It will be restored and it should have its original architectural values preserved. We will open spaces with the demolition of all the non-original walls and divisions, with the aim of valuing and highlighting the details and materials employed in construction.

The decision to create a lengthwise axis defined by and aligned with the Château, parallel to the water's edge, will increase the open areas of the park and configure a large green plaza. The long wall, besides providing structural support to the new buildings, will have the task of defining and organizing the occupation of the terrain.

We named the great central hollow of the larger building ágora. It will be the neuralgic center of circulation and communication. It will serve as a meeting stage for employees, visitors, and passersby. A set of ladders and exclusive elevators will give access to the external walkways of the great wall, so that the visitors can enjoy the view of the park and are able to touch the stones set on the concrete of the wall, representing each nation. Also, through the ágora, we will capture light and provide ventilation to all levels of the edifice.

In contrast to the great concrete and stone wall facing the Southwest, the Northeast façade will be enclosed by glass and aluminum frames, fixed on the support structure. It will resemble a cut crystal, with its multifaceted design of triangular and trapezoidal shapes. The large structural gaps and the long transversal 12 meter overhang will accentuate the lightness of this great floating crystal and, as a consequence, provide contrast with the great concrete wall.

All areas of business will be punctuated by coffee/meeting spots, placed along the building in all floors. The gym should be placed on the ground floor, in immediate contact with the park. On the roof, a restaurant surrounded by a garden terrace will allow the enjoyment of the beautiful view of the city and the mountains, on one side, and the park and lake, on the other. That will be the ultimate meeting spot of the entire complex, on business days or when there are events. All of these project decisions are aimed at searching for gentler spaces.

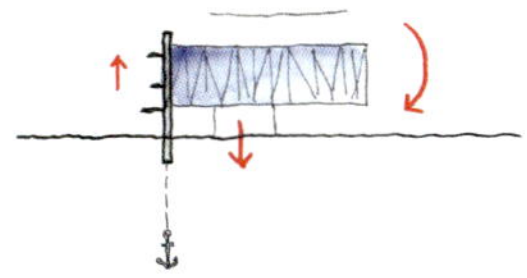

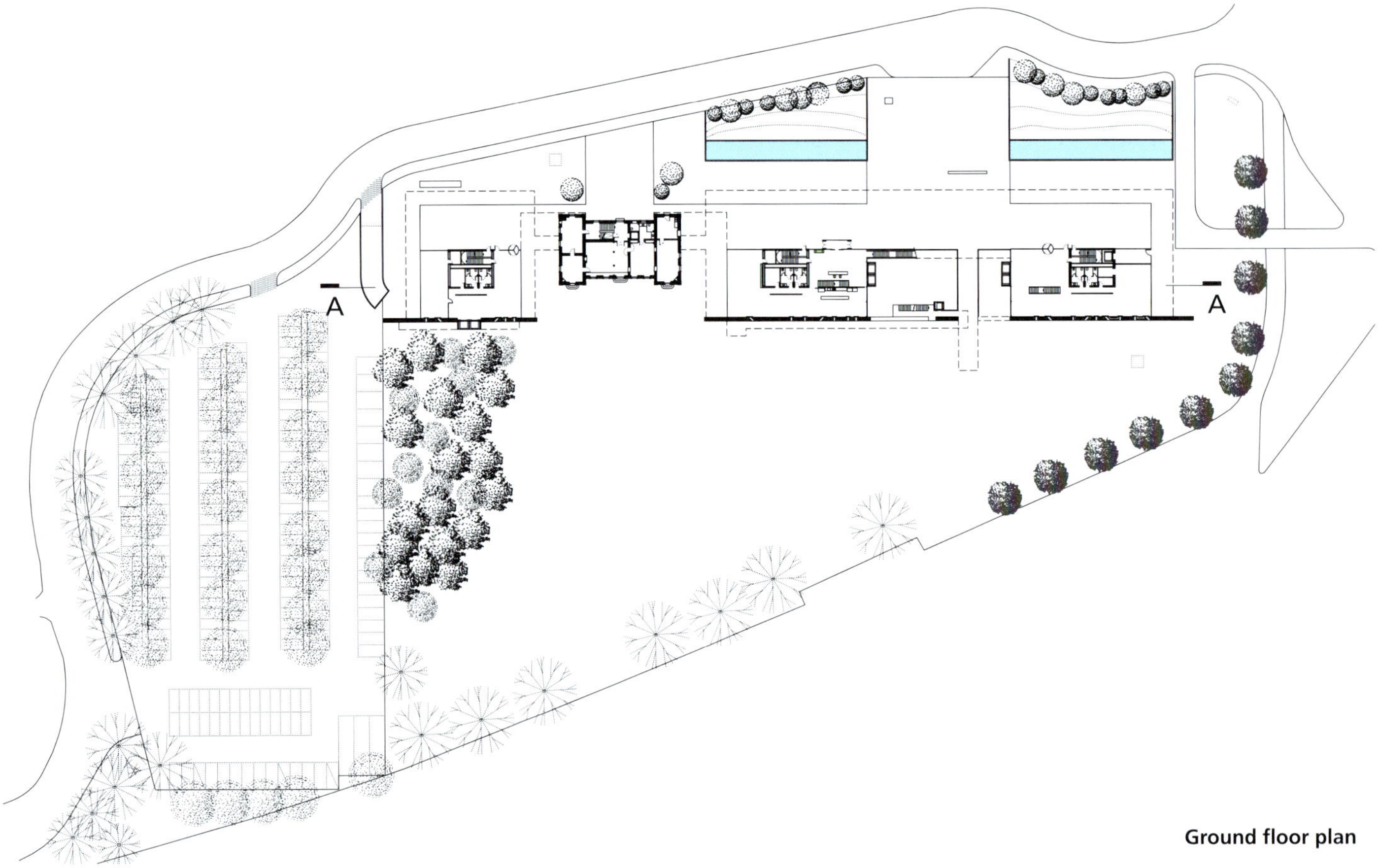

Ground floor plan

0 5 15 30 60

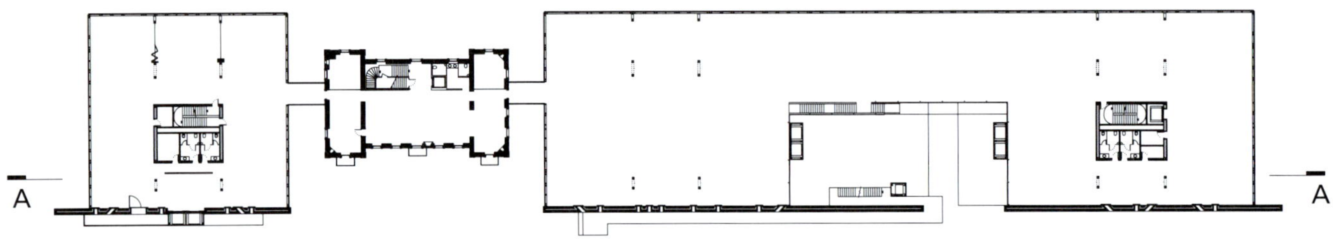

First floor plan

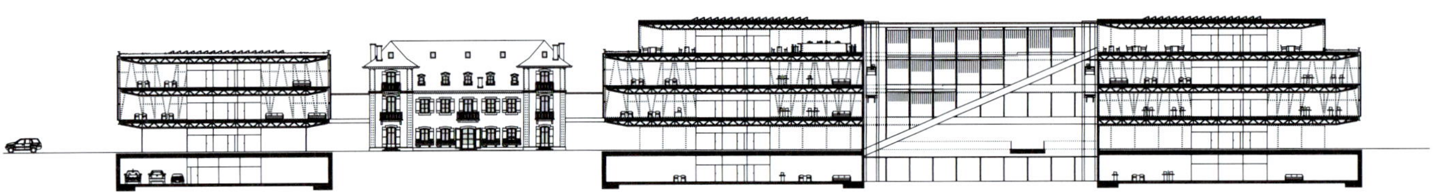

Longitudinal section

0 5 15 30

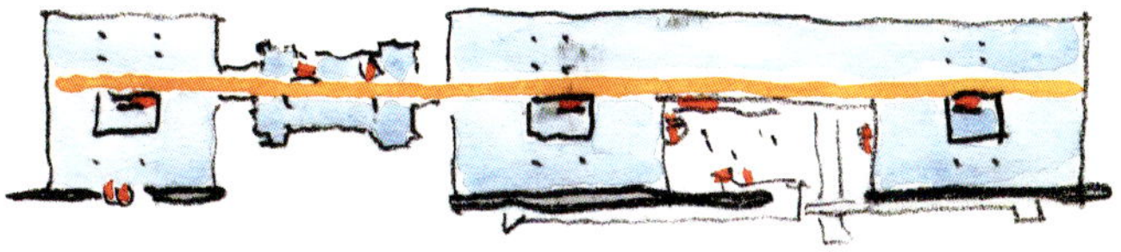

Holocaust Museum and Memorial

São Paulo, 2013

The future Holocaust Museum and Memorial of São Paulo should express the theme in its integrity, displayed in its spaces, walls, and gardens. Architecture and museology will play in unison. Together, they should convey the message of remembrance and honor to those who fell and fought against one of the most horrific atrocities in the history of the world. It should also serve as a clear warning against similar events that could take place in the future. Memory and search for peace should guide this project.

A great challenge posed to the creative team in this project is the need to speak to the Brazilian public with originality, without repeating or copying exiting formulas already adopted in other Holocaust museums around the world. In spite of dealing with a well-known and publicized theme, a universal theme, our museum must find its own original language; a Brazilian museum in the center of the metropolis of São Paulo.

It is in the interest of the content that the architecture should be designed, from the plans and setup of the building to the choice of materials; from the rooms and areas that clearly open themselves to the visitors to those that create uneasiness and might shock; from the studied and directed entrances of light in different environments to the colors and textures of employed materials.

The entire complex will be in exposed concrete. Closed units, with a slight golden pigmentation, will be supported by blackened walls and slabs. Entering from Consolação Street, we should see a large golden cuboid, supported by two black walls that progressively draw closer together, to create a surprising entryway. The impact is derived from the fact that, as we enter the main gateway, we should find ourselves in a great lobby, very well lit, by the effect of the transparent glass roof. A coffee house, a store, and an information booth welcome the visitor, but, most of all, one is received by the sensation to have entered a very specific thematic tour, leaving the world and all street noise outside.

A new experience waits for us. From this lobby, we can understand the structure that organizes the museum in its integrity. We can visually reach the basement, which should hold temporary exhibits, a small auditorium, a media library, technical facilities, and we can visualize the upper levels as well; they will hold the permanent exhibits. Still on the ground floor, a rock garden of various sizes and colors occupies the entire terrain. The garden will constitute an invitation to reflect upon the exhibitions or, simply, a place for gatherings.

Top, externals and internal views of the final design; bottom, study model

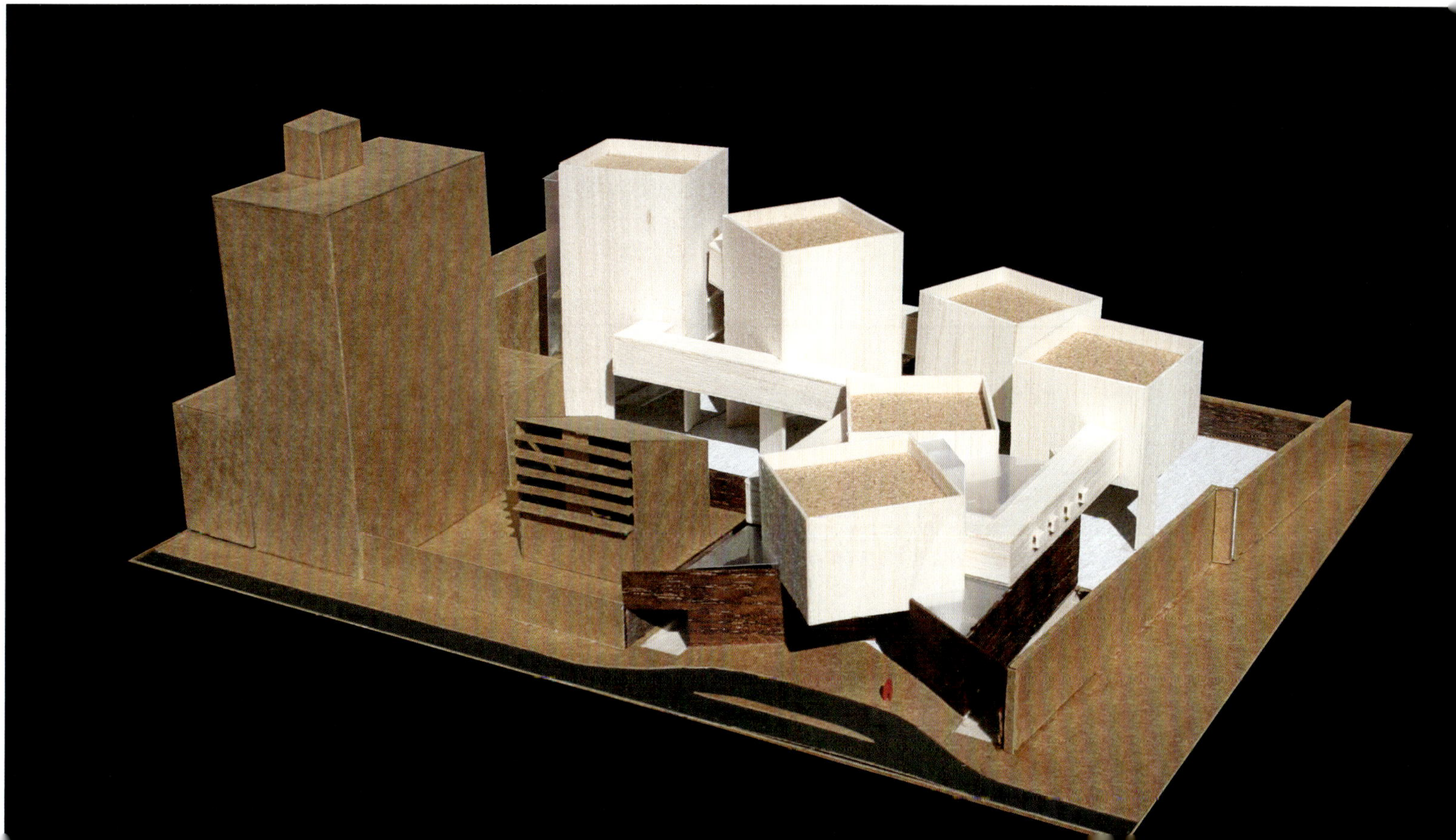

Mission Museum

with Carlos Eduardo Comas

São Miguel das Missões, Rio Grande do Sul, 2014

After the interventions by Lúcio Costa in the historical site of São Miguel das Missões, when an assertive project built the small museum (today entitled Lúcio Costa Pavillion), it is very clear that all new interventions must follow the directives put forth by him explicitly and subjectively. These directives relate to the manner of respect and conformity to the heritage one seeks to preserve from a material stand point (ruins, walls, stonework, and the museum itself), but they also relate to the perspective one tends to adopt when reconstituting what were the epic Guarani missions of the 18th century, by gathering elements from the remnants of the landscape.

The immense blue skies of the pampa flatlands, the exuberant green of the vegetation, and the iron oxide red of the ruinous church stones and the Lúcio Costa Pavillion dominate the visual memory of all visitors. These are colors that stand-out as almost unique in the landscape, painting the canvas of our imagination.

An intervention project at a historic site such as São Miguel must consider the current needs of the socioeconomic life of a community whose foundation is agrarian. It must also consider the particularity of carrying on a legacy of enormous cultural wealth. This territory of historical heritage must have its touristic potential activated in favor of the community. It must claim history as an ally in the construction of the contemporary city. And, on the other hand, it must allow this heritage to come alive with uses, needs, and relationships of the present day.

Just as they influenced the designs of the museum by Lúcio Costa in 1938, the urban occupations of the São Miguel reduction, laid down in the 18th century, help us find a starting point for the project of the architectural ensemble now.

The rigid mesh of the Spanish urban grid utilized by the Jesuits in the reduction gives us hints of the new project, despite appearing only in the remnants of the constructions, on the markings left on the terrain, and on the drawings and documents of old. These give us a sense of security, as we adopt concepts and designs, images and shapes. Even if the hints are symbolic and distant, they support our modulated reordering of the missionary citadel.

The red rock of the ruins suggests the path to be followed, weather it is on the employment of cyclopic concrete in the stonework or on the use of reinforced concrete with iron oxide pigment to create a tectonic continuum of respect to the heritage. The utilization of current building techniques highlights the distinction of time, and the concrete reaffirms itself as our contemporary stonework.

We chose the Northwest flank on the edge of the park to set up the group of buildings that will hold the rich, varied brief and its use classes. This site had been previously suggested by the IPHAN studies. Thus, the sight of the church to the North will continue to dominate the view. This visual voyage across time is one of the great riches of the place and it reveals the wisdom of the Jesuits that choose the hills of the region as the foundation site.

The brief proposed by IPHAN and the township serves as the basis of our project, especially as it pertains to the ideas of providing refuge and acquaintanceship. The complex boasts a great welcoming for tourists, visitors, and for the local inhabitants; a care facility for the demands of comfort and adequacy to the communal activities of the Centro de Tradições Nativistas (or nativist tradition center, in free translation), for the technical and administrative activities of the Municipal Tourism Secretary, and for the offices of the IPHAN and the Brazilian Institute of Museums – IBRAM, with its labs, library, and research center. All of it integrated and in consonance with the workings of a new museum that comes to enrich the visiting experience of the historic site.

All of these activities will be allocated in the architectural set with new structures connected and separate, that is, with working autonomy for each sector, but in collaborative proximity of the neighboring buildings, when necessary; in the mirrored image of a citadel.

As it occupies two city blocks that are sliced by São Nicolau Street, the new complex will be articulated by a large plaza in its center. This plaza, surrounded by reddish edifices in concrete and stone, will bring forth the memory of the cloisters and terraces of the Jesuit schools. The fronts of these two sliced halves, one more in touch with local everyday life and the other more geared towards touristic visitation, should create a healthy tension in their programs, due to the mixture of uses and services that will be available and shared.

Beside the museum, there will be a new shelter for the indigenous M'biá Guarani people. As an extensive part of the citadel ensemble, this building will be integrated to the set, but it should also provide privacy for the families. This will be accomplished by the possibility of physically isolating the premise with walls and gardens

R Tebiquay
S. Miguel
Pueblos de los
Guaranis
S. Thomé
Cordillera del Bosque

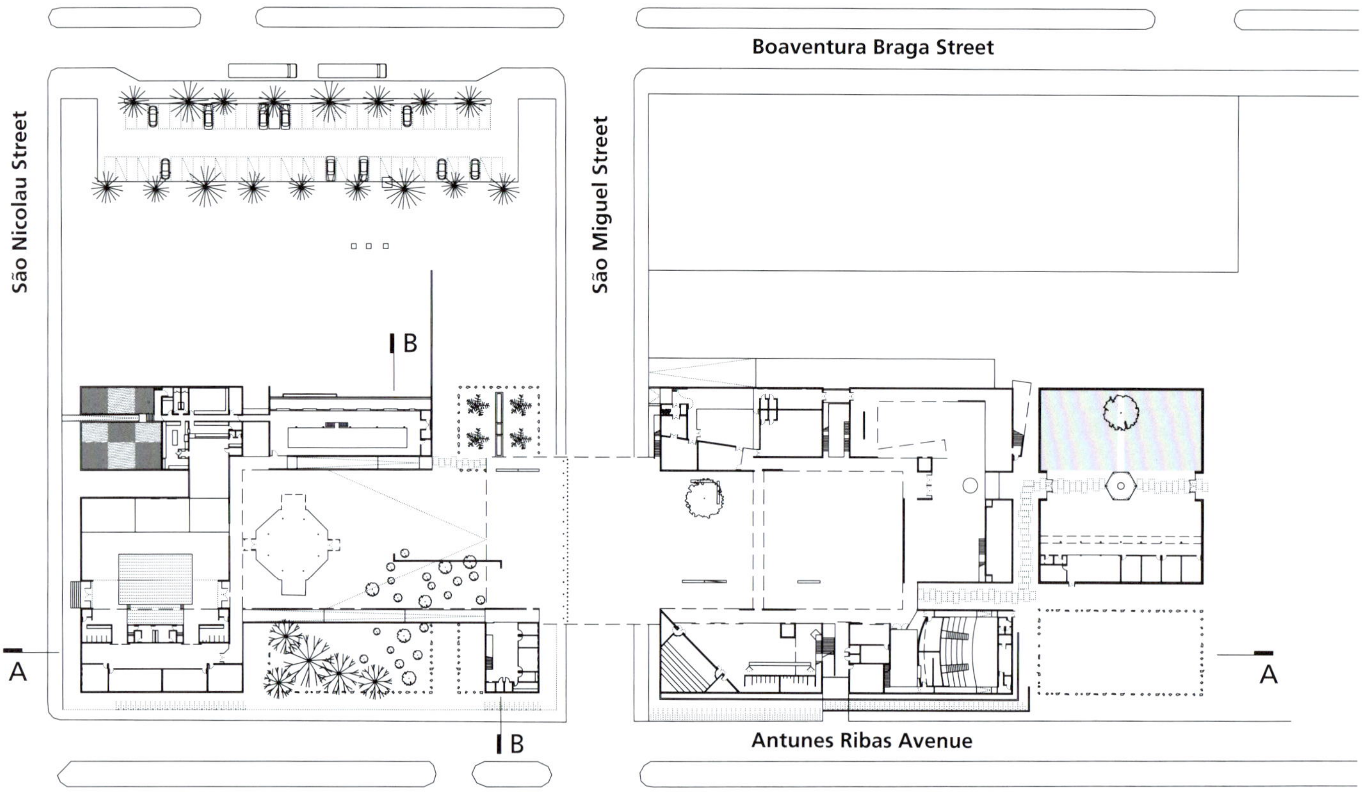

Ground floor plan

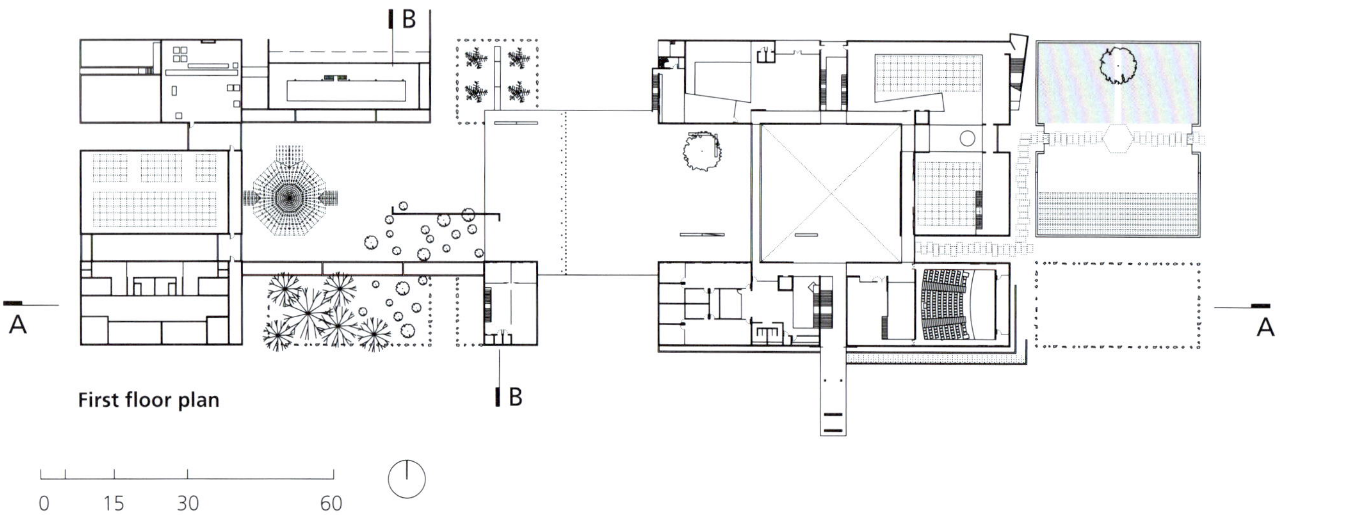

First floor plan

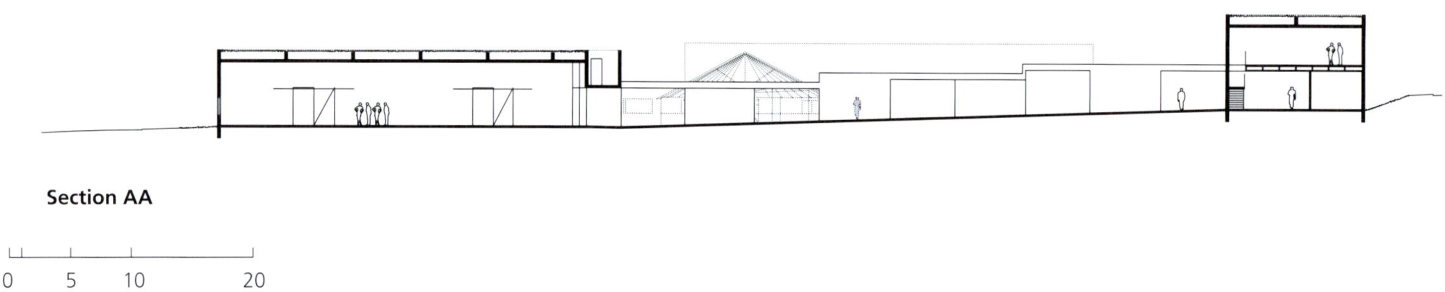

Section AA

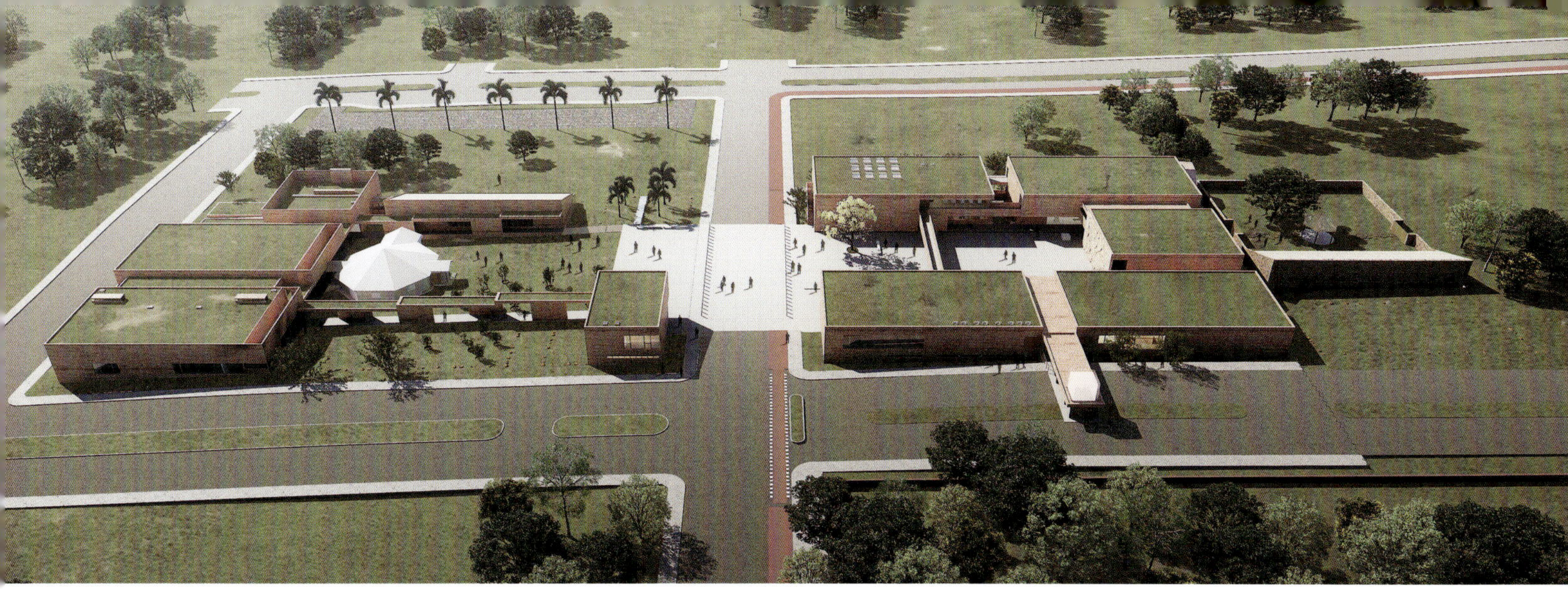

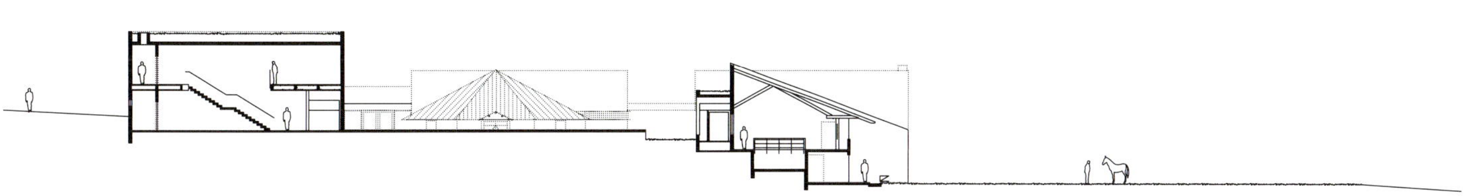

Section BB

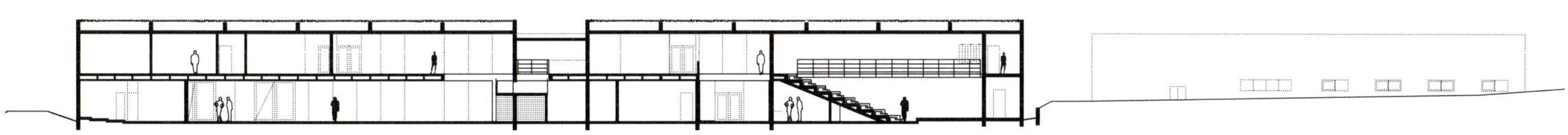

Rio Verde Farm

Conceição do Rio Verde, Minas Gerais, 2015

We might say that this project, commissioned by the Ipanema Coffees Company, consisted in acting to restore the historic buildings, rehabilitate obsolete equipment towards new ends, and build new high technology equipment for preparing and processing coffee.

From a master plan, we stablished several projects in consonance with the brief and use class definitions. The old headquarters of the Rio Verde Farm, built in stone with wattle and daub, was restored and made into a memorial in honor of the family that founded the business and their 130 years of production in farming and livestock in South Minas Gerais, on the outskirts of the Mantiqueira Region. The old out-of-use yards for drying coffee grains were turned into gardens for Brazilian grape trees, surrounding the old coffee stock bins – also out of use. These were restored and adapted to hold administrative offices.

The remaining warehouse of the old chicken farm was, likewise, restored and adapted to be the Concept House of the Ipanema brand and also a guest house for visitors – it is a huge shed of masonry and clay tiles. Finally, we designed a new yard for drying coffee at the top of a sunny hill, with 14 thousand square meters, and, around that, sophisticated washing, drying, and processing equipment in three large structures of approximately five thousand square meters each, to hold all the necessary machinery to produce coffee.

It is important to highlight that these buildings, built with corten steel and coated in galvanized alloy, resulted in arched shapes almost by an internal adequacy to the machinery sheltered there and its designed workings. In other words, the given necessity of a 15 meter height ceiling for the elevators – unnecessary in the remainder of the facilities – and the accommodation to the 3 meter gap between the yard and the lower floor suggested the curve-fitting design. The metallic arcs, besides constituting structural shapes by excellence, execute their functions with efficiency and delineate a gentle presence in the landscape, among coffee plantations, natural forests, and hills.

This is a multifaceted project (or multiple projects in one) that aims at not defacing any of the architectural sets. On the contrary, the ample project, through the designed master plan and the adopted architectural solutions, has created and reinforced a rich dialogue between four distinct time periods. The new Rio Verde Farm, with its deep historic roots, is a centennial testimony of the transformations the period saw in labor and technique, but it aims at the future of the coffee business, with its vocation attuned to the special *terroir* of the region.

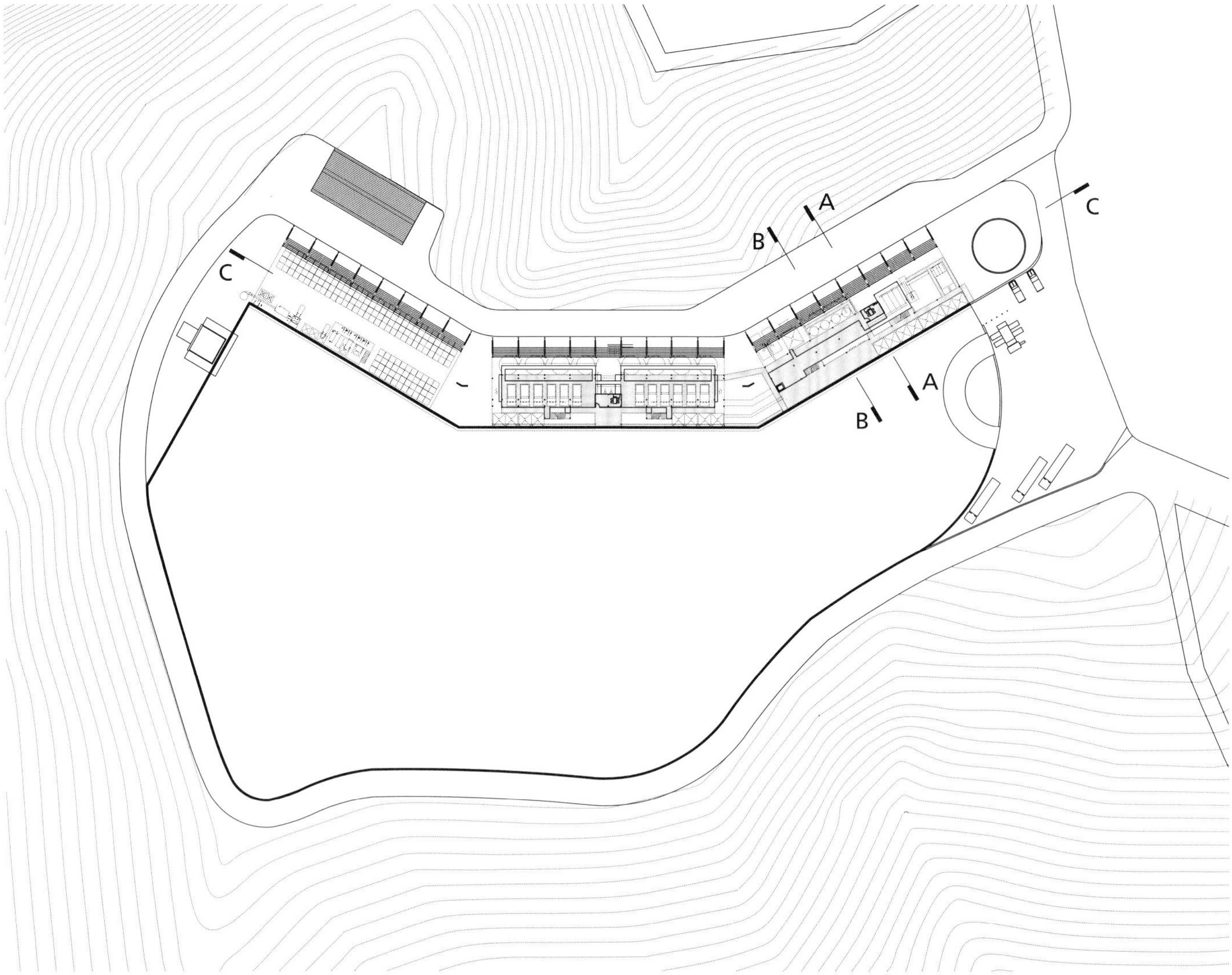

Ground floor plan

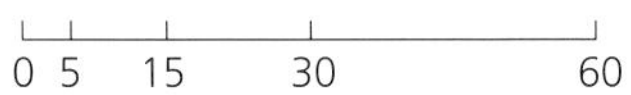

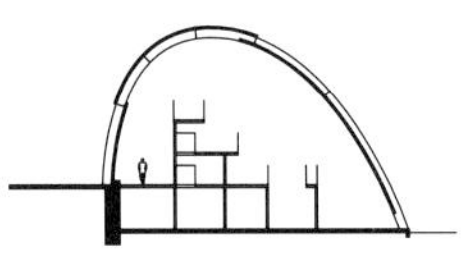

Section AA

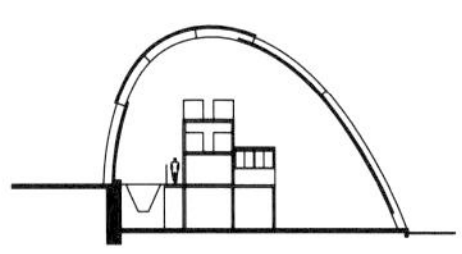

Section BB

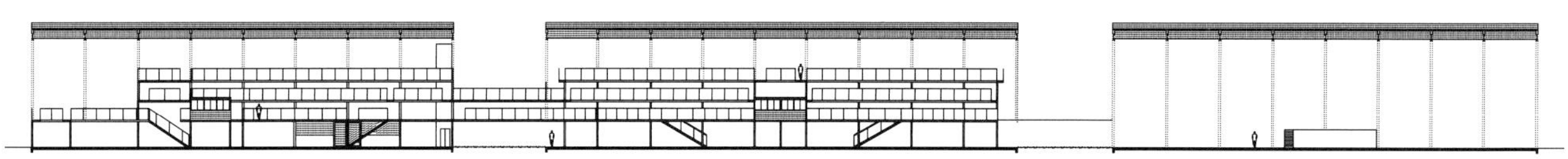

Section CC

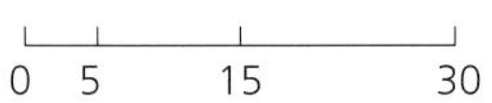

Pure and Applied Mathematics Institute – IMPA

Rio de Janeiro, 2015

The new head-offices of the Pure and Applied Mathematics Institute – IMPA should express the city we desire, in terms of human integration with the natural landscape. The word coexistence sums up our ideals in this project: Coexistence between man and nature; between the Tijuca Forest and the necessary urbanization of Rio de Janeiro, part of a dialogue of respect and integration in the construction of edifices and streetways.

We tried, in our proposal, to align sharpness and delicacy in a subtle, but assertive design. We planted buildings all across the terrain – slopes, clearings, and plateaus –, intertwined by pathways, gardens, and small plazas, ensuring tranquility and privacy for the researchers of the Institute in their daily life, as they are also able to enjoy the landscape and the forest from numerous viewpoints.

Our modulated buildings, multiple in their structure, should occupy the spaces and the gaps between the trees in a rarefied manner, in complete accord with the topography of the terrain. The contour lines are the basis of the project of this small citadel set up on levels. Elongated buildings, as ribbons, will snake across the steep hillsides, landing gently over the terrain and supported by central pillars that touch ground every 12 meters.

We assembled the communal areas on the high grounds: The library, the restaurant, the auditorium, and the large exhibition hall; all arranged for researchers, professors, students, and eventual visitors. Thus, all may enjoy the incantation and grandiosity of the old stone quarry on one side and the view of the Botanical Gardens and the Rodrigo de Freitas Lagoon on the other.

No cars. The entire area will be destined for pedestrians. The cars should stay outside or on the peripheral areas of the complex, in a discreet parking lot, built in leveled slabs, under a *velarium* garden.

No elevators. A unique system of funicular transportation on slanted planes will provide vertical circulation, replacing the elevators. It will connect the lower levels, at the entrance, to the highest grounds, servicing comfortably all the built areas for living and studying, from Stone Station (a reference to the great granite boulders on the entryway) to Beacon Station (a reference to the luminous installation that will light the quarry on special occasions at night). This lighthouse should be a new landmark in the city landscape.

The auditorium of the new IMPA will crown the entire complex. Immersed in the quarry, at times introspective with black curtains, at times extrovert and integrated with the exterior, it will be the greatest stage for the slate blackboard, the irreplaceable tool of mathematicians.

From the stone to the stone.

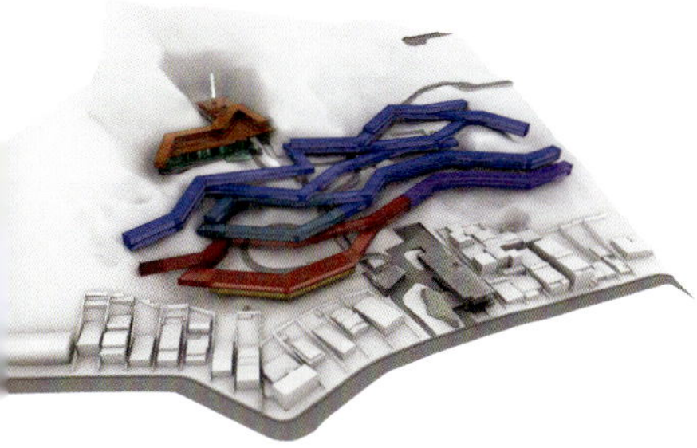

Plan

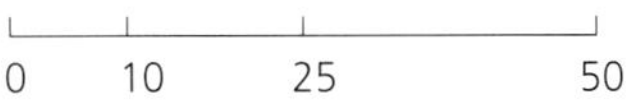

Section

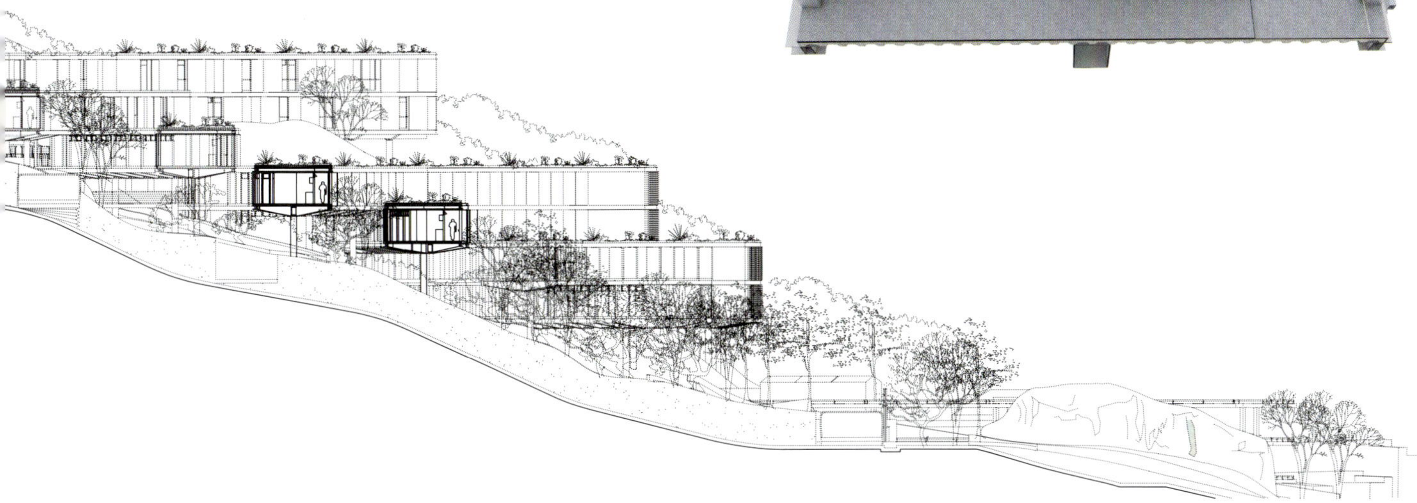

Brick Museum

Arvorezinha, Rio Grande do Sul, 2015

The Brick Museum is a realist project in terms of costs and constructive solutions, without giving up the poetic and spatial richness that a museum should have. With 530 square meters and structured in repetitive 5m x 5m modules, the museum has its rationality and hardness moderated by the inflection of the auditorium module, by the sinuous and crimped columns, and by the basalt rock that traverses the terrain from side to side and is highlighted in the interior of the building as well.

The basalt defines a 3-meter gap between the high ground, at street level, and the back of the lot. This naturally suggests a difference in structure, from a simple height in the frontal portion of the building to a double height ceiling in the posterior section. The idea of the project was to land the building on the terrain such as it is, without great groundworks.

The Fachinetto's ceramic brick was employed as a basic material of construction in the entire structure. At times exposed, at times whitewashed, the brick defines the personality of the museum. The concrete, in turn, is used on the foundation, on the beams and on the floor slabs. The prominent columns were executed one at a time in irregular and organic shapes, combining whole bricks with incomplete ones. They became great sculptures that support the concrete slabs.

A thick brick wall regulates the entire design and the use classes displayed in the museum, as a great backbone, 35 meters long, in the North-South direction. A sequence of applications accompanies the development of this wall, marking its presence as a structuring element in the design. Beginning with the reception, where the old company truck bids the visitors welcome, the permanent exhibition tells the story of the pottery produced by the Fachinetto family since the early 20th century. Along the wall, a timeline shows the objects and panels that delineate the history of brick across human history.

On the lower level, the museum holds a library, research facilities, a pottery atelier, a coffee house, and spaces for didactic and leisure activities. Near the staircase, there is a small auditorium that takes advantage of the contour gap to provide seating for 48 people. Large glass panels illuminate the inner spaces of the museum and allow for the enjoyment of the external landscape from inside and vice-versa. The whole edifice has high strength cement floors. They are low maintenance and very efficient in high flow environments. On the roof, lastly, a garden functions also as a low maintenance device for thermal insulation.

The Pottery Museum integrates the Route of the Mills and it should attract visitors from the region and from all over the country (much like the Bread Museum), but it should primarily be a cultural facility designed to serve the local community of Arvorezinha.

0

1

2

3

MUSEU
DO TIJOLO

Lagoa House

Florianópolis, Santa Catarina, 2016

In a small corner lot, with a three level foundation implanted on a steep slope, we designed a small building in front of Casarão Branco (the oldest remaining structure of the Conceição Lagoon region). The house we designed is a mixture of home and atelier that seeks to pose a dialogue with its noble neighbor and with the lagoon on the background. It is set up in the existing three levels without altering the terrain, as if it was wedged into the retaining stonewall structure. The design takes advantage of the uneven ground to implant a pair of two-story units connected by a walkway and an internal patio.

We applied concrete as a basic building material in the slabs and in the supporting wall along the entire terrain. There are whitewashed walls, floors of goiás white stone, and wooden frames. The continuous and sequential employment of glass in all frames, from the street front to the back of the lot, creates an intentional transparency in search of the landscape view of the mountains and the blue lagoon on the distance.

Small details are very meaningful in this project. One of them is the painting of three blind wooden panels in some of these frames, two in the living room and one in the back bedroom. They are painted in the same shades of red and blue employed on the small boats traditional all along the Brazilian coast and especially marked on the Island of Santa Catarina.

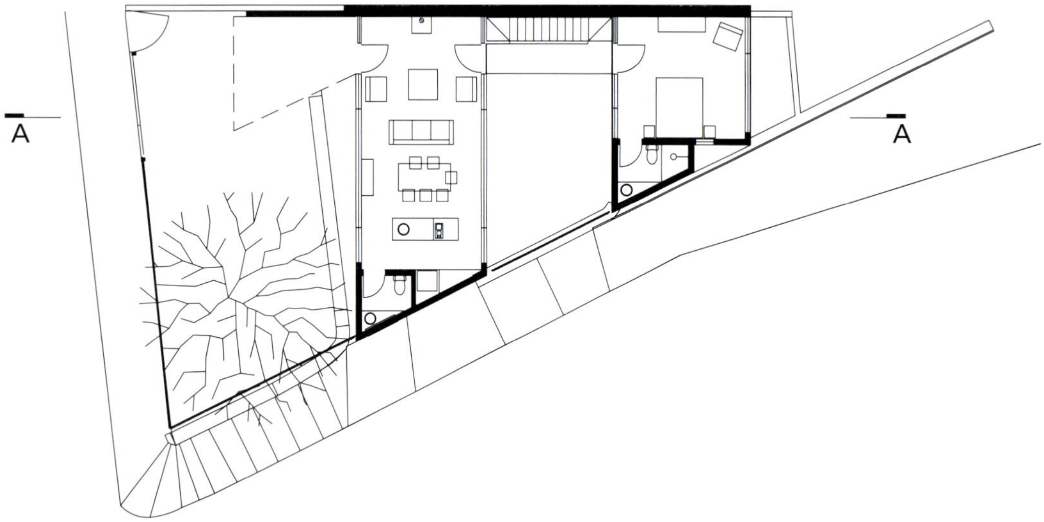

Ground floor plan

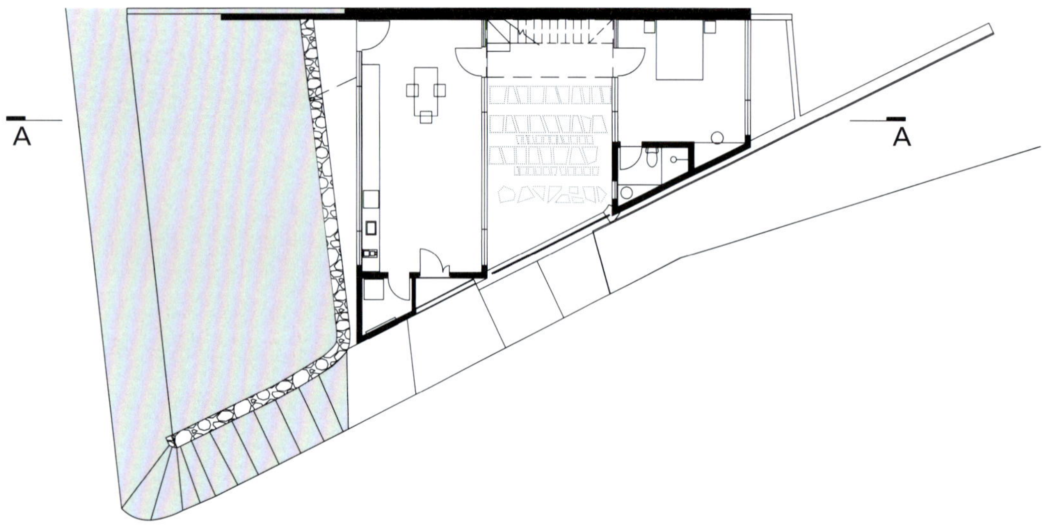

First floor plan

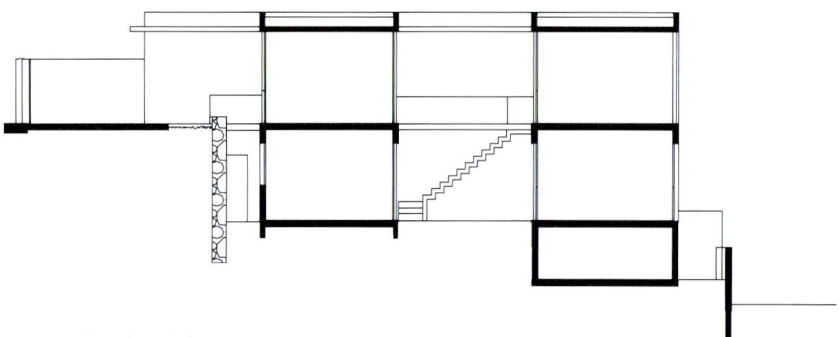

Section AA

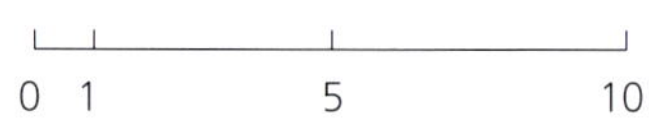

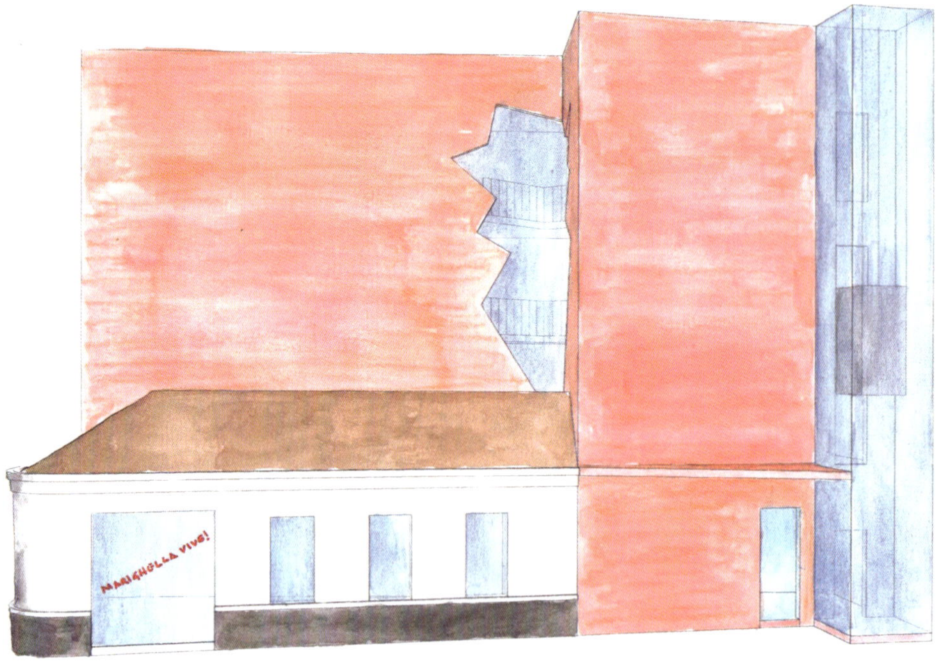

Marighella Memorial

Salvador, Bahia, 2016

One of the most visited touristic attractions in the city of Prague is the house where Franz Kafka lived. Whoever goes to Mexico City does not miss a visit to Frida Kahlo's house. In Berlin, the home where Bertolt Brecht lived is a spot of international pilgrimage. It seems visiting these places brings us closer to those icons we admire and respect; being there, somehow, makes them more human.

In Brazil, the name Carlos Marighella is finally being rescued from obscurity to occupy an important place in the pantheon of Brazilians who fought for a better, more equal nation. In Marighella's case, the fight cost him his life. Over the last few years, books, movies, songs, and other honors have attested his condition as a national hero.

A natural-born citizen of Salvador, Marighella lived, from a tender age, in a small house in Barão do Desterro Street, at Baixa dos Sapateiros (or cobblers' downtown, in free translation), in Salvador. This was, without a doubt, the place where he spent the longest time in his short and intense existence – a large portion of it, in hiding. The place served as his bunker in the victorious electoral campaign for the National Constituent Assembly of 1946. The Marighella family home also served as his father's mechanical workshop and it stands as historic testimony of all of it to this day.

Considering the symbolic importance of this landmark in the history of Salvador and the history of Brazil, we are proposing the implantation of the Marighella Memorial in this house, a building that will, not only pay him respect, but also hold all documents referring to his life and political strife. It should also serve as a reference and research center. Our proposal is to create a museum in situ there, open to public visitation.

The place where the house is situated has a rich past and boasts a noble neighborhood: Baixa dos Sapateiros and the Historic Center listed by UNESCO as a World Heritage Site. Despite its centrality, the house is situated in a small streetway that gives its surroundings an atmosphere of almost bucolic urbanity, an oasis of tranquility in the agitated Baixa dos Sapateiros. The building of plain construction has a character of its own and strong traces of a specific time period, the early 20th century. However, it can be easily restored and expanded to incorporate all the necessary installations required for the workings of a museum.

In order to accomplish that, an annex will be built in an adjoining building devoid of architectonic or historic value. The annex will display a markedly contemporary language, with working condition and apt installations, collection storage, and other services. Thus, we will have the new building anchored to the old house, which will remain as artifact and testimonial of the past, with intangible and irreplaceable value. Its symbolic force is the greatest wealth of this unique patrimony.

The old home will be restored, maintaining its constructive qualities. The new edifice will be done all in reinforced exposed concrete with red pigmentation. A large free-form tear, designed as if it were a shattered windowpane, will serve as opening for the three upper floors and will provide lighting for the stairs and circulation areas. This tear will certainly be a hallmark, an emblematic image of the ensemble.

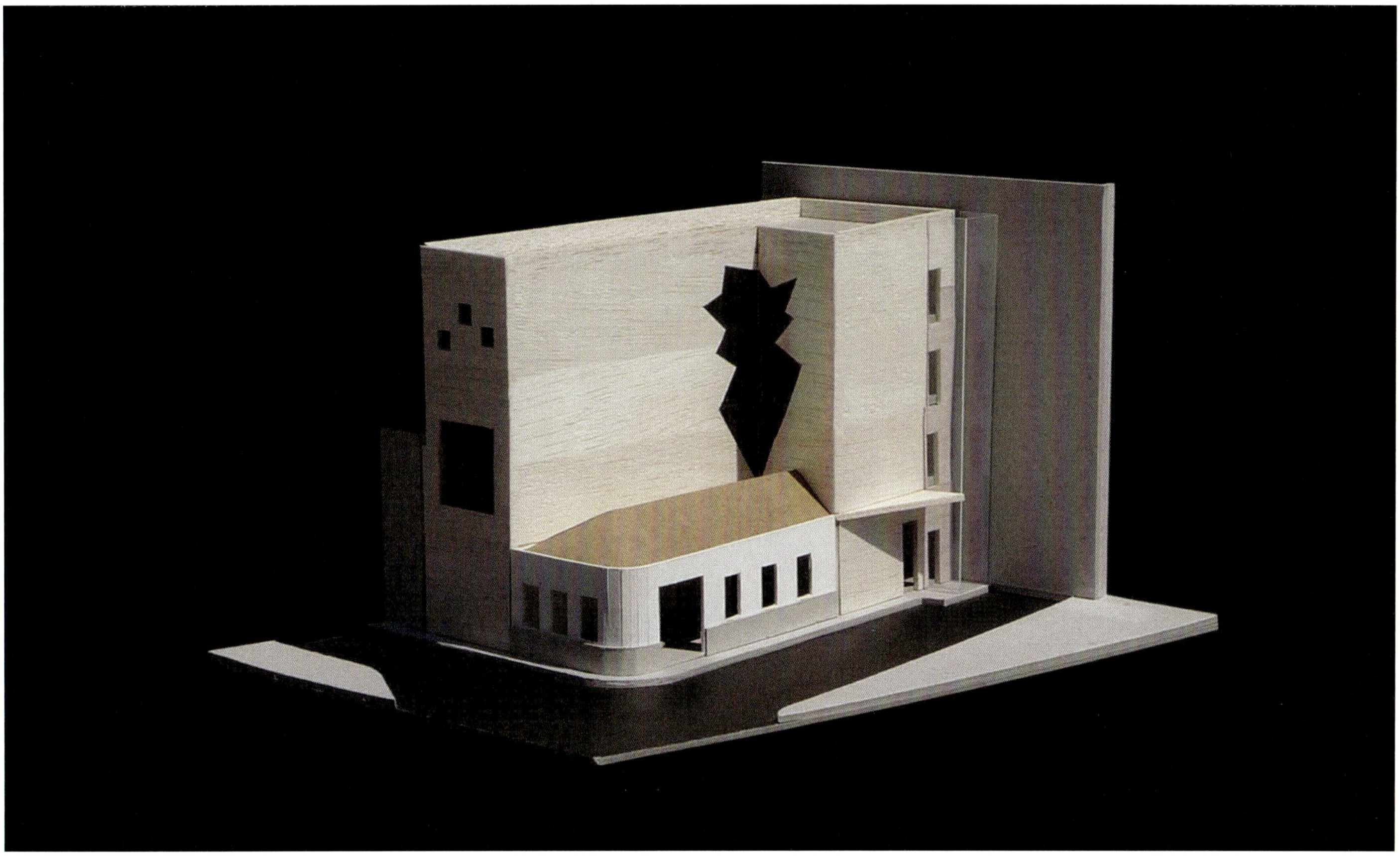

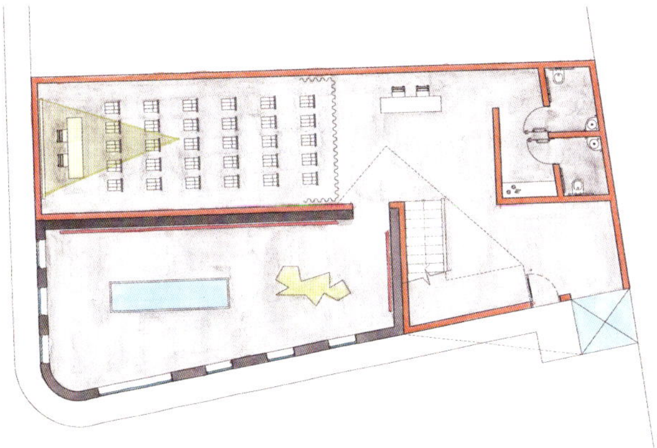

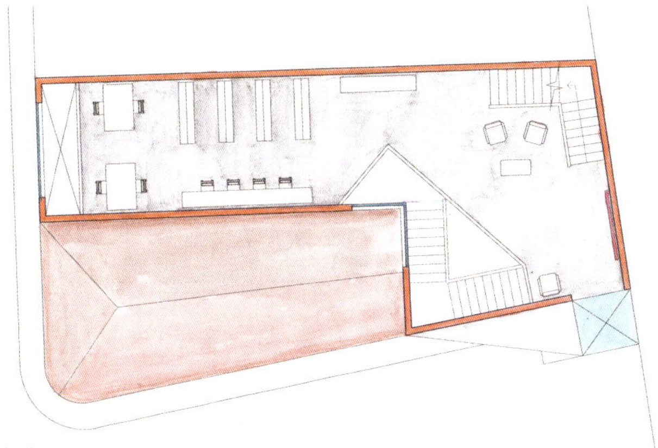

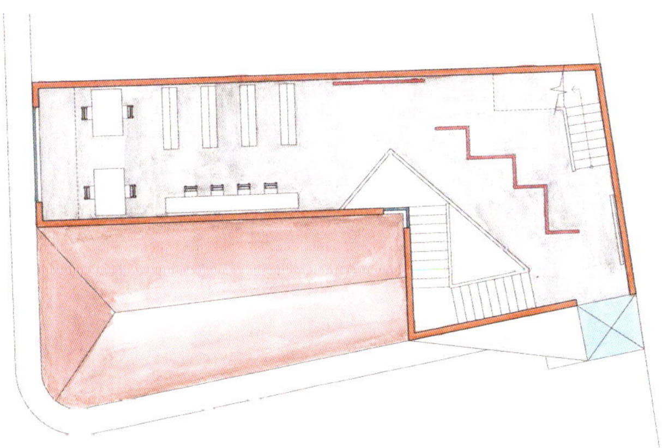

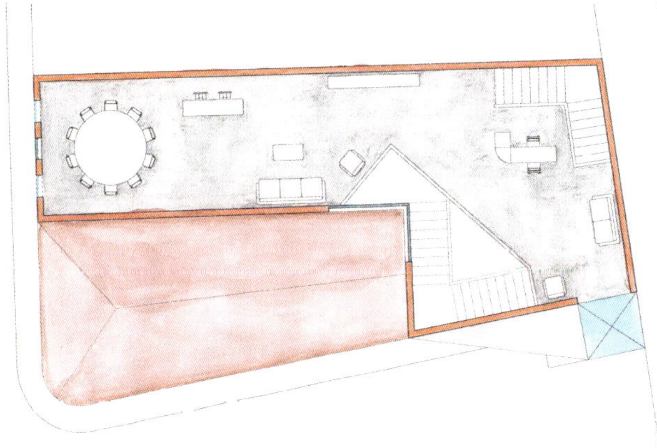

Lima Art Museum – MALI

Lima, Peru, 2016

Passageways have always fascinated men. These are search spaces – whether the searches are systematic or random. They are spaces for surprises and discoveries, fortuitous or arranged encounters, simple wonderings, exercises in urbanity. Passageway and coexistence are terms that express the spirit of our project for the new contemporary art wing of the Lima Art Museum – MALI. It will be, at one time, a great urban passageway and a meeting ground for subway users and visitors of the museum and the park.

The project creates a respectful and subtle dialogue, a tense and silent coexistence between two buildings that are almost a 150 years distant in time, allowing each of them to speak the language of its era. Flexibility and freedom are guidelines of the project, with the goal of taking advantage of the spaces to the fullest, with multiple usage possibilities, as any contemporary art museum requires. The complex should be geared towards the present and future, open to new ways of expression and manners of exposition.

A large entryway, 40 meters wide, in a soft decline welcomes the visitors and passersby, to lead them into the new annex of the MALI. In a vertical organization pattern, the use classes go from most public on the upper levels to the most private and introspective on the lower floor.

A great cleft slices the unit vertically, across its entire expanse and all its floors, bringing controlled lighting and ventilation to the entire edifice. The cleft will hold a vertical garden of rustic outlook and a water garden. These gardens are structuring the entire project and they are fundamental to the creation of a gentle and welcoming atmosphere for the users of the museum's several facilities, all designed completely underground.

The entire structure of the complex will be of exposed concrete. A rigorous design of forms will give the piece its final projected outlook, at times emphasizing the vertical lines, at times the horizontal ones. Vertical structural plates provide support for the ribbed, prestressed slabs. The structure is fundamental in defining the architecture we intend, as free and versatile. Once the structure is done, so will be the architecture.

The pigmented cement – Andean earthy – employed in the preparation of the concrete, with high fixation and strength technology, will avoid the need for maintenance painting and future repairs. Glass will be utilized in all the floors to capture daylight, with the possibility of control through the use of blackout systems and curtains.

The dense and vibrant landscape of downtown Lima will continue to display the grand white palace shinning in the distance, with its reflection mirrored in a water blade, announcing something new down below the earth: The MALI contemporary art wing.

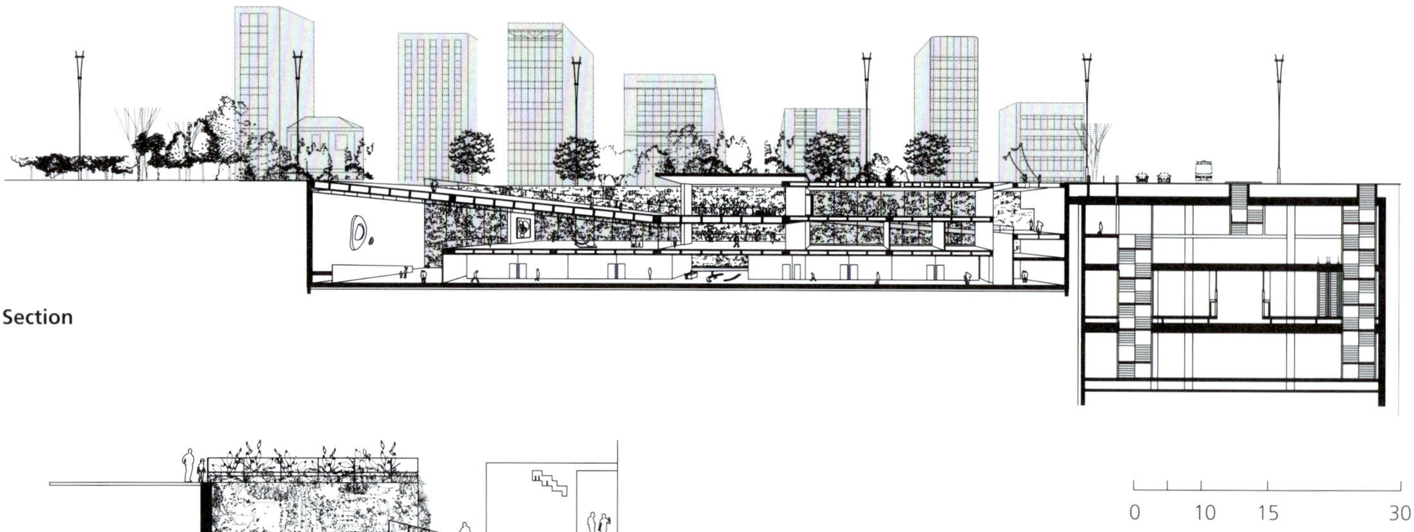

Section

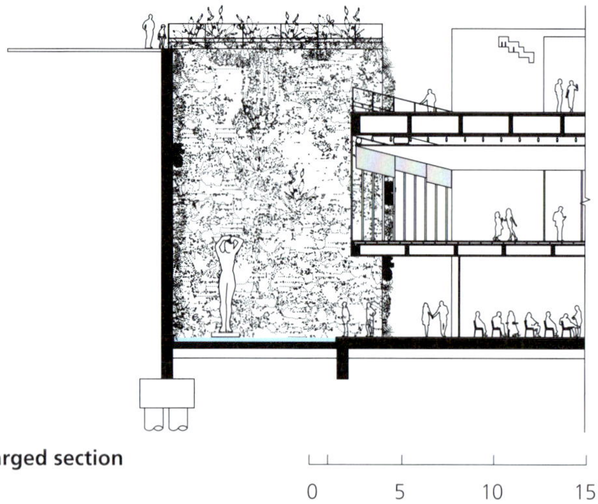

Enlarged section

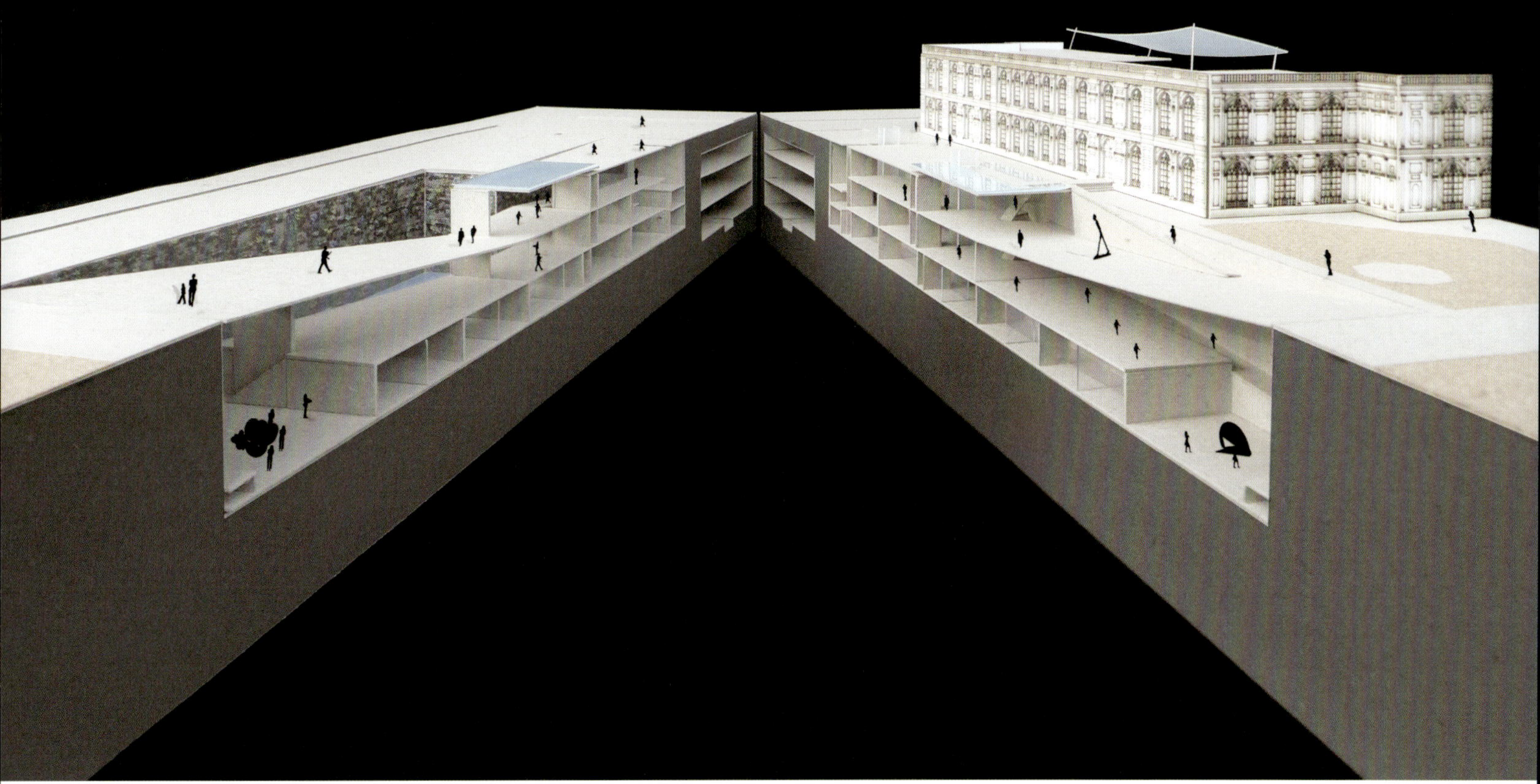

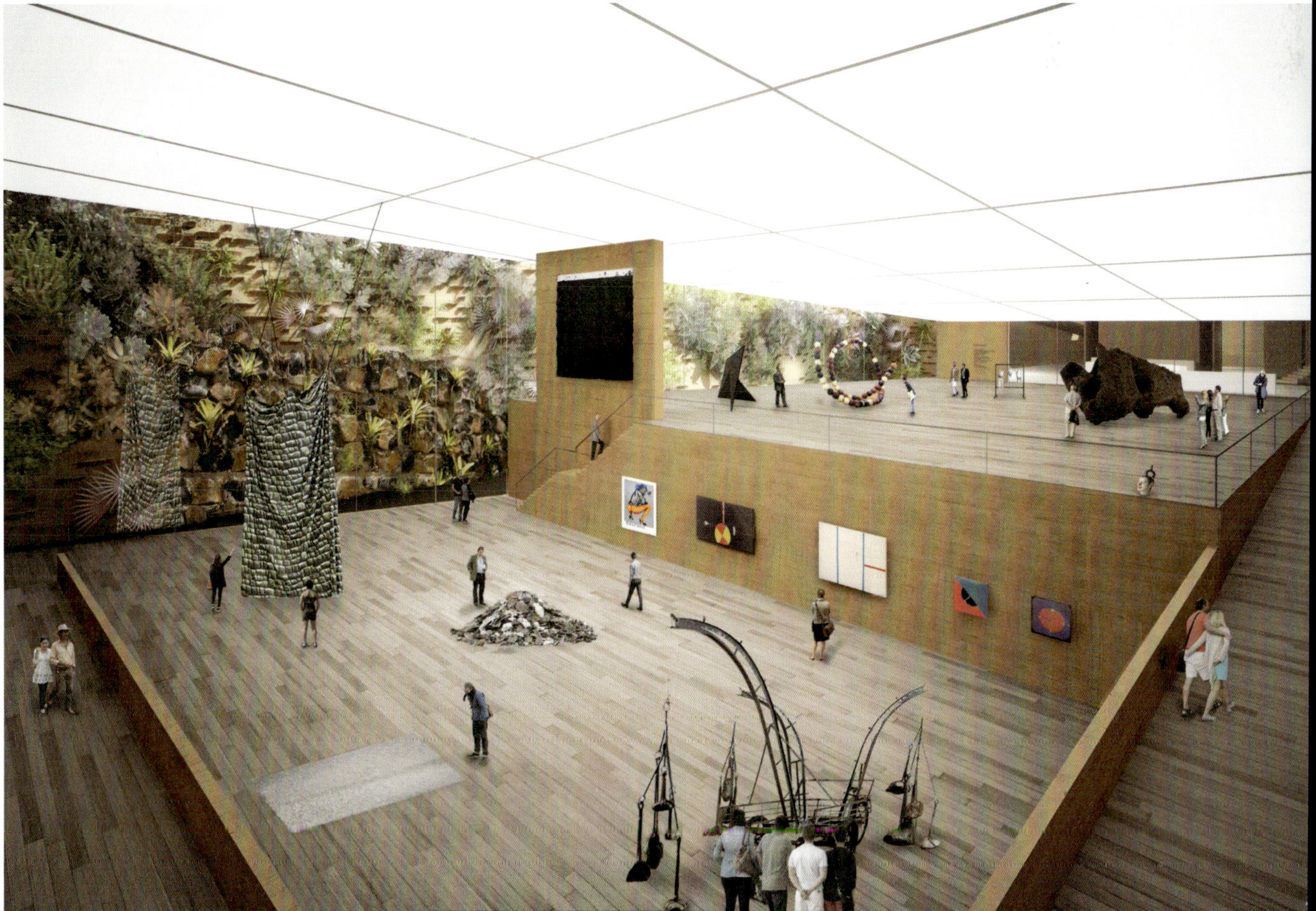

Terreiro de Òsùmàrè

Salvador, Bahia, 2017

From a larger scale, the green spot delineated by Terreiro de Òsùmàrè, on the hillside of Vasco da Gama Avenue, represents what has been the logic of occupation of the irregular territory of Salvador for the past few centuries: Small constructions at the tops of hills along with access paths, surrounded by the exuberant vegetation set on slopes, until the valleys and streams are reached.

This previous model has been slowly fading in the last decades, destroyed by the massive and unbridled urbanization process. However, Terreiro de Òsùmàrè, as a recognized national historical heritage site, preserves this original logic and its features. The logic is that of mediating construction with the preservation of nature. In the urban area of Salvador, this is one of the last remaining examples of that occupation method, adapted to the topography and the geographical features of the city. Òsùmàrè has withstood thanks to the traditions of the *candomblé* religion.

The intervention we project can be divided in three nuclei corresponding to the three levels of contour lines. In the superior nucleus, a new building should be erected in ocher yellow, earthly shades. The ground floor there will have an industrial size kitchen. The upper floors will hold a laundry room, quarters, the residence of the babalorixá,[1] and administrative offices. The staircase of this nucleus will connect the upper streetway to the central contour level where the main shed is. Much like the current stairwell of the lower level, the new staircase will constitute a strong symbolic landmark of the *terreiro*.

For the mid-level nucleus, the project outlines reformations, with a few demolitions and some small constructions. The ritual space of the main shed will be expanded and the surrounding areas will be reworked. An important demand of this nucleus should also be highlighted: The expansion of the frontal terrace of the shed, which works as a roof for the lower nucleus. It should now be able to accommodate a large number of people with comfort and security on days of celebration.

The lower nucleus was designed to hold the Terreiro de Òsùmàrè Memorial. It will be built on the lower floors of the new building, along with an auditorium, exhibition rooms, a library, and service areas. This new representational and institutional block should be entirely coated in pigmented mortar of an earthy reddish hue of iron oxide, in order for it to stand out in relation to the other buildings.

The long white staircase that penetrates the woods and leads into the frontal terrace will be kept and restored. It is a strong symbolic element of the *terreiro*. Taking into account the contour lines, the new designs of the adjoining areas are defined, in order to make the access to the woods and the sacred trees of worship easier. One of these levels should hold a large plaza connected to Exu's House. It will be another place for rites, gatherings, and leisure.

Mata Escura (as this area of the city was known until the beginning of the 20th century) will be restored, and it will grow in density. It will receive pathways, in gentle ramps for walking and for the contemplation of nature and the holly.

In the lower part of the terrain, at the level of Vasco da Gama Avenue, the House of Arts will be a new space prepared for the execution of cultural and social projects that the *terreiro* already oversees, to benefit the local and the general community.

As a general guideline, the project aims at a unity of language across all the interventions, trying to maintain the integrity and strong character of the existing buildings and spaces, in consonance with future constructions.

We attempted to introduce elements of nature with our architecture, such as the stone employed in the retaining walls; the different shades of ochre and red used in the plastered walls of the new units, in contrast with the whitewashed coating utilized currently in the houses of the saints; the clay used on the floors of the future Exu Yard; and, finally, the gravel on the pathways to the woods.

With the collaboration of guest artists, symbolic elements will inhabit the many niches of the future institutional block building, in the manner of the figures of the Royal Palaces of Abomey in Benin.

Today, the blue and white colors bring light into the worship grounds and they should continue to do so after the reformation. New *cogobós* were designed to protect the terraces and verandas of the entire complex, inspired by the symbolic coiled snake. Seen from above or from below, the winding staircase should, likewise, represent the long snake/path to cross the holly lands of Ilê Òsùmàrè.

Note

1. T.N.: Title given to the male priests of *candomblé* meaning father of orixás or father of saints.

Section

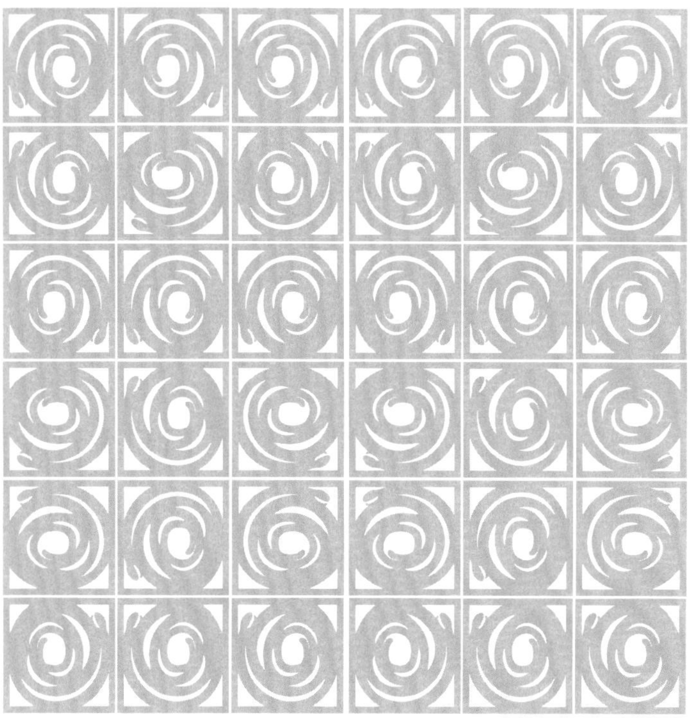

Left, Òsùmàrè *cobogó* module used for ventilation of the vertical circulation block, as well as short walls etc.; top, Òsùmàrè's Throne, study with wood relief od the snake/*cobogó*

Left, niches in the walls of Ghezo Royal Palace, Abomey, Benin, design reference

Araucaria Museum

Countryside of Rio Grande do Sul, 2018

The creation of a museum to give reverence and deal with the theme of the araucaria (araucaria angustifolia) in the South of Brazil is an imperative. Better put, it is a debt that must be repaid to one of the oldest vegetal species of the planet, whose presence both physically and symbolically is so poignant in human occupation and goes well beyond our territory and borders.

Projected as occupation of, but also entanglement with, the wooded area typical of the Araucaria Forest – once a strong presence in the subtropical region, it is now nearly extinct –, this study is born out of the generative logic of the woods themselves. This logic leads us to occupy the terrain with several buildings meandering through the grounds, dodging the trees, and intertwining with them.

A great concrete marquee leads into the museum, which is made up of blocks of different sizes. We enter the ensemble in the first of these, a welcoming area with information and gathering facilities, restrooms, a small coffee/gift shop that should provide products and treats related to the theme, eatable and otherwise.

Like concrete boxes or pillboxes camouflaged in the woods, each of the ensuing blocks will house an exhibition room that will deal with specific themes: The araucaria and its scientific and botanical aspects; the occupation of the territory, from the first human settlements to the pioneer forest explorers; the presence of this wood in the Brazilian historical and socioeconomic context, especially in housing; the universe of pine nuts as ancestral food and its gastronomic possibilities today. These units will be interconnected by covered walkways, at times more closed-off, at times less so. The walkways will serve as exposition galleries as well, and walking through them should feel like strolling through the woods.

The entire ensemble of the museum will have the araucaria as a basic building material. The concrete (laid in different designs and geometrical shapes), the frames, the insulation panels, and even the furniture shall be produced from this wood, within the current parameters of recycling and ecological management.

Besides the thematic units, the museum will also display a small multipurpose auditorium, connected directly to the welcoming area. This block, unlike the rest of them, will be entirely open to the surrounding landscape, with glass casing and optional blackout curtains.

Climate, contour lines, fauna, flora, water, and, especially, human creation in the construction of new landscapes and new life, all of it should serve as thematic subject of the new museum, which will radiate energy and transmit its message of celebration for the araucaria tree.

Plan

CAPTION

1. Access marquee
2. Hall
3. Module 1 (araucaria)
4. Module 2 (araucaria)
5. Module 3 (water)
6. Module 4 (railroad and great hotel)
7. Module 5 (music)
8. Module 6 (theater)
9. Auditorium
10. Technical reserve
11. Administration
12. Warehouse

Japanese Immigration Museum

Registro, São Paulo, 2016

Given the donation of the KKKK Complex to the Sesc Institution, the Japanese Immigration Museum, that previously occupied the mill, is due to be transferred to another building in town. A gentrified area in the center of Beira Rio Park was granted for the construction of the new museum, which will house the collection, exhibition areas, and a small auditorium.

The collection is made up of objects, photographs, and documents of the pioneer immigrants that came to the region starting in 1913. It also features several works of art donated in 2002, when the KKKK Complex was inaugurated. These are sculptures and paintings produced by Japanese-Brazilian artists, among them are contemporary works and older ones dating back to the generation that first arrived here in the beginning of the past century.

A pavilion with 650 square meters was designed in exposed concrete and glass. It was implanted lengthwise between the water's edge and the avenue that runs parallel to the river. It is an elongated and low-ceiling unit, supported by stilts, as a way of allowing the structure to scape eventual floods that affect the area from time to time.

The Southern façade, which is towards the city, since it never receives direct sunlight, was designed fully in glass. This allows the collection displayed within to be showcased to the city outside. The Northern side, which faces the river and the riparian woodland, is an almost blind façade, with concrete insulation to protect from the heat. So as to not loose completely the possibility of gazing at the river, small openings were put there, each flanked by two Thonet style benches. Each opening also features a different symbolic shape derived from Japanese culture, with meanings such as fortitude, patience, prosperity, beauty, good harvest, protection, and poetry.

In summary, the Japanese Immigration Museum of Registro will serve as a new communal center, once it is set in Beira Rio Park. It will further reinforce the operation started there with the restoration of the KKKK Complex, that is, the reclaiming of the river bed as an urban centrality. Such a move is based on the history of the place, since the city was founded there, but also on the construction of a future of healthy and amiable relations with the river waters.

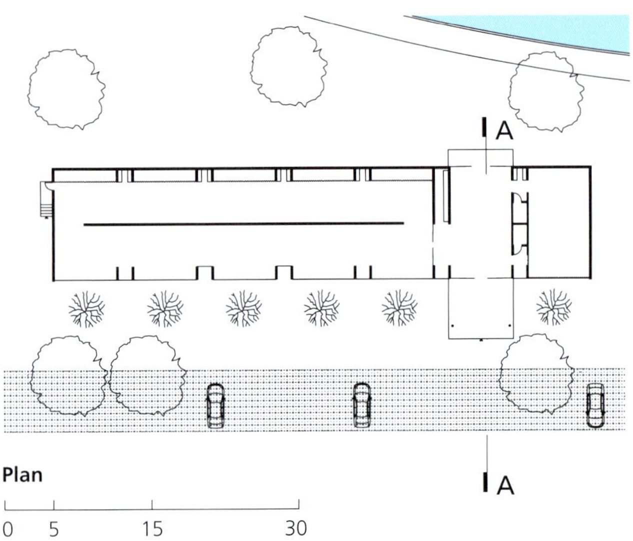

Plan

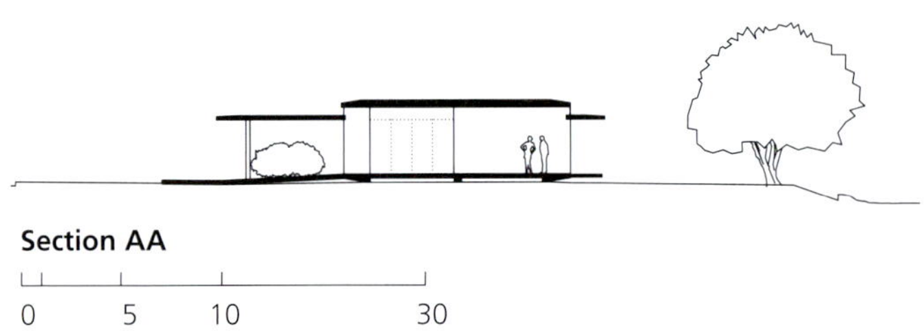

Section AA

Sesc Registro

Registro, São Paulo, 2018

In 2016, the town of Registro donated the historic complex known as KKKK to the Sesc SP institution, so that a new Sesc unit could be implanted there.

Unlike what happens in the other units of the institution, whether they are on the metropolitan area of São Paulo or in smaller cities, the Sesc unit of Registro has a set of peculiarities that makes it a unique case. In large part, this has to do with the geography of the place, whether we analyze it from a wider regional scale or from a local micro scale.

The Registro unit presents itself with a vocation and a duty to fulfil its mission as a cultural, sporting, and leisure center for the entire Ribeira Valley. In the past few decades, this region was seen and treated as a second-class territory by the state authorities and the politicians in general. The Ribeira Valley has been in isolation.

This isolation, however, could also be explained by its natural landscape of mountains and floodplains, aggressively hot and humid tropical weather, and by the strong presence of the Atlantic Forest. These factors certainly make the access to the valley more difficult.

Registro is prominent as the capital city of this small universe of the Ribeira Valley, composed all together of 23 towns and a population of 443 thousand people. And, yet, it is the Ribeira de Iguape River that reins in the area. It dictates the cycles and rhythms of the lives of these communities.

The local micro scale of the Sesc Registro makes it singular. Once the second module is finished, it will constitute a set divided into two separate blocks of buildings, organized by a central public plaza, and occupying two lots that do not reach each other, even as they are both on the same riverbank. One of the modules is already in working condition, the historic KKKK Complex. It is totally open and integrated to the city, with no fences, walls, or gates; as will be the second module, on the other side of the plaza.

This is done not only for the continuation of the historic complex, but also by the decision to expand the plaza into the domains of the Sesc unit. The design is, in the same measure, a product of the need to protect against the recurring floods that affect the area. This made us decide to elevate the building from the soil level and to create a large urban terrace, a shelter from sun and rain, for visitors and passersby, a public stage for the most diverse activities.

These distinctive aspects of the Sesc Registro establish their own way of relating spatially to the urban and public environment. With the construction of the second module, the exuberant nature and the cultural spring of human occupation that surround the majestic Ribeira de Iguape River will be more strongly represented: upstream, to the slopes of Eldorado and Iporanga; downstream, to Iguape, Cananeia, and the rich waters of the Atlantic Ocean.

Once completed, this unit should be the urban epicenter of encounters between the cultures of different origins that make up the contemporary life of the city: *caipira*, *caiçara*, *quilombola*, indigenous-Guarani, Japanese-Brazilian.[1] And the city of Registro assumes more and more its role as capital city of the Ribeira Valley Region.

A long concrete marquee/walkway will connect the first module, the historic KKKK, with the second module, traversing the Beira Rio Plaza and signaling the presence of the Sesc Registro on both sides. Undoubtedly, the urban intervention created in the river landscape will reorganize the accesses, the limits, and the flow of pedestrians to the plaza, besides constituting a new landmark that will frame the river bend.

We will employ concrete pigmented with iron oxide on the new structures of the walkway and on the building, as well as on the foundations of the pool, ramps, and ladders. We are looking for the same shade of red that the bricks of the KKKK Complex have, so that a visual unity can be created with the Sesc building. A similar process will be delineated with the use of wooden *muxarabi* framework, already employed in the historic edifice.

However, the efforts to create unity do not seek to undermine the hundred year division in time that separates both constructions – the KKKK was built in 1920. This period gap will be present and highlighted in the architectural solutions, in the building techniques, and in the materials employed in each time period, without causing superposition or submission of one to the other.

Note

1. T.N.: These are all identities related to the roots of local culture, in a mixture of Native-American, African, European and Asian immigrant ethnicities.

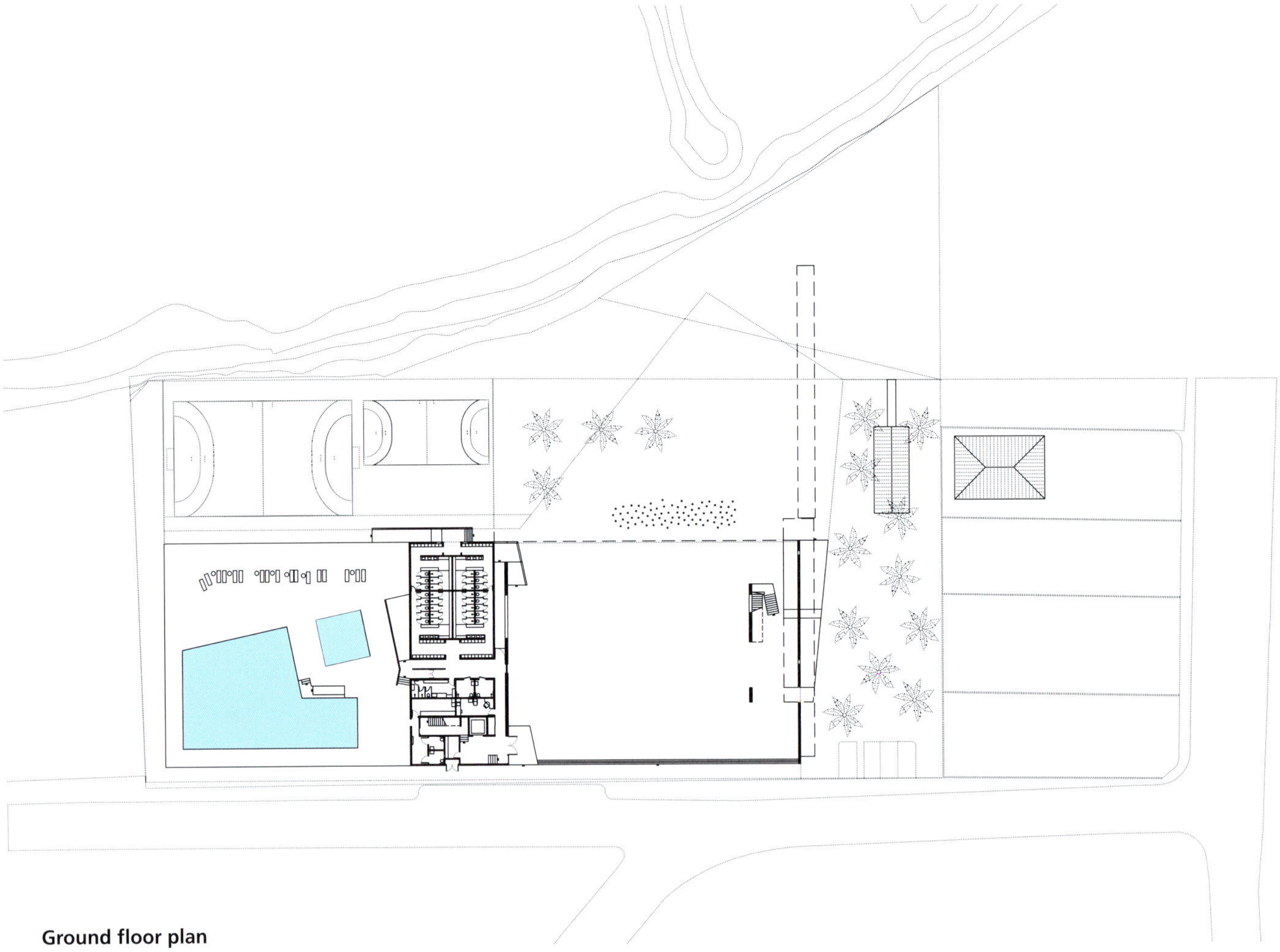

Ground floor plan

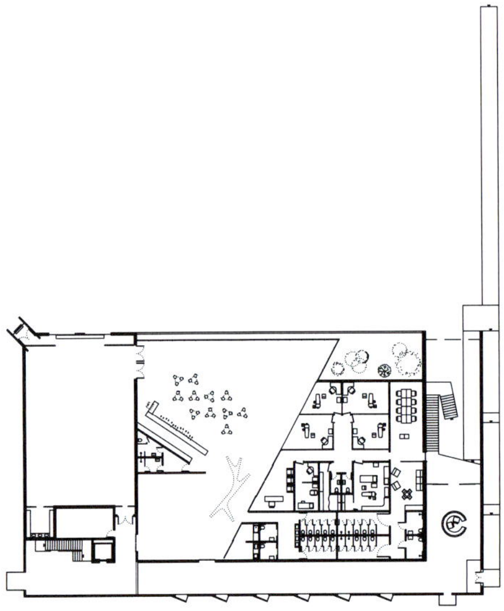

First floor plan

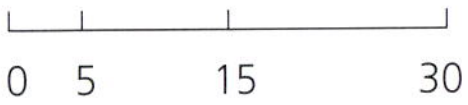

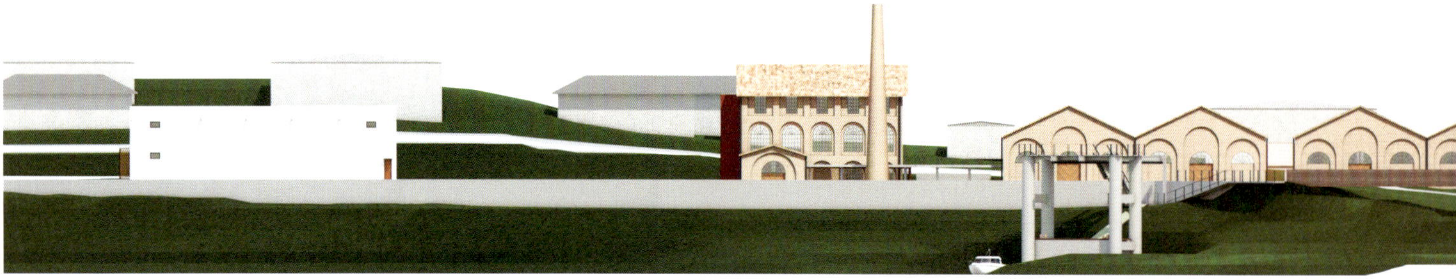

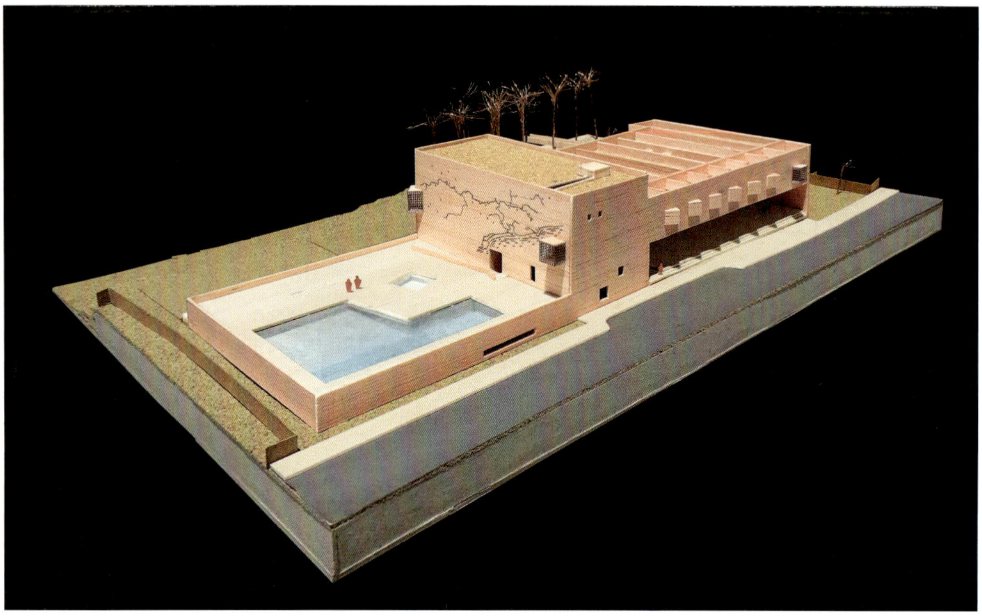

Bibliography

Books by Francisco Fanucci and Marcelo Ferraz

Fanucci, Francisco, and Marcelo Carvalho Ferraz. *Francisco Fanucci, Marcelo Ferraz. Brasil Arquitetura*. São Paulo: Cosac Naify, 2005.

Fanucci, Francisco, and Marcelo Carvalho Ferraz. *Theatro Polytheama de Jundiaí*. Jundiaí: Prefeitura Municipal de Jundiaí, 1996.

Ferraz, Marcelo Carvalho. *Arquitetura Conversável*. Rio de Janeiro: Azougue, 2011.

Ferraz, Marcelo Carvalho. *Arquitetura Rural na Serra da Mantiqueira*. 1st edition. São Paulo: Instituto Quadrante, 1992.

Ferraz, Marcelo Carvalho. *Arquitetura Rural na Serra da Mantiqueira*. 2nd edition. Translated by C. Stuart Birknishaw. São Paulo: Instituto Bardi, 1996.

Ferraz, Marcelo Carvalho. *Arquitetura Rural na Serra da Mantiqueira*. 3rd edition. Translated by C. Stuart Birknishaw. São Paulo: Romano Guerra, 2020.

Ferraz, Marcelo Carvalho, ed. *Lina Bo Bardi*. 5th edition. São Paulo: Instituto Bardi/Romano Guerra, 2018.

Ferraz, Marcelo Carvalho, ed. *O conjunto KKKK*. São Paulo: Takano, 2002.

Articles by Francisco Fanucci and Marcelo Ferraz

Fanucci, Francisco, Marcelo Carvalho Ferraz, and Marcos Cartum. "Praça das Artes, São Paulo." *Monolito*, no. 18 (2013 annual), December 2013/ January 2014, 72-85.

Fanucci, Francisco, and Marcelo Carvalho Ferraz. "Cais do Sertão." *Projetos* 18, no. 216.02, December 2018. http://www.vitruvius.com.br/revistas/read/projetos/18.216/7193.

Fanucci, Francisco, and Marcelo Carvalho Ferraz. "Casa da Lagoa." *Projetos* 19, no. 222.01, June 2019. http://www.vitruvius.com.br/revistas/read/projetos/19.222/7403.

Fanucci, Francisco, and Marcelo Carvalho Ferraz. "Comunidade se Prepara para a Cidade Formal. Brasil Arquitetura, Habitação Social, São Paulo." *Projeto Design*, no. 396, February 2013, 66-69.

Fanucci, Francisco, and Marcelo Carvalho Ferraz. "Escuela del Parque Santo André." *Arquine*, no. 49, September 2009, 60-613.

Fanucci, Francisco, and Marcelo Carvalho Ferraz. "Fiesta del Pan." *Summa+*, no. 96, September 2008, 36-41.

Fanucci, Francisco, and Marcelo Carvalho Ferraz. "Jardín de Infantes de la Escuela San Andrés." *Trama*, no. 110, January 2012, 22-25.

Fanucci, Francisco, and Marcelo Carvalho Ferraz. "Ocupando Espaços para Deixá-los Livres. Brasil Arquitetura – Praça das Artes." *Summa+*, no. 135, May 2014, 80-89.

Fanucci, Francisco, and Marcelo Carvalho Ferraz. "Praça das Artes." *Projetos* 13, no. 151.03 (July 2013). http://www.vitruvius.com.br/revistas/read/projetos/13.151/4820.

Fanucci, Francisco, and Marcelo Carvalho Ferraz, "Sede do Instituto Socioambiental – ISA." *Projetos* 16, no. 191.0, November 2016. http://www.vitruvius.com.br/revistas/read/projetos/16.191/6284.

Fanucci, Francisco, Marcelo Carvalho Ferraz, and Marcelo Suzuki, "Casa em Tamboré." *AU – Arquitetura e Urbanismo*, no. 48, June/July 1993, 35-37.

Fanucci, Francisco, Marcelo Carvalho Ferraz, and Marcelo Suzuki, "Casa em Tamboré, Barueri, São Paulo." *Architécti*, no. 19/20, August/September 1993, 42-45.

Fanucci, Francisco, and Marcelo Carvalho Ferraz, "Acción Arquitectónica." In *Brasil – Documentos del Colegio de Arquitectura de la UFSQ*, edited by Diego Oleas Serrano and Abilio Guerra, 57-60. Quito: El Colegio de Arquitectura de la Universidad San Francisco de Quito, 2010.

Fanucci, Francisco, and Marcelo Carvalho Ferraz, "Museu Rodin Bahia." *Projetos* 6, no. 070.01, October 2006. http://www.vitruvius.com.br/revistas/read/projetos/06.070/2721.

Fanucci, Francisco, and Marcelo Carvalho Ferraz, "Requalificação do Bairro Amarelo." *Arte!Brasileiros*, no. 2, November 2009, 46-47.

Fanucci, Francisco, and Marcelo Carvalho Ferraz, "Praça das Artes. Urbanismo Hecho de Arquitectura." *ARQ*, no. 92, April 2016, 26-31.

Fanucci, Francisco, and Gianfranco Vannucchi, "Desenhando Conceitos, Construindo Manifestos." *Arc Design*, no. 10, July/August 1999, 28-33.

Fanucci, Francisco. "Arquitetura em Sítios Históricos." *Arquiteturismo* 02, no. 020.03, October 2008. http://www.vitruvius.com.br/revistas/read/arquiteturismo/02.020/1466.

Fanucci, Francisco. "Brasília 50 Anos – Edifício Antac, 2004 – Brasil Arquitetura." *Projeto Design*, no. 362, April 2010, 96.

Fanucci, Francisco. "Praça das Artes." *Alecrim*, April 2018, 7-8.

Ferraz, Marcelo Carvalho, Marcelo Suzuki, José Sales Costa Filho, and Tâmara Roman. "Paço Municipal de Cambuí." *Projeto*, no. 131, April/ May 1990, 36-37.

Ferraz, Marcelo Carvalho. "An Idea of a Museum / Uma Ideia de Museu." In *Museu Art Today / Museu Arte Hoje*, edited by Martin Grossmann, and Gilberto Mariotti, 19-23, 123-126. São Paulo: Hedra, 2011.

Ferraz, Marcelo Carvalho. "Arquitetura em Vão? Sobre Exposição da Arquitetura Brasileira em Matosinhos, Portugal." *Resenhas Online* 18, no. 205.04, January 2019. http://www.vitruvius.com.br/revistas/read/resenhasonline/18.205/7231.

Ferraz, Marcelo Carvalho. "Casa in Città." *Abitare*, no. 374, June 1998, 214-215.

Ferraz, Marcelo Carvalho. "Desenho e Projeto." In *Disegno. Desenho. Desígnio*, edited by Edith Derdyk, 221-228. São Paulo: Senac São Paulo, 2007.

Ferraz, Marcelo Carvalho. "Desenho, Projeto, Arquitetura..." *Projetos* 17, no. 201.06, September 2017. http://www.vitruvius.com.br/revistas/read/projetos/17.201/6708.

Ferraz, Marcelo Carvalho. "França, Bahia e Rodin." *S/N° – Sem número*, no. 8, Spring/ Summer 2006-2007, 132-135.

Ferraz, Marcelo Carvalho. "Graças e Desgraças de Nossas Cidades." *Cult*, no. 113, May 2007, 47-50.

Ferraz, Marcelo Carvalho. "Graças e Desgraças de Nossas Cidades." *Drops* 07, no. 019.03, September 2007. http://www.vitruvius.com.br/revistas/read/drops/07.019/1721.

Ferraz, Marcelo Carvalho. "Minha Experiência com Lina." *AU – Arquitetura e Urbanismo*, no. 40, February/March 1992, 39.

Ferraz, Marcelo Carvalho. "Museus têm Novos Papéis na Vida Urbana." *Folha de S.Paulo*, January 8, 2010, E5.

Ferraz, Marcelo Carvalho. "Numa Velha Fábrica de Tambores. Sesc Pompeia Comemora 25 Anos." *Minha Cidade* 08, no. 093.01, April 2008. http://www.vitruvius.com.br/revistas/read/minhacidade/08.093/1897.

Ferraz, Marcelo Carvalho. "O Pelourinho no Pelourinho." *Minha Cidade* 08, no. 096.02, July 2008. http://www.vitruvius.com.br/revistas/read/minhacidade/08.096/1885.

Ferraz, Marcelo Carvalho. "O Rio e a Cidade." In *Piracicaba, o Rio e a Cidade: Ações de Reaproximação*, 92-102. Piracicaba: Instituto de Pesquisa e Planejamento de Piracicaba – IPPLAP, 2011.

Ferraz, Marcelo Carvalho. "Obra Poética de uma Humanística." *O Estado de S. Paulo*, April 29, 2012, D4.

Ferraz, Marcelo Carvalho. "Olho Sobre o Bexiga." *Arquitextos* 08, no. 087.00 (August 2007). http://www.vitruvius.com.br/revistas/read/arquitextos/08.087/215.

Ferraz, Marcelo Carvalho. "Sesc Pompeia – Conferencia Dictada el 31 de Mayo de 2013." *Colección Conferencias*, no. 6 (August 2013).

Ferraz, Marcelo Carvalho. "Stones Against Diamonds." *AA Files*, no. 64, 2012, 78-79.

Ferraz, Marcelo Carvalho. "Útil, Bela e Cheia de Vida." *A&D – Arte e Decoração*, no. 225, October 1998, 64-73.

Ferraz, Marcelo Carvalho. "Volumes Articulados e Materiais Rústicos Definem Projeto com Inspiração em Arquitetura Rural Mineira." *Projeto Design*, no. 219, April 1998, 64-67.

Ferraz, Marcelo. "Arquitetura de Palavras: A Escrita Livre e Exata de Lina Bo Bardi." *Folha de S.Paulo*, March 3, 2013, 6.

Ferraz, Marcelo. "Graces and Disgraces of Our Cities." In *Liber Amicorum Max Risselada*, edited by Dick Van Gameren and Dirk Van Den Heuvel, 112-115. Delft: Delft University of Technology, 2014.

Ferraz, Marcelo. "Haicai – Casa de Arquiteto / Hai Kai – Architect's House." *Monolito*, no. 14, April/May 2013, 8-9.

Ferraz, Marcelo. "Marcelo Ferraz – Casa Ubiracica (1996-1997), São Paulo." *Monolito*, no. 14, April/March 2013, 108-115.

Ferraz, Marcelo. "Memória do Futuro." *Folha de S.Paulo*, February 25, 2003, A3.

Ferraz, Marcelo. "São Nossas Periferias uma Causa Perdida?" In *O Arquiteto e a Cidade Contemporânea*, edited by Abilio Guerra and Roberto Fialho, 42-45. São Paulo: Romano Guerra, 2009.

Ferraz, Marcelo. "Sonhos Não Envelhecem / Dreams Do Not Age." *Monolito*, no. 18 (2013 annual), December 2013/January 2014, 60-65.

Ferraz, Marcelo. "Um Centro de Referência para o Pampa." *Arqtexto*, no. 15 (2009), 146-149.

Books

Almeida, Cícero Antônio Fonseca de. *Museu de Porto Seguro*. Brasília: IPHAN/Ministério da Cultura, 2000.

Almeida, Daniel, Rogério Trentini, and Baba Vacaro. *O Cais do Sertão de Gonzagão – Quando Arquitetura Rima com Música*. Collection Arranha Céu, vol. 4. São Paulo: Editora C4, 2018.

Andrade, Mário (1928). *Ensaio Sobre a Música Brasileira*. 3rd edition. São Paulo: Martins/INL, 1972.

Andreoli, Elisabetta, and Adrian Forty. *Arquitetura Moderna Brasileira*. London: Phaidon, 2004.

Augustat, Claudia, and Carolina de West. *Copyright by Kadiwéu – Von der Körperbemalung* im *Mato Grosso zur Fassadenfliese in Berlin*. Berlin: SMPK, 1998.

Bachelard, Gaston. *A Poética do Espaço*. Collection Os Pensadores. São Paulo: Abril Cultural, 1978.

Bardi, Lina Bo. *Tempos de Grossura – O Design no Impasse*. São Paulo: Instituto Bardi, 1994.

Bastos, Maria Alice Junqueira. *Pós-Brasília – Rumos da Arquitetura Brasileira*. São Paulo: Perspectiva, 2003.

Cavalcanti, Lauro, and André Corrêa do Lago. *Ainda Moderno? Arquitetura Brasileira Contemporânea*. Rio de Janeiro: Nova Fronteira, 2005.

Correa, Maria Elizabeth Peirão, Mirela Geiger de Mello, and Helia Mari Neves. *Arquitetura Escolar Paulista: 1890-1920*. São Paulo: FDE, 1991.

Cruz, Eneida Carvalho Ferraz. *Cambuí, 20 Casas do Século 20*. São Paulo: Ferrari Artes Gráficas, 2006.

Ferraz, João Grinspum, ed. *Museu do Pão – Caminho dos Moinhos*. Ilópolis: Associação dos Amigos dos Moinhos do Vale do Taquari, 2008.

Ferreira, Avany de Francisco, Maria Elizabeth Peirão Corrêa, and Mirela Geiger de Mello. *Arquitetura Escolar Paulista – Restauro*. São Paulo: FED, 1998.

Finotti, Leonardo. *Brasil Arquitetura – Praça das Artes*. São Paulo: Blurb, 2013.

Fortes, Alexandre, Mônica Almeida Kornis, and Paulo Fontes, eds. *Trabalho e Trabalhadores no Brasil*. Rio de Janeiro: CPDOC/FGV, 2006.

França, Elizabete. *Arquitetura em Retrospectiva – 10 Bienais de São Paulo*. São Paulo: KPMO Cultura e Arte, 2017.

Governo do Estado da Bahia. *Sociedade Cultural Auguste Rodin. Museu Rodin Bahia: Estratégia de Ação e Desenvolvimento*. Serie Obras Institucionais. Salvador: Secretaria da Cultura e Turismo, 2003.

Governo Do Paraná. *Programa de Valorização Cultural do Paraná – Novo Museu. Apresentação ao BID Banco Interamericano de Desenvolvimento.* Curitiba: Secretaria de Estado para Assuntos Estratégicos, 2002.

Jatobá, Waldick. *Desafios do Design Sustentável Brasileiro.* São Paulo: Versal, 2014.

Jordan, Kátia ed. *De Villa Catharino a Museu Rodin Bahia 1912-2006: Um Palacete Baiano e Sua História*. Salvador: Solisluna, 2006.

Koolhaas, Rem. *Nova York Delirante: Um Manifesto Retroativo para Manhattan*. São Paulo: Cosac Naify, 2008. Original publication: Koolhaas, Rem. *Delirious New York: Retroactive Manifesto for Manhattan*. New York: Oxford University Press, 1978.

Melo, Luiz Emanuel Limeira de, and Gabriel Loureiro Pereira da Mota Ramos. *Cais do Sertão. Prodetur & Pernambuco – Relato de uma Parceria de Sucesso*. Recife: Provisual, 2018.

Neves, José Manuel, ed. *Brasil Arquitetura + Marcos Cartum – Praça das Artes*. Collection Brazilian Architects. Lisbon: Uzina Books, 2013.

Nosek, Victor, ed. *Praça das Arte*s. Rio de Janeiro: Azougue, 2013.

Nosek, Victor. *Teatro Polytheama de Jundiaí*. Jundiaí: Prefeitura do Município de Jundiaí, 2011.

Rocca, Luísa Duran. *Breve Histórico Sobre os Moinhos para Produzir Farinha na América*. Porto Alegre: Author's edition, 2004.

Rutman, Jacques, ed. "Brasil Arquitetura." *Estruturas Metálicas – Projetos e Detalhes*. São Paulo: JJ Carol, 2014.

Santinelli, Cecília. *Escola-obra Moinho "Colognese" de Ilópolis*. Rome: Instituto Ítalo-Latino Americano, 2006.

Schlee, Aldyr Garcia. *Dicionário da Cultura Pampeana Sul-Rio-Grandense*. 2 volumes. Pelotas: Fuctos da Paiz, 2019.

Schlee, Aldyr Garcia. *Uma Terra Só*. 2nd edition. Porto Alegre: Ardotempo, 2011.

Segre, Roberto. *Casas Brasileiras*. Rio de Janeiro: Viana & Mosley, 2010.

Segre, Roberto. *Museus Brasileiros*. Rio de Janeiro: Viana & Mosley, 2010.

Sennett, Richard. *O Artífice*. Rio de Janeiro: Record, 2008.

The Phaidon Atlas of 21st Century World Architecture. London: Phaidon, 2008.

Tomazello, Maria Guiomar L. *Plano Diretor e Projetos para Implantação do Engenho da Ciência*. Piracicaba: Prefeitura Municipal de Piracicaba/UNIMEP/IPHAN, 2003.

Winkler-Kühlken, Bärbel. *Brasilianisches Flair Prägt ein Quartier: Das Gelbe Viertel. Dokumentation*. Berlin: WoGeHe, 1998.

Book Chapters

Anelli, Renato. "Museo del Pane." In *Architettura Contemporanea: Brasile*, 136-137. Milan: Motta Architettura, 2008.

Benjamin, Walter. "O Narrador." In *Obras Escolhidas*. Vol. 1 of Magia e Técnica, Arte e Política. São Paulo: Brasiliense, 1986.

Bogéa, Marta. "Territorio – Tiempo." In *Brasil – Documentos del Colegio de Arquitectura de la UFSQ*, edited by Diego Oleas Serrano and Abilio Guerra, 54-56. Quito: El Colegio de Arquitectura de la Universidad San Francisco de Quito, 2010.

Bonesio, Luisa. "Habitar a Terra e Reconhecer-se Nos Lugares." In *Filosofia e Arquitetura da Paisagem: um Manual*, edited by Adriana Verísssimo Serrão, 203-210. Lisbon: Centro de Filosofia da Universidade de Lisboa, 2012.

"Brasil Arquitetura, Brazil. The Novo Zepelin Complex." In *Houses of Steel*, edited by Stephen Crafti, 78-79. Victoria: Images Publishing, 2009.

Cecília, Bruno, Laurence Kimmel, and Anke Tiggemann. "Teatro Engenho Central; Museu das Missões; Museu do Pão." In *Architectural Guide Brazil,* 96, 282-283. Berlin: Dom, 2013.

Cunha, Aguinaldo. "Arquitetura 2012." In *APCA 60 anos*, 31. São Paulo: Monolito, 2017.

Ferraz, Marcelo. "O Interior do Interior." In *Bloco 5 – Arquitetura de Interior*, edited by Ana Carolina Pellegrini and Juliano Vasconcelos, 10-20. Novo Hamburgo: Universidade Feevale, 2009.

Finotti, Leonardo. "Casa na Finlândia." In *10+10 Contemporary + Modern Brazilian Houses*, 50-59. São Paulo: Obra Comunicação, 2013.

Gorjão, José Duarte. "O Tempo da Cidade." In *Filosofia e Arquitetura da Paisagem – Intervenções*, Serrão, edited by Adriana Verísssimo, 179-186. Lisbon: Philosophy Center of University of Lisbon, 2012.

Hiriart, Gustavo, and Álvaro Marques. "Arquitetura Poética – Entrevista a Marcelo Ferraz." In *Entrevistas*, 3rd volume, 158-172. Montevidéu: Facultad de Arquitectura, Diseño y Urbanismo/Universidad de la República, 2017.

Koolhaas, Rem. "Conferência 21/1/1991." In *Conversas com Estudantes*, by Rem Koolhaas, 10-11. Barcelona: Gustavo Gili, 2002.

Melo Neto, João Cabral de (1966). "A Educação pela Pedra." In *Antologia Poética*. 3rd edition. Rio de Janeiro: José Olympio, 1975.

Oiticica, Hélio (1967). "Esquema Geral da Nova Objetividade." In *Hélio Oiticica: Museu é o Mundo*, edited by César Oiticica, 87-101. Rio de Janeiro: Beco do Azougue, 2011.

Pellegrini, Ana Carolina. "Pão e Circo – Caminho dos Moinhos." In *Bloco 4 – O Arquiteto e a Sociedade*, edited by Ana Carolina Pellegrini and Juliano Vasconcelos, 17-27. Novo Hamburgo: Universidade Feevale, 2008.

Ribeiro, Maria de Fátima Bento, and Alan Dutra de Melo. "Centro de Interpretação do Pampa em Jaguarão – RS." In *Espaços Culturais e Turísticos em Países Lusófonos: Cultura e Turismo*, edited by Luiz Manuel Gazzaneo. Rio de Janeiro: UFRJ/FAU/PROARQ, 2011.

Santos, Cecília Rodrigues dos. "Arquiteturas do Brasil – Brasil Arquitetura." In *Francisco Fanucci, Marcelo Ferraz: Brasil Arquitetura*, edited by Francisco Fanucci and Marcelo Carvalho Ferraz, 14-23. São Paulo: Cosac Naify, 2005.

Segawa, Hugo. "O Vale do Ribeira e a KKKK." In *O Conjunto KKKK*, edited by Marcelo Carvalho Ferraz, 13-21. São Paulo: Takano, 2002.

Solà-Morales, Ignasí de. "Terrain Vague." In *Territorios*, by Ignasí de Solà-Morales, 181-193. Barcelona: Gustavo Gili, 2002.

Monographies, Ph. D. Dissertations and Master's Thesis

Anticoli, Audrey Migliani. "Brasil Arquitetura – Construindo uma Trajetória." Master's thesis, USJT, 2016.

Dieterich, Anne. "Brasil Arquitetura – Plano Estratégico." MBA monography, FGV Management, 2016.

Gonçalves, Simone Neiva Loures. "Museus Projetados por Oscar Niemeyer de 1951 a 2006 – o programa como coadjuvante." PhD diss., FAU USP, 2010.

Gorski, Joel. "Reciclagem de Uso e Preservação Arquitetônica." Master's thesis, PROPAR UFRGS, 2003.

Kinies, Carolina Gottert. "Brasil Arquitetura – Projetos e Obras no Sul." Master's thesis, UNIRITTER/MACKENZIE, 2015.

Martins, Elisa Toschi. "Sítios Saturados – Intervenções em Vazios Urbanos." Master's thesis, PROPAR UFRGS, 2015.

Nahas, Patrícia Viceconti. "Brasil Arquitetura – memória e contemporaneidade. Um percurso do Sesc Pompeia ao Museu do Pão (1977-2008)." Mastter's thesis, FAU MACKENZIE, 2009.

Osterkamp, Guilherme. "O Brasil Arquitetura e a Invenção do Patrimônio." Master's thesis, PROPAR UFRGS, 2015.

Regiani, Luana Espig. "Modernos e Brasileiros – o Diálogo do Brasil Arquitetura com o Trabalho de Lina Bo Bardi e Lúcio Costa." Master's thesis, FEC UNICAMP, 2014.

Romio, Ramona. "Moinho de Ilópolis – Dossiê de Informações para Processo de Tombamento." Graduation Monography, CAU UCS, 2003.

Villas Bôas, Alexandre dos Santos. "Centro de Interpretação do Pampa (RS) – a Revitalização de um Patrimônio Cultural." Master's thesis, UFSM, 2014.

Viotti, Giovanna. "Projeto em Relação com Pré-Existências Arquitetônicas: A Obra do Escritório Brasil Arquitetura." Research monography, FAU Mackenzie, 2018.

Specialized magazines

"7ª Bienal Internacional de Arquitetura de São Paulo – Arquitetura de Convivência." *Arc Design*, no. 57, December 2007, 67-69.

"A Marca Contemporânea do Concreto." *Cimento Hoje*, no. 48, March 2004, 6-7.

Abolafio, Beto. "Cinco Vezes Cultura." *Casa Vogue*, no. 308, April 2011, 92-94.

"Acessos Controlados e Palco na Praça das Artes." *Projeto Design*, no. 396, February 2013, 18.

"Adiós a uma Exitosa Bienal – Marcelo Ferraz (Brasil)." *Entre Rayas*, no. 125, July 2018, 32.

Alcântara, Denise de. "A Restauração do Teatro Preserva o que é Essencial, Abrindo Espaços para a Vida Cultural Contemporânea." *Projeto Design*, no. 210, July 1997, 32-39.

Almeida, Eneida de, and Marta Bogéa. "Esquecer para Preservar." *Arquitextos* 08, no. 091.02 (December 2007). http://www.vitruvius.com.br/revistas/read/arquitextos/08.091/181.

Almeida, Eneida de. "Incursões de Lina Bo Bardi pelo Território da Memória e Possíveis Relações com a Teoria da Restauração." *Contraste*, no. 1, January/June 2013, 73-79.

Alves, Letícia de Almeida. "Beleza em Ascensão – Leves Fluidas e com Desenhos Inovadores, as Escadas Metálicas Alcançam o Status de Escultura – Aço Corten e Ipê." *Arquitetura e Construção*, no. 4, April 2011, 113.

Anelli, Renato. "Grave Urbanidade." *Projeto*, no. 172, March 1994, 56-58.

"Anos 90 – Terminais de Transportes. Aeroportos e Metrôs, Ampliados, Atendem Tráfego Crescente." *Projeto Design*, no. 251, January 2001, 70-73.

"Antena – De Repente 30. Brasil Arquitetura Completa Três Décadas de História." *Casa Vogue*, no. 288, August 2009, 19.

Apiacás Arquitetos, Brasil Arquitetura. "Containers. Estação Natureza, São Paulo." *Arquine*, no. 49, September 2009, 36-39.

"Após Encerramento, a Hora de Avaliar a 7ª Bienal de Arquitetura – Categoria Obra Construída 1° Premio Museu Rodin." *Projeto Design*, no. 335, January 2008, 32-33.

"Arquiteturas do Mundo. No Caminho da Roça..." *Arquitetura e Construção*, no. 10, October 1994, 12-13.

"Arte de Ser Simples." *Casa Claudia*, no. 8, August 1998, 52-53.

Astorga Garros, Jorge. Archeiros. "Sobre o Lançamento dos Livros de Marcelo Ferraz e Cyro Lyra no Paço Imperial." *Resenhas Online* 16, no. 179.03, November 2016. http://www.vitruvius.com.br/revistas/read/resenhasonline/16.179/6279.

Barda, Marisa. "Brasiliani a Berlino." *Costruire*, no. 173, October 1997, 241.

Barda, Marisa. "Regionale e Cosmopolita." *Construire*, no. 165, February 1997, 112-115.

Bardi, Lina Bo. "Uma Casa no Litoral." *AU – Arquitetura e Urbanismo*, no. 32, October/November 1990, 58-61.

Barrero, Vera, and Nuria Uliana. "Era uma Vez uma Cozinha Escura." *Arquitetura e Construção*, no. 5, May 1997, 102-103.

Bastian, Winnie. "Raízes Brasileiras." *Arc Design*, no. 43, July/August 2005, 44-46.

Bava, Cristina, and Joana Baracuhy. "O Melhor da Terra." *Arquitetura e Construção*, no. 6, June 2005, 37-43.

Bava, Cristina, and Marilia Scalzo. "A Casa Não Tem Vista, Mas o Muro Deixa Tudo Azul." *Arquitetura e Construção*, no. 11, November 1996, 56-65.

Belchior, Camila. "Rodin ao Dendê." *Casa Vogue*, no. 261, May 2007, 60-61.

Bertho, Beatriz Carra. "Conversa com Francisco Fanucci e Marcelo Carvalho Ferraz. A Trajetória do Brasil Arquitetura." *Entrevista* 12, no. 045.01, January 2011. http://www.vitruvius.com.br/revistas/read/entrevista/12.045/3725.

"Biblioteca – Arquitetura Conversável." *Projeto Design*, no. 380, October 2011, 42.

"Biblioteca – Praça das Artes." *Projeto Design*, no. 399, March 2013, 42.

Bis, Keila. "O Anexo do Municipal." *Arquitetura e Construção*, no. 7, July 2011, 146.

Bogéa, Marta, and Abilio Guerra. "Algo Muito Humano Além de Belo. Exposição Território de Contato, Módulo 1: Cao Guimarães e Brasil Arquitetura." *Arquitextos* 12, no. 144.00 (May 2012). http://www.vitruvius.com.br/revistas/read/arquitextos/12.144/4365.

Bogéa, Marta. "Imaginar o Passado, Com Saudade do Futuro." Arquitextos 20, no. 229.00 (June 2019). http://www.vitruvius.com.br/revistas/read/arquitextos/20.229/7417.

Bogéa, Marta. "Brasil Arquitetura – Uma Partilha das Distâncias, Construindo Convívios." *Arquitextos* 14, no. 159.01 (August 2013). http://www.vitruvius.com.br/revistas/read/arquitextos/14.159/4844.

Borges, Adelia. "Reich an Zukunft." *Form – Zeitschrift fur Gestaltung*, no. 147, July/August 1994, 44-46.

Bottura, Roberto. "Brasil Arquitetura. Entre-Deux / In Between." *L'Architecture d'Aujourd'hui*, no. 407, June 2015, 64-65.

Brandão, Ignácio de Loyola. "A Poesia Íntima de um Povo." *Casa Vogue*, no. 254, October 2006, 46-50.

Brandão, Ignacio de Loyola. "Brasileiros Vão Mudar a Cara de Berlim." *Casa Vogue*, no. 142, 1997, 24-25.

"Brasil Arquitetura – Centro Culturale KKKK." *Casabella*, no. 723, June 2004, 48-53.

"Brasil Arquitetura – Entrevista com Marcelo Feraz e Francisco Fanucci." *Contraste*, no. 1, January/June 2013, 41-72.

"Brasil Arquitetura – Square of Arts, São Paulo, Brazil, 2012." *AU – Architecture and Urbanism*, no. 532, January 2015, 44-49.

Brasil Arquitetura. "Museo del Pan." *Arquine*, no. 44, June 2008, 76-79.

Brasil Arquitetura. "Residencial Bamburral (2011/_)." *Monolito*, no. 7, February 2012, 116-121.

Brendle, Betânia, and Natália Miranda Vieira. "Cais do Sertão Luiz Gonzaga no Porto Novo do Recife. Destruição Travestida em Ação de Conservação." *Arquitextos* 13, no. 150.03 (November 2012). http://www.vitruvius.com.br/revistas/read/arquitextos/13.150/4460>

Brito, Adriana. "Todas as Tribos." *Casa Vogue*, no. 289, September 2009, 86-87.

Calsavara, Katia. "Transformadores de Paisagens." *Docol Magazine*, no. 12, October/December 2010, 10-15.

Camargo, Ana Carolina F. de. "Alvenaria de Elementos Vazados." *AU – Arquitetura e Urbanismo*, no. 224, November 2012, 86.

Camargo, Mônica Junqueira de. "Arquitectura del Lugar: Un Viaje por las Obras Recientes de Brasil Arquitetura." *Diseño en Síntesis: Reflexiones Sobre la Cultura del Diseño* 22, no. 50/51 (2014). http://bidi.xoc.uam.mx/tabla_contenido_fasciculo.php?id_fasciculo=680.

"Cantina Famiglia Facin." *AU – Arquitetura e Urbanismo*, no. 252, March 2015, 30.

Cardoso, Katia. "Lar dos Japoneses." *Claudia Cozinha*, no. 13, May 2002, 64-65.

Carrasco, André de Oliveira Torres. "Um Breve Comentário sobre o Bexiga, o Teatro Oficina e o Centro Cultural e Comercial do Bixiga." *Minha Cidade* 06, no. 064.03, November 2005. http://www.vitruvius.com.br/revistas/read/minhacidade/06.064/1960.

Carta, Silvio. "New History, New Life to Exiting – Ilópolis Bread Museum." *C3*, no. 305, January 2010, 136-143.

Castroviejo, Alessandro, and Vasco Caldeira. "Casas do Brasil – Casa Ubiracica." *AU – Arquitetura e Urbanismo*, no. 84, June/July 1999, 59-61.

Castroviejo, Alessandro, and Vasco Caldeira. "Casas do Brasil – Residência Kapaz." *AU – Arquitetura e Urbanismo*, no. 69, December 1997/January 1998, 53-55.

Carvalho, Luiz. "Quay Change." *The Architectural Review*, no. 1465, October 2019, 6-13.

Cella, Luisa. "Perceber a Natureza do Lugar." *Casa Claudia Luxo*, no. 28, April/May 2012, 34-35.

"Cenário – 9° Bienal Seleciona Obras Finalistas e Premiadas." *AU – Arquitetura e Urbanismo*, no. 243, June 2014, 12.

"Cenário – Brasil Arquitetura Vence Concurso para o Novo Centro Comunitário Shalom." *AU – Arquitetura e Urbanismo*, no. 159, June 2007, 10.

"Cenário – Cores Brasileiras em Berlim." *AU – Arquitetura e Urbanismo*, no. 72, June/July 1997, 22-23.

"Cenário – Escritório Brasil Arquitetura Divulga Projeto do Memorial da Democracia." *AU – Arquitetura e Urbanismo*, no. 221, August 2012, 12.

"Cenário – Favelas Paulistanas Sediam Mostra Internacional de Arquitetura." *AU – Arquitetura e Urbanismo*, no. 215, February 2012, 12.

"Cenário – IAB-SP Premia Projetos Paulistas – Mas Muitas Categorias Não Tiveram Vencedores – Requalificação e Restauros de Edifícios de Caráter Histórico." *AU – Arquitetura e Urbanismo*, no. 225, December 2012, 10.

"Cenário – IAB/RJ Anuncia Vencedores de sua 50ª Premiação Anual – Premio Especial Teatro Engenho." *AU – Arquitetura e Urbanismo*, no. 227, February 2013, 10.

"Cenário – Lição Maior." *AU – Arquitetura e Urbanismo*, no. 24, June/July 1989, 30-31.

"Cenário – Premiação IAB/SP-98. Os Vencedores." *AU – Arquitetura e Urbanismo*, no. 84, June/July 1999, 25.

Colontonio, Allex. "No Vale dos Moinhos." *Casa Vogue*, no. 272, April 2008, 68-72.

Comas, Carlos Eduardo. "Cidade, Praça e Artes." *Summa+*, no. 135, May 2014, 68-69.

"Concreto Amarelo Simboliza Cor do Sertão (Publicidade)." *Projeto*, no. 446, November/December 2018, 92-93.

"Concurso Fechado Escolherá Projeto para Museu Judaico." *Projeto Design*, no. 304, June 2005, 30-33.

Corbioli, Nanci. "Assimétrico, Conjunto Organiza-se por Meio de Muros de Concreto Ciclópico." *Projeto Design*, no. 287, January 2004, 52-57.

Corbioli, Nanci. "Conjunto Fabril Dará Lugar a Centro de Atividades Culturais." *Projeto Design*, no. 312, February 2006, 96-99.

Corbioli, Nanci. "Escala Doméstica da Cultura, Ateliês Têm Inspirações Diversas." *Projeto Design*, no. 364, June 2010, 54-59.

Corbioli, Nanci. "Livre de Divisórias, Espaços Integram-se Visualmente." *Projeto Design*, no. 364, June 2010, 60-63.

Corbioli, Nanci. Obra Premiada Cria Opções de Transporte e Ajuda a Revitalizar Região Industrial. *Projeto Design*, no. 250, December 2000, 46-51.

Corbioli, Nanci. "Recuperados, Armazéns Transformam-se em Centro de Informação e Cultura." *Projeto Design*, no. 265, March 2002, 40-46.

Corbioli, Nanci. "Revitalização em Unidade do Sesc Preserva Projeto Original de Lina Bo Bardi." *Projeto Design*, no. 276, January 2003, 78-80.

"Cultura Leva Milhões de Pessoas a Visitarem Espaços Reciclados." *Projeto Design*, no. 371, January 2011, 66-69.

Cunha, Aline. "Praça das Artes – Arquitetura Atende Tanto os Novos Usos Ligados a Musica e Dança Como Abre Espaço de Convivência a Partir do Histórico Local." *Construção – Arquitetura* (annual), no. 12, December 2012, 15-20.

Cypriano, Fábio. "Teuto-Brasilis – Conjunto Habitacional, em Berlim, Restaurado Com Projeto de Arquitetos Brasileiros Incorpora Artes Gráficas da Tribo Kadiwéu." *Construção*, no. 2635, August 1998, 22-23.

Dêgelo, Marilena. "À Prova do Tempo." *Casa e Jardim*, no. 638, March 2008, 94-101.

Dêgelo, Marilena. "Fluidez e Visão Total." *Casa e Jardim*, no. 649, February 2009, 90-97.

Degêlo, Marilena. "Poesia Concreta – A Vida Corre Sob Lajes em Balanço Nesta Casa de 360m² Projetado pelo Brasil Arquitetura." *Casa e Jardim*, no. 730, August 2013, 114-123.

Dêgelo, Marilena. "Simples Assim." *Casa e Jardim*, no. 607, August 2005, 70-77.

"Design Brasiliano per la Falegnameria." *Ufficiostile*, no. 4, 1993, 37-40.

"Design de Mobiliário no Brasil – Uma Explosão de Novos Talentos." *Architécti*, no. 28, 1995, 114-122.

Dieterich, Anne. "Interpretacija Povijesti Svakidašnjice – Everyday History Interpretation." *Oris*, no. 57, November/December 2009, 100-107.

Dino, Claudia. "À Serviço da Arte." *Construir*, no. 127, February 2010, 110.

Duarte, Juliana. "Família Ferraz." *Construir*, no. 129, April 2010, 40-41.

Duduch, Jane Victal Ferreira. "Um Pouquinho de Brasil em Berlim." *Boletim Óculum* 4, no. 34, August 1999, 3.

Dussel, Susanne. "Tres Posiciones Frente a la Tradición Moderna: Arquitectos Latino-Americanos Proyectam a la Remodelación del "Barrio Amarillo" de Berlín-Hellersdorf." *GALA – Grupo de Arquitectos Latinoamericanos* 6, no. 42. June/July 1997, 5-8.

EDELWEISS, Roberta Krahe; BORTOLI, Fábio; VOLPATTO, Carlla Portal. "O Museu do Pão e o Caminho dos Moinhos: preexistência, intervenção e produção do lugar regional." *Prumo* 3, no. 4, November 2018. https://bit.ly/2RkFJqG.

Ekerman, Sergio Kopinski. "The Struggle for Dialogue Within a Heritage City." *Architectural Design* 241, May/June 2016, 106-111.

"Em Área Urbana, Isolada dos Ruídos Externos." *Finestra Brasil*, no. 16, 1999, 104-106.

"Em Dia – Bienal Ibero-Americana em Medellín." *Projeto Design*, no. 368, October 2010, 30.

"Em Dia – Brasil Arquitetura Desenha Museu do Trabalho." *Projeto Design*, no. 371, January 2011, 19.

"Em Dia – Brasileiros Ganham Concurso em Berlim." *Projeto Design*, no. 210, July 1997, 16.

"Em Dia – Centro Comunitário Judaico." *Projeto Design*, no. 328, June 2007, 19.

"Em Dia – Cine Marrocos Será Teatro na Praça das Artes." *Projeto Design*, no. 366, August 2010, 18.

"Em Dia – Democracia no Centro de São Paulo." *Projeto Design*, no. 390, August 2012, 32.

"Em Dia – Excelência e Diversidade no Prêmio IAB/SP." *Projeto Design*, no. 347, January 2009, 8-9.

"Em Dia – Finalmente Praça das Artes se Abre para o Anhangabaú." *Projeto*, no. 448, March 2019, 24.

"Em Dia – IAB/RJ Anuncia Vencedores da Sua 50ª Premiação Anual." *Projeto Design*, no. 396, 2013, 17.

"Em Dia – O sertão Vai Ver o Mar." *Projeto Design*, no. 384, February 2012, 30.

"Em Dia – Sede do MIS/RJ é de Diller Scofidio + Renfro." *Projeto Design*, no. 355, September 2009, 18-19.

"Em Dia – Vencedores do Prêmio IAB/SP 2012." *Projeto Design*, no. 395, January 2013, 28.

"Especial Anos '00 – Em Formas Contidas ou Arrojadas, Casa Brasileira Ainda é Laboratório." *Projeto Design*, no. 371, January 2011, 92-95.

"Especial Museu – K.K.K.K. Museu da Imigração Japonesa." *Registro Des!* (special edition), January 2009, 40-41.

"Expositions – Brasil Arquitetura." AMC – *Le Moniteur Architecture*, no. 202, December 2010/ January 2011, 20.

"Fato & Opinião – Até que Ponto Concursos de Arquitetura São Necessários? – Marcelo Carvalho Ferraz." *AU – Arquitetura e Urbanismo*, no. 194, May 2010, 14.

"Fato & Opinião – Concursos de Arquitetura Cancelados Após Entrega de Propostas – Marcelo Carvalho Ferraz." *AU – Arquitetura e Urbanismo*, no. 205, April 2011, 17.

"Fato & Opinião – Desapropriações e Revitalização Urbana: Como Fazer? – Marcelo Ferraz." *AU – Arquitetura e Urbanismo*, no. 207, June 2011, 21.

"Fato & Opinião – Existe Conflito de Gerações na Arquitetura? – Marcelo Ferraz." *AU – Arquitetura e Urbanismo*, no. 230, May 2013, 20-21.

Fernández, Antonio. "Intervenciones – Museo Rodin Bahia." *Enlace*, no. 3, March 2008, 50-57.

Figuerola, Valentina. "Concreto, Poesia e Niemeyer." *AU – Arquitetura e Urbanismo*, no. 106, January 2003, 38-45.

Figuerola, Valentina. "Herança Restaurada." *AU – Arquitetura e Urbanismo*, no. 136, July 2005, 42-49.

Figuerola, Valentina. "Qual Seria o Significado – Social e Arquitetônico – Do Fechamento do Vão do MASP?" *AU – Arquitetura e Urbanismo*, no. 106, January 2003, 38-45.

Figuerola, Valentina. "Rodin em Salvador." *AU – Arquitetura e Urbanismo*, no. 106, January 2003, 34-37.

Fiori, Mylena. "Concreto no Oásis." *Casa e Jardim*, no. 592, May 2004, 64-73.

Fleiss, Elein. "Lina Bo Bardi." *X-Knowledge Home*, no. 22, December 2003, 54-59.

"Fotógrafos – Daniel Ducci." *Projeto Design*, no. 400, June 2013, 116-117.

Frajndlich, Rafael Urano. "A Arte Está por Toda a Casa." *AU – Arquitetura e Urbanismo*, no. 237, December 2013, 32-39.

Frajndlich, Rafael Urano. "Flexibilidade Azul." *AU – Arquitetura e Urbanismo*, no. 214, January 2012, 22-29.

Frajndlich, Rafael Urano. "Sonoro Monolito." *AU – Arquitetura e Urbanismo*, no. 227, February 2013, 24-33.

Frajndlich, Rafael Urano. "Tem Palco no Engenho." *AU – Arquitetura e Urbanismo*, no. 221, August 2012, 54-61.

Frajndlich, Rafael Urano. "Vila no Alto da Serra." *AU – Arquitetura e Urbanismo*, no. 221, August 2012, 26-31.

Gasperini, Valéria. "Use e Abuse da Cor." *Reforma Fácil & Acabamento*, no. 30, January 2001, 36-43.

Gelinski, Gilmara. "Marquise em Balanço Integra Espaços." *Finestra*, no. 73, March/April 2012, 44-53.

Glažar, Tadej. "Adijo Evropa! Pozdravljena Brazilija." *Oris*, no. 49, 2008, 72-79.

Goh, Hyunkyung. "Cais do Sertão Museum." *Architecture & Culture*, no. 460, September 2019. 128-137.

Gorelik, Adrián. "The Metropolitan Demand." *AU – Architecture and Urbanism*, no. 532, January 2015, 24-27.

Goytia, Noemí, and Miguel Roca. "Museo Rodin." *30-60 – Cuaderno Latinoamericano de Arquitectura*, no. 14, September 2007, 60-69.

Grunow, Evelise. "Dois Dias e Uma Noite." *Projeto Design*, no. 356, October 2009, 76-83.

Grunow, Evelise. "Galpão Modernizado Com Engenho e Arte." *Projeto Design*, no. 390, August 2012, 58-65.

Grunow, Evelise. "Na Boa Arquitetura, a Subtração de Espaço." *Projeto Design*, no. 377, June 2011, 86-89.

Grunow, Evelise. "Perfil – Brasil Arquitetura." *Projeto*, no. 446, November/December 2018, 76-81.

Grunow, Evelise. "Perfil – O Sertão Ancora no Porto." *Projeto*, no. 446, November/December 2018, 82-89.

Grunow, Evelise. "Perfil – Três Tempos." *Projeto*, no. 446, November/December 2018, 90-91.

Grunow, Evelise. "Rigor e Plasticidade São Guiados pelas Referências Modernas." *Projeto Design*, no. 335, January 2008, 48-55.

Grunow, Evelise. "Vittorio Garatti." *Projeto Design*, no. 389, July 2012, 10-13.

Guerra, Abilio. "A Universidade e a Crítica de Arquitetura no Brasil." *Arquitextos* 15, no. 173.02 (November 2014). http://www.vitruvius.com.br/revistas/read/arquitextos/15.173/5332.

Guerra, Abílio. "Arquitectura Brasileña – Espacio Público, Identidad y Democracia." *Arquine*, no. 49, September 2009, 84-95.

Guerra, Abilio. "Los Diez de Quito." *Arquiteturismo* 03, no. 025.04, March 2009. http://www.vitruvius.com.br/revistas/read/arquiteturismo/03.025/1503.

Guerra, Abilio. "Modernistas na Estrada." *Arquiteturismo* 01, no. 008.02, October 2007. http://www.vitruvius.com.br/revistas/read/arquiteturismo/01.008/1366.

Guerra, Abilio. "Praça das Artes. Complexo Arquitetônico Brasileiro Começa a ser Reconhecido no Exterior." *Minha Cidade* 14, no. 161.02, December 2013. http://www.vitruvius.com.br/revistas/read/minhacidade/14.161/4984.

Guerra, Abilio. "Prêmio APCA 2012 – Categoria "Obra de Arquitetura." Premiado: Praça das Artes / Brasil Arquitetura e Marcos Cartum." *Drops* 13, no. 063.08, December 2012. http://www.vitruvius.com.br/revistas/read/drops/13.063/4629.

Guerra, Abilio. "Quadra Aberta. Uma Tipologia Urbana Rara em São Paulo." *Projetos* 11, no. 124.01, April 2011. http://www.vitruvius.com.br/revistas/read/projetos/11.124/3819.

Guerra, Abilio. "Sobre o Escritório Brasil Arquitetura. A Obra Maior de Francisco Fanucci e Marcelo Ferraz." *Resenhas Online* 15, no. 180.04, December 2016. http://www.vitruvius.com.br/revistas/read/resenhasonline/15.180/6333.

Guerra, Abilio. "Universidad y Crítica de Arquitectura en Brasil / Universidade e Crítica de Arquitetura no Brasil." *Summa+*, no. 134, February 2014, 94-99.

Haegele, Steffen. "Tanz in den Strassen." *Archithese*, no. 43, July/August 2013, 10-14.

Hartman, Hattie. "Seeds of Change: Urban Transformation in Brazil." *Architectural Design* 86, no. 3, May 2016, 10-19.

Hennigan, Tom. "Spotlight on Brazil. Then and Now: A Country Builds Its Future." *Architectural Record*, no. 197, May 2014, 71-77.

Hennigan, Tom. "Spotlight on Brazil. Lina Bo Bardi: Architect for the Ages." *Architectural Record*, no. 197, May 2014, 90-94.

Herrera, Jorge Sánchez. "Museu Rodin Bahia." *Enconcreto*, no. 1, May 2012, 44-53.

Horta, Maurício. "A Celebração da Madeira." *AU – Arquitetura e Urbanismo*, no. 168, March 2008, 38-47.

Horta, Maurício. "Arquitetura da Convivência." *AU – Arquitetura e Urbanismo*, no. 150, September 2006, 34-45.

Hossbach, Benjamin. "As Cores do Brasil." *Bauwelt*, no. 17/18, May 1997, 876.

Ibarra, Thadeo. "Do Brasil para o Mundo: Conheça os Projetos Selecionados para Representar o País na Bienal Iberoamericana de Arquitetura e Urbanismo, na Colômbia." *Docol Magazine*, no. 9, January/March 2010, 32.

"Interiores – Sertão no Cais." *Projeto Design*, no. 414, September 2014, 76-83.

"Jardim Interior. Brasil Arquitetura – Casa Pepiguari." *Summa+*, no. 140, January 2015, 74-77.

Jordão, Claudia. "Cenário Fluído." *Casa e Design* (annual), 2015/2016, 104-109.

"Jornal da Casa – 5 Coisas Que Você Precisa Saber Sobre... Museu Rodin." *Casa Claudia*, no. 9, September 2010, 46.

Kere, Alex. "Interview with Marcelo Carvalho Ferraz." *X-Knowledge Home* 22, December 2003, 59.

Klintowitz, Jacob. "Hellersdorf: Arquitetura Brasileira em Berlim." *Arc Design*, no. 5, May/June 1998, 46-53.

Kon, Nelson. "Ensaio Fotográfico / Photographic Essay." *Monolito* (annual), no. 18, December 2013/January 2014, 66-71.

Lage, Ana Luisa. "Aberto para Visitas – Um Lugar para Relaxar." *Construir*, no. 137, November 2010, 35.

Lage, Ana Luiza. "Solte a Imaginação! Contemporane, o Conceito Aparente Chama a Atenção e Destaca os Elementos da Estrutura – Efeito Fotográfico." *Construir*, no. 124, November 2009, 35.

Larsen, Patrícia, and Cléa Martins. Convivência Harmônica. *AU – Arquitetura e Urbanismo*, no. 191, February 2010, 22-27.

Leal, Ledy Valporto. "Cultura Retraçada." *AU – Arquitetura e Urbanismo*, no. 158, May 2007, 30-35.

Lima (Lelé), João Filgueiras. "Brasil Arquitetura. Respeito à Memória, Tradições e Características Climáticas Brasileira." *Drops* 07, no. 016.02, September 2006. http://www.vitruvius.com.br/revistas/read/drops/07.016/1693.

Lima, Juliana Saboia de Almeida, and Maria Conceição Wenzel. "Histórias do Brasil." *A&D – Arte e Decoração*, no. 220, May 1998, 32-41.

Lira, José. "Un Teatro nella Giungla." *Domus*, no. 958, May 2012, 54-55.

"Living Steel Anuncia os Vencedores do 2º Concurso Internacional de Arquitetura para Habitação Sustentável." *Projeto Design*, no. 332, October 2007, 1-8.

"Living Steel Divulga os Finalistas." *AU – Arquitetura e Urbanismo*, no. 162, September 2007, 10.

Luz, Maturino da. "Museo del Pan." *30-60 – Cuaderno Latinoamericano de Arquitectura*, no. 26, September 2010, 12-23.

Macedo, Raquel Palhares de. "Diário de Viagem: Viga Berlin." *Arq Informa*, no. 4, September 2002, 20-24.

Macinnes, Kathenne. "Playing the Game." *World Architecture*, no. 63, February 1998, 31.

Mahfuz, Edson. "Poesia e Construção – A Obra Como Paradigma da Qualidade Arquitetônica." *AU – Arquitetura e Urbanismo*, no. 40, February/March 1992, 40-41.

"Marcenaria Baraúna." *Design & Interiores*, no. 16, September/October 1989, 58.

Martins, Rosele. "Feitiço do Tempo." *Casa Claudia Luxo*, no. 29, June/July 2012, 114-125.

Mazza, Márcio. "Com a Singeleza de uma Oca." *AU – Arquitetura e Urbanismo*, no. 56, October/November 1994, 128.

Melendez, Adilson. "Brasil Arquitetura e Marcos Cartum: Praça das Artes, SP, Uma Praça Abrigada no Coração Paulistano." *Projeto Design*, no. 395, January 2013, 42-51.

Melendez, Adilson. "Desenho do Centro Educacional Rompe Caos Urbano Desolados." *Projeto Design*, no. 325, March 2007, 58-65.

Melendez, Adilson. "Edifício Voltará as Origens, Depois de Sediar Legislativo, Delegacias e Prefeitura." *Projeto Design*, no. 265, March 2002, 98.

Melendez, Adilson. "Em Dois Edifícios, Museu Combina o Passado e o Presente, de Olho no Futuro." *Projeto Design*, no. 275, January 2003, 40-55.

Melendez, Adilson. "Memoria Projeto – Centenário, Teatro Polytheama Quer Espaço para Encenar Terceiro Ato." *Projeto Design*, no. 385, March 2012, 110.

Melendez, Adilson. "Negros Vencem Imigrantes em "Briga" por Pavilhão Paulistano." *Projeto Design*, no. 305, July 2005, 110.

Melendez, Adilson. "Sesc Pompeia Completa Vinte Anos e É Modelo para Obras de Reciclagem." *Projeto Design*, no. 98, August 2002, 270.

"Memorial do Vinho – Sabor da Tradição." *Decor*, no. 70, 2012, 66-70.

Montaner, Josep Maria, and Zaida Muxí. "A Praça das Artes. Reconstruindo São Paulo." *Minha Cidade* 14, no. 159.04, October 2013. http://www.vitruvius.com.br/revistas/read/minhacidade/14.159/4914.

Monteiro, Flora. "Casa – Morada Escultural." *Wish Casa*, no. 28, April 2014, 77-83.

"Museo del Pan em Ilópolis, Rio Grande do Sul, Brasil." *En Blanco*, no. 9, May 2012, 30-35.

"Museo del Pan y Escuela de Confiteros." *Escala E*, no. 213, 2009, 56-60.

"Museu Rodin Bahia." *Escala E*, no. 213, 2009, 67-71.

Nahas, Patricia Viceconti. "O Novo e o Velho – A Experiência do Escritório Brasil Arquitetura nos Programas de Intervenção em Edifícios e Sítios Históricos." *Revista de Arquitectura*, no. 12 (January/December 2010), 58-67. https://bit.ly/2K57nUC.

Nalio, Alessandra. "A Vida É Azul." *Reformar e Construir*, no. 30, November 2000, 58-63.

"News – Tradição Brasileira em Roma." *Arc Design*, no. 70, May/June 2010, 6.

"O Conjunto KKKK." *Architécti*, no. 59, July/September 2002, 76-83.

"O Melhor Design." *Casa Vogue*, no. 145, August 1997, 11.

Obata, Sasquia Hizuro. "Aulas de Projeto." *AU – Arquitetura e Urbanismo*, no. 237, December 2013, 68-73.

Oliveira, Monelli. "Simples Como a Vida no Campo." *Construir Mais por Menos*, no. 28, February 2013, 56-61.

Oliveira, Raíssa de. "Marcelo Carvalho Ferraz." *Entrevista* 08, no. 030.02, April 2007. http://www.vitruvius.com.br/revistas/read/entrevista/08.030/3295.

Ortiz, Andréa. "A Casa Moderna dos Anos Noventa." *Arquitetura e Construção*, no. 11, November 1993, 30-39.

Paiva, Cida. "Novo Olhar Sobre a Cidade." *Finestra Brasil*, no. 32, January/March 2003, 40-51.

"Panorâmica – Arquitetura Como Meio de Transformação Social." *Arc Design*, no. 58, March 2008, 74.

Pearson, Clifford. "South America's Building Boom – Brazil Growth Is Spreading from Rio and São Paulo to a Second Tier of Cities." *Architectural Record*, no. 9, September 1998, 96-97.

Pedreira, Lívia. "Lembranças da Bahia." *Arquitetura e Construção*, no. 149, September 1999, 94-103.

Pereira, Suzane Luíse. "Preservando Nossas Tradições." *Revista Univates*, no. 1, May 2012, 19-21.

Perrotta-Bosch, Francesco. "Dissatisfied São Paulo. Special Edition Brazil – Restructuring the Urban." *Architectural Design* 86, no. 3, May/June 2016, 68-69.

"Pesquisa de Preços – Laje Flutuante." *AU – Arquitetura e Urbanismo*, no. 228, March 2013, 74.

"Plaza de las Artes." *DQ Manus*, no. 2, November 2013, 150-167.

Polisseni, Katja. "Contemporâneo e Eclético." *Sua Casa*, no. 7, June 2009, 22-24.

Porfírio, Luciana. "Cinquentenário." *Casa & Mercado*, no. 135, 2013, 76-77.

"Praça das Artes / Art's Square – Brasil Arquitetura + Marcos Cartum." *Monolito*, no. 17, October/November 2013, 86-87.

"Praça das Artes." *Plot*, no. 14, August/September 2013, 50-65.

"Prancheta – Hotel Fazenda Tem Arquitetura Simples e Linguagem da Serra da Mantiqueira." *Projeto Design*, no. 234, August 1999, 92.

"Prancheta – Memorial Contará Trajetória de Família no Mundo do Vinho." *Projeto Design*, no. 381, November 2011, 42-45.

"Prêmio Asbea 2012 – Na Chapada, as Lembranças do Garimpo. Brasil Arquitetura, Centro de Referência e Memória. Igatu, BA. Edição Especial: Prêmio Asbea 2012." *Projeto Design*, no. 394, December 2012, A44.

"Prêmio o Melhor da Arquitetura – Edifícios Uso Misto – Museu do Pão, em Ilópolis, RS." *Arquitetura e Construção*, no. 11, November 2008, 115.

"Projeto Beira-Rio (2004/_), Piracicaba, SP." *Monolito*, no. 23, December 2013/January 2014, 38-45.

"Projetos Futuros – Museu para Revelar a Memória das Missões." *Projeto Design*, no. 429, January/February 2016, 78-85.

"Propostas Buscam Soluções para Melhorar Relações Com a Cidade." *Projeto Design*, no. 371, January 2011, 52-55.

"Proyectos – Plaza de Las Artes." *Escala E*, no. 231, December 2014, 60-67.

"Proyeto Internacional – Plaza de las Artes." *Arkinka*, no. 237, August 2015, 58-63.

Pugliese, Maria Helena. "Arrojada Simplicidade." *Casa e Jardim*, no. 480, January 1995, 80-85.

"RevistaAU no Instagram – Foto da Praça das Artes." *AU – Arquitetura e Urbanismo*, no. 238, January 2014, 6.

Rocha, Flávia. "A Arquitetura que Sopra Moinhos." *Casa Vogue*, no. 262, June 2007, 62-64.

Rocha, Laura. "Traço Brasileiro." *Dcasa*, no. 13, March/April 2008, 96-103.

Rocha, Silvério, and Fernando Serapião. "A Alma da Arquitetura Contemporânea Está Indo Embora, Perdendo o Sentido. Entrevista de Marcelo Carvalho Ferraz." *Projeto Design*, no. 265, March 2002, 6-8.

Rodríguez, Claudia, and Beatrice Vico-Morán. "Una Propuesta Delicada. Entrevista a Marcelo Ferraz y Francisco Fanucci." *GALA – Grupo de Arquitectos Latinoamericanos* 6, no. 42. June/July 1997, 8-10.

Sabbag, Haifa Yazigi. "Edifício-Rua." *AU – Arquitetura e Urbanismo*, no. 94, February/March 2001, 58-61.

Sabbag, Haifa Yazigt. "Espaço-Sentinela." *AU – Arquitetura e Urbanismo*, no. 76, February/March 1998, 88-90.

Sabbag, Haifa Yazigi. "Versão Brasileira em Berlim." *AU – Arquitetura e Urbanismo*, no. 80, October/November 1998, 40-46.

Sabbag, Haifa Yazigi. "Vitrine do Futuro." *AU – Arquitetura e Urbanismo*, no. 94, February/March 2001, 61.

"Sala de Estar – Escritório Brasil Arquitetura Cria Projetos Com Olhar Mais Humanista e Amplo." *Espaço K*, no. 8, March 2014, 28-34.

Santos, Cecilia Rodrigues dos. "Encuentro en el Tempo." *Summa+*, no. 96, September 2008, 28-35.

Santos, Cecilia Rodrigues dos. "Grisbi Industrias Têxteis. Camaçari, Bahia, 1980." *Caderno de Boas Práticas*, no. 12, 2009, 17-18.

Santos, Cecilia Rodrigues dos. "Lucio e Lina." *Projeto Design*, no. 400, June 2013, 56-57.

Santos, Cecilia Rodrigues dos. "Morada Paulista." *AU – Arquitetura e Urbanismo*, no. 48, 1993, 35-37.

Santos, Cecilia Rodrigues dos. "Opera Interrotta." *AU – Arquitetura e Urbanismo*, no. 51, December 1993/January 1994, 38-45.

Santos, Cecilia Rodrigues dos. "Quando o Concurso Comanda o Debate." *AU – Arquitetura e Urbanismo*, no. 54, June/July 1994, 74-76.

Sayegh, Simone. "Praça das Artes." *Infraestrutura Urbana*, no. 23, February 2013.

Sayegh, Simone. "Preservação da Vida. Entrevista de Marcelo Carvalho Ferraz." *AU – Arquitetura e Urbanismo*, no. 130, January 2005, 48-51.

Schneider, Clarissa. "Estilo Zen." *Casa Vogue*, no. 141, April 1997, 103-115.

Schneider, Clarissa. "News – Tradição Brasileira em Roma." *Arc Design*, no. 70, May/June 2010, 6.

Schneider, Clarissa. "Ponto de Vista." *Casa Vogue*, no. 262, June 2007, 161.

Segawa, Hugo. "Brasil Arquitetura: Convívio Entre o Contemporâneo e o Tradicional." *Resenhas Online* 05, no. 060.01, December 2006. http://www.vitruvius.com.br/revistas/read/resenhasonline/05.060/3123.

Segawa, Hugo. "Suave Rudeza." *Projeto*, no. 172, March 1994, 59.

Segre, Roberto. "Sobriedade Apaixonada." *Projeto Design*, no. 319, September 2006, 42-53.

Serapião, Fernando. "A Década da "Geração de Sevilha", do Pritzker de Mendes da Rocha, dos Estrangeiros e do Novo Milagre." *Projeto Design*, no. 371, January 2011, 30-33.

Serapião, Fernando. "Anexos Semelhantes Têm Materialidade e Uso Diversos." *Projeto Design*, no. 337, March 2008, 42-51.

Serapião, Fernando. "Brasil Arquitetura: Museu Rodin. Relação Entre Edifícios de Séculos Diferentes Dá Mote ao Desenho." *Projeto Design*, no. 319, September 2006, 42-53.

Serapião, Fernando. "Building Brasil." *The Architectural Review*, no. 1465, October 2019, 6-13.

Serapião, Fernando. "Cinquentenário da FAU/USP – A Influência de Lina Bo Bardi – Marcelo Ferraz (1978) Marcelo Suzuki (1980), Francisco Fanucci (1977) e Roberto Guitarrari / Brasil Arquitetura – Escola Superior de Administração e Negócios. São Paulo, 1989/93." *Projeto Design*, no. 228, January/February 1999, 78.

Serapião, Fernando. "Conjuntos Habitacionais Revelam Valorização do Desenho Urbano." *Projeto Design*, no. 251, January 2001, 119.

Serapião, Fernando. "Desenho do Brasil Busca Diálogo Com Arquitetura Finlandesa." *Projeto Design*, no. 358, December 2009, 44-51.

Serapião, Fernando. "Espaço Cultural Ajudará a Revitalizar Recife Antigo." *Projeto Design*, no. 372, February 2011, 65-71.

Serapião, Fernando. "Novos Edifícios Escolares Atenderam Maior Demanda do Ensino Privado." *Projeto Design*, no. 251, January 2001, 114-115.

Serapiao, Fernando. "Orgânico e Racional Contrastam em Planos Horizontais e Verticais." *Projeto Design*, no. 282, August 2003, 53-57.

Serapião, Fernando. "Prêmio Dá Destaque aos Prismas Regulares – Categoria Habitação Pública de Interesse Social (Projeto): Vila Nova Esperança, Salvador, 2008." *Projeto Design*, no. 348, February 2009, 62.

Serapião, Fernando. "Prêmio Dá Destaque aos Prismas Regulares – Prêmio Rino Levi Museu do Pão." *Projeto Design*, no. 348, February 2009, 56.

Serapião, Fernando. "Qualidade e Diversidade da Produção São Destaques em Concorrida Edição. Revitalização de Edifícios (Executado). Prêmio: Conjunto KKKK, Registro, SP." *Projeto Design*, no. 276, January 2003, 33.

Serapião, Fernando. "Racionalismo e Cultura Indígena no Rio Negro." *Projeto Design*, no. 349, March 2009, 54-61.

Serapião, Fernando. "Sete Obras e 365 Dias – 29 de Novembro." *Monolito*, no. 18, December 2013/January 2014, 22-23.

Serapião, Fernando. "Teatro Polytheama: O Último Ato de Lina Bo Bardi." *Projeto Design*, no. 251, January 2001, 102-103.

Serapião, Fernando. "Torres de Alvenaria Branca Ladeiam Núcleo de Madeira." *Projeto Design*, no. 349, March 2009, 62-67.

Serapião, Fernando. "Três Impressões de um Projeto Atípico." *Projeto Design*, no. 265, March 2002, 46.

Serapião, Fernando. "Ventos do Norte." *Projeto Design*, no. 347, January 2009, 20.

Silva, Vânia. "5a Bienal Internacional de Arquitetura e Design, SP – Representações Nacionais." *AU – Arquitetura e Urbanismo*, no. 115, October 2003, 35.

Simonelli, Nádia. "A Arquitetura da Liberdade Segundo Lina." *Casa Claudia Luxo*, no. 34, May/June 2013, 14-15.

Simonelli, Nádia. "Síntese do Morar Urbano." *Casa Claudia Luxo*, no. 36, October/November 2013, 80-89.

Suzuki, Marcelo, and Maria Cecília Loschiavo dos Santos. "Gli Oggetti e le Etnie." *Abitare*, no. 374, June 1998, 62-64.

Suzuki, Marcelo. "Casa del Muro Azul / The Blue Wall House." *Arquine*, no. 3, Spring 1998, 32-33.

Suzuki, Marcelo. "Despojamento na ESAN." *Projeto*, no. 172, March 1994, 55-56.

"Talento – Madeira da Boa." *Casa e Jardim*, no. 593, June 2004, 24-25.

"Tecnologia e Inovação – Marcelo Ferraz (Brasil). VI Bienal de Arquitectura de Santa Cruz – BASC18." *Entre Rayas*, no. 123, March 2018, 18.

"Terminal Rodoferroviário Santo André." *Arquitetura e Aço*, no. 3, September 2004, 15-17.

Terna, Diego. "The Scene That Buids a Community – The Square of Arts: Brasil Arquitetura. Special edition Community and the City." *C3*, no. 357, January 2010, 178-193.

Testa, Catarine. "Conservatorio Drammatico e Musicale – Music and Drama Conservatory, Praça das Artes – Sao Paulo, Brazil." *The Plan – Architecture & Technologies in Detail*, no. 67, August 2013, 108-118.

"Textures Vernaculaires pour une Demeure Urbaine." *L'Architecture d'Aujourd'hui*, no. 320, January 1999, 109-111.

Tonon, Carlotta. "Fanucci e Ferraz. Bread Museum, Ilópolis, Brasile. Um Abrigo da Chuva Brasileira." *Casabella*, no. 787, March 2010, 38-47.

"Urdimbre Vernácula." *Arquitectura Viva*, no. 4, August 2012, 64-65.

Villac, Maria Isabel. "Arquitetura como Experiência e Apropriação. Prêmio APCA 2018 – Categoria "Contribuição à Cultura Brasileira:" Brasil Arquitetura / Marcelo Ferraz e Francisco Fanucci." *Drops* 20, no. 142.07, July 2019. http://www.vitruvius.com.br/revistas/read/drops/19.142/7422.

Weiss, Ana. "Ruínas Reinventadas." *Casa Claudia Luxo*, no. 34, May/June 2013, 138-143.

Weiss, Ana. "Uma Praça para a Música." *Arc Design*, no. 66, May/June 2009, 58-60.

Wenzel, Maria Conceição, and Débora M. de Carvalho. "O Espelho D'água Brilha Também à Noite." *Casa Claudia*, no. 12, December 1994, 56-57.

Wenzel, Maria Conceição. "Diga Não à Convenção." *Casa Claudia*, no. 10, October 1994, 92-99.

Wenzel, Maria Conceição. "Opção pelo Simples." *Arquitetura e Construção*, no. 2, February 1993, 60-65.

Wenzel, Mariane. "Ponto Pacífico." *Arquitetura e Construção – Edição Top*, no. 1, January 2007, 20-21.

Wisnik, Guilherme. "Prêmio APCA 2012 – Categoria "Cliente / Promotor." Premiado: Carlos Augusto Calil / Secretaria de Cultura da Prefeitura de São Paulo." *Drops* 13, no. 063.07, December 2012. http://www.vitruvius.com.br/revistas/read/drops/13.063/4619.

Wisnik, Guilherme. "Trópico Emergente." *Arquitectura Viva*, no. 144, August 2012, 20-25.

Zancan, Roberto, João Batista Martinez Correa, Daniela Castro, and José Lira. "La Strada è un Teatro." *Domus*, no. 958, May 2012, 42-53.

Zein, Ruth Verde. "Residência em Ilha e Campo." *Projeto*, no. 73, March 1985, 82-83.

Zunino, Maria Giulia. "News – Museo Rodin in Brasile." *Abitare*, no. 466, November 2006, 100.

Non-Specialized Magazines

"50 Razões para Amar São Paulo – 8. Temos Praça das Artes." *Época São Paulo*, no. 68, May 5, 2014, 20-21.

Adler, Mario, Rabino Adrián Gottfried, and Marcelo Steuer. "Inauguração da Nova Sinagoga da Comunidade Shalom." *Hineni* 15, no. 1, May 2011, 6-15.

"Agenda – Passagem Aberta." *Select*, no. 23, April/May 2015, 28.

Almeida, Samira. "Bossa Brasileira." *Bamboo*, no. 6, September 2011, 62-65.

Altman, Fábio. "Boniteza e Precisão – Livro e Exposição em São Paulo Celebram a Obra de uma Dupla de Criadores que Virou Referência na Arquitetura Brasileira." *IstoÉ Dinheiro*, no. 425, November 2005, 82-83.

Altman, Fábio. "Rodin à Baiana." *Época*, no. 244, January 2003, 81.

Antonio, Alexandre. "Rodin à Baiana." *Wish Report*, no. 35, 2010, 126-131.

Áquila, Marcella. "Lições do Passado e Olho no Futuro." *Brasileiros*, no. 61, August 2012, 34.

Araium, Cíntia, and Deborah Apsan. "Caipira com Orgulho." *ViverBem*, no. 10, 2003, 128-138.

Araium, Cíntia. "Simplicidade Planejada." *ViverBem*, no. 10, October 2000, 52-57.

"Arquitetura e Turismo." *AAI em Revista*, no. 38, September/October 2008, 6.

"Arquitetura Modernista Ainda Tem Algo a Dizer?" *Select*, no. 23, April/May 2015, 52.

"Autor do Projeto Diz que KKKK Colocará Registro no Mapa do Brasil." Section Resgate da História. *Jornal em Revista*, no. 68, January 2002, 12.

"Bairro Moinho Começa a Ser Revitalizado." *Eco Regional*, no. 336, January 31, 2008, 12.

Bardi, Pietro Maria. "Estilo que Funciona." *IstoÉ Senhor*, no. 1146, 1991.

Barrero, Vera. "A Praça é Nossa." *Revista Gol*, no. 137, August 2013, 50-51.

"Beleza com Simplicidade." *Marcenaria Moderna*, no. 27, 1988, 16-19.

Bezerra, Julio. "Pão Nosso de Cada Dia." *Revista de História da Biblioteca Nacional*, no. 40, January 2009, 12.

Brandão, Ignácio de Loyola. "Dos Arquitectos Brasileños Retocan la Cara de Hellersdorf, un Barrio en el Norte de Belin." *Humboldt*, no. 127, November 1999, 42.

"Brasilianishes Architekten Verschönern Plattenbauten." *Berliner Kurier*, no. 96/97, April 9, 1997.

"Brasilinisches Flair Pragt ein Quartier Wogehe." *Die Drei Arbeiten*, May 1998, 18-25.

Bruno, Cássia Barreto, ed. "Azulejos Kadiwéu." *Revista Ide – Sociedade Brasileira de Psicanálise de SP*, no. 32, May 2000, 9-15.

Cartum, Marcos. "Pauliceia Renovada." *Bamboo*, annual 2013, 66-68.

Chagas, Luiz. "Rodin, à Baiana." *Brasileiros*, no. 28, November 2009, 26-27.

Chut, Eliahu. "Pouquíssimo Noticiado em Nossa Imprensa a Vitória em Concurso Mundial." *O Hebreu*, no. 212, December 1997, 40.

Cicere, Jackson. "Famiglia Facin – Tradição Historia e o Sabor da Itália à Mesa." *Revista da Cameron*, no. 7, July/August/September 2015, 24-26.

"Cidades Arquitetura – Icon para Praça das Artes." *Brasileiros*, no. 78, January 2014, 88.

Corbioli, Nanci, and Martha Lébeis. "Liberdade Experimental." *Espaço D'*, no. 8, August 1999, 60-65.

"Em Área Urbana, Isolada dos Ruídos Externos." *Esquadrias de PVC*, June 2000, 29-31.

"Espaço do Arquiteto – Entrevista com Francisco Fanucci." *Revista Hitachi*, no. 2, July/September 2003, 5.

Ferraz, Marcos Grinspum. "Bienal de Arquitetura Ocupa São Paulo para Discutir Urbanismo." *Arte!Brasileiros*, no. 18, March/April 2013, 80-81.

Fontes, Flávio. "Teatro da Força." *TAM Magazine* 2, no. 13, March 2005, 60-63.

Fraia, Emílio. "Palco do Saber." *Private Brokers*, no. 9, December 2005, 62-63.

França, Raphael. "As Linhas de Lina." *Bamboo*, no. 12, April 2012, 48-49.

Girardi, Giovana. "Na Trilha dos Moinhos – Projeto de Restauração no Vale do Taquari Recupera a Tradição Histórica dos Imigrantes Italianos de Fazer Farinha e Pão." *Horizonte Geográfico,* no. 116, April 2008, 22-29.

Gonçalves, Marcos Augusto. "Pauliceia Renovada." *Bamboo*, 2013, 66-68.

Guedes, Regina. "Arquitetura que Transforma." *360°*, no. 4, November 2015, 24-29.

Heathcote, Edwin. "Building of the Year – Praça das Artes." *Icon*, no. 127, January 2014, 72-76.

Hollstein, Miriam. "Südamerikanische Balkons in Hellersdorf Umstritten." *Marzahn-Hellersdorf-Rundschau*, no. 171, July 25, 1997, 18.

"Im Gelben Viertel Geht's Voran." *WoGeHe*, no. 148, June 1997.

Junior, Gonçalo. "Templo de Rei." *Brasileiros*, no. 76, November 2013, 22-23.

Kaiser, Millos. "Praia de Paulista." *Revista Itaú Personnalité*, no. 21, January/February/March 2013, 25-30.

Kato, Gisele. Museu de Novidades – Curitiba Discute a Matéria da Arte Brasileira em uma das Seis Exposições que Inauguram o Novo Museu. *Bravo!*, no. 62, November 2002, 26-31.

"Lateinamerikanische Details für das, Gelbe Viertel." *Verlags Thema*, November 1997, 67.

Lavigne, Nathalia. "Bahia de Todas as Artes." *TAM nas Nuvens*, no. 22, October 2009, 100-104.

Leal, Sheila. "Conheça a Praça das Artes." *Projeto São Paulo City*, January 17, 2017. https://bit.ly/2Q0xrUE.

Leão, Renata. "De Cara Lavada." *Private Brokers*, no. 22, July 2009, 57-65.

Leme, Renata Toledo, ed. "Projeto Beira Rio. PAE – Plano de Ação Estruturador." Piracicaba: Prefeitura do Município de Piracicaba; Secretaria Municipal de Defesa do Meio Ambiente; Secretaria Municipal de Planejamento; Polis. https://bit.ly/2Q7dZWj.

Leue, Gunnar. "Rio in Hellersdorf." *Taz*, June 12, 1997. https://taz.de/!1396849.

Longo, Giovanna. "Praça das Artes." *Em Cartaz – Revista da Secretaria Municipal de Cultura de São Paulo*, no. 64, December 2012, 4-5.

"Moinho Castamán Começa a Ganhar Vida Novamente." *Eco Regional* 7, no. 336, January 31, 2008, 15.

Molitor, Andreas. "Der Wohnungs-Riese Von Hellersdorf." *Berliner Beitung*, no. 83, April 10, 1997.

Muylaert, Roberto. "O Brasil pela Arte." *Ícaro*, no. 194, October 2000, 100-101.

"Novo Museu: Referência de Cultura e de Arquitetura." *O Vidroplano*, no. 360, December 2002, 38-41.

"O Bairro Amarelo: Cultura Brasileira em Berlim Oriental." *Office* 13, no. 70, 2002, 48-53.

Oliveira, Fran. "Jóia Negra." *Wish Report*, no. 2, April/May 2005, 58-67.

Orlandi, Ana Paula. "Onda Étnica – Marcenaria Baraúna." *Private Brokers*, no. 8, September/November 2005, 98

Parente, Ediana. "Estética e Inserção Social – Obra de Arquitetura: Praça das Artes." *Revista APCA*, 2013, 8.

Penna, José Luiz. "Entrevista – Arquitetos da Vila Projetam Prédios e Mobiliário." *Guia da Vila Madalena*, no. 229, September 2016, 8-12.

Piza, Daniel. "Razão. Dialogar com o Espaço – Fazer Parte do Todo em Harmonia." *Eurobike Magazine*, no. 10, December 2009, 10-18.

"Projeto Nova Vera Cruz." *Cinema em São Paulo*, 1998, 7-11.

"Quem Te Viu, Quem Te Vê: Dupla Paulista Dá Cor e Graça à Velha Berlim Oriental de Honecker." *Bravo!*, no. 1, October 1997.

Rabelo, Carina. "A Bahia do Futuro." *IstoÉ*, no. 2099, February 2010, 68-69.

Rodrigues, Cinthia. "Berlim em Cores Vivas – Dupla de Arquitetos Brasileiros Inaugura Reforma Que Mudou a Cara de um Bairro na Alemanha." *Época*, no. 4, June 1998, 88.

Rodrigues, Cinthia. "Os Pioneiros." *Quem Acontece*, no. 188, April 2004, 91.

Rodrigues. Cinthia. "Berlim em Cores Vivas." *Época*, no. 4, June 15, 1998, 88.

Rudhart, Werner. "Índio, Arte e Memória." *Ícaro Brasil*, no. 177, May 1999, 60-66.

Salema, Isabel. "O Arquiteto que Fez uma Cadeira para Maria Bethânia." *Ipsilon*, October 27, 2017, 22-24.

Santos, Joel Rufino dos. "Presença Negra." *Ícaro*, no. 194, October 2000, 132-140.

Santos, Priscilla. "É Velho, Mas Tá Novo." *Vida simples*, no. 83, September 2009, 42-47.

"São Paulo Tem Jeito." *Revista Kalunga*, no. 85, January 1998, 100-103.

Schelp, Diogo. "Feito por Niemeyer." *Veja*, no. 1.779, November 27, 2002, 138.

Schelp, Diogo. "Oscar Refaz sua Obra." *Veja*, no. 1.734, January 16, 2002, 56.

Schneider, Clarissa. "Arquitetura de Refúgio – Resumo de Vida." *Bamboo*, annual 2014, 138-143.

Schneider, Clarissa. "Brasil, Mostra a Tua Cara." *Bamboo*, annual 2012, 144-149.

Schneider, Clarissa. "Conhecimento – Marcelo Ferraz." *Casa Vogue*, no. 2, 1997, 102.

Schneider, Clarissa. "Sertão à Beira-Mar." *Bamboo*, no. 38, August 2014, 84-85.

Serapião, Fernando. "Favela: Moderna ou Contemporânea?" *Select*, no. 5, April/May 2012, 108-113.

Silveira, Faiga. "Design.Br." *Bamboo*, no. 6, September 2011, 47-53.

Stathaki, Ellie. "Next in Line." *Wallpaper – The Great Brazilian Modernists Are a Hard Act to Follow. But a New Geration Have Big Ideas of Their Own*, no. 135, June 2010, 140-144.

Stefani, Arlindo. *Projeto Beira Rio – Diagnóstico*. Piracicaba: Prefeitura Municipal de Piracicaba, 2001.

"Südamerikaner Wollen Hellersdorf Bunter, Schooner Machen – 90 Mio Für Die Alten Platen." *Hauptstadt Berlin*, April 9, 1997, 11.

"Teatro Polytheama de Jundiaí é Tombado Como Patrimônio Histórico." *G1*, October 18, 2012. https://glo.bo/2NwMDaK.

"Trabalho de Índio." *IstoÉ Dinheiro*, no. 44, July 1998, 14.

Weiss, Ana. "Fim das Fronteiras – Novas Gerações Resgatam Engajamento dos Anos 1970 e Aproximam Cada Vez Mais a Arte e o Urbanismo." *Pesquisa Fapesp*, no. 214 (December 2013): 86-89.

Yuri, Débora. "Prefeitura Começa Atendimento às Famílias do Bamburral." *Renova SP*, no. 1, July 2011, 13.

Newspapers

"1º Museu do Pão da América Latina Será Inaugurado Hoje." *Jornal Notiserra*, February 22, 2008, 9.

"A Berlim de Ares Tropicais." *Jornal da Tarde*, April 15, 1997.

Abreu, Gilberto. "Brasil +500 em Fragmentos." *Jornal do Brasil*, October 9, 2000, 1.

ACS. "Polyhteama renasce como espaço cultural." *Gazeta Mercantil*, October 19, 1996, 6.

Angiolillo, Francesca. "Futuro em Ruínas." *Folha de S.Paulo,* April 30, 2019, C1.

"Argos Deixou Marcas e Saudades para Trás." *Jornal da Cidade*, June 11, 1996, 15.

"Argos Industrial, a Primeira Fábrica de Brins do Brasil." *Jornal da Cidade*, August 3, 1995, 13.

"Argos Não É Mais Problema para Ampliação da José do Patrocínio." *Jornal da Cidade*, August 31, 1994, 7.

"Argos, o Fim de um Império." *Jornal da Cidade*, March 13, 1991, 2.

Arruda, Roldão. "Acervo de Lula Será Separado de Memorial em SP." *O Estado de S. Paulo*, June 26, 2012, A13.

"Autor do projeto diz que KKKK colocará Registro no mapa do Brasil." Section Resgate da História. *Jornal em Revista*, no. 68, January 2002, 12.

Barros, Mariana. "Vizinha ao Municipal, Praça das Artes Sai do Papel no 2º Semestre." *Folha de S.Paulo*, May 29, 2008, C13.

Becker, Adreane. "Preservada Memória os Imigrantes Italianos." *O Informativo do Vale*, March 4, 2007, 13.

Bergamo, Mônica. "Chapelaria." *Folha de S.Paulo*, October 27, 2005, E2.

Bergamo, Mônica. "Kassab Projeta Praça das Artes." *Folha de S.Paulo*, January 5, 2008, E2.

"Berlim – Botoquena und Zurück." *Mieter Journal*, no. 16, 1997.

Bianco, Dante. "Novo Museu em Curitiba." *Gazeta do Povo*, November 23, 2002, 17.

Biderman, Iara. "Guia Reunirá História e Informações Sobre as 70 Sinagogas da Grande SP." *Folha de S.Paulo*, August 17, 2019, B5.

Brasil, Ubiratam. "APCA Escolhe os Melhores de 2012." *O Estado de S. Paulo*, December 12, 2012, D5.

"Bunkio Busca Peças Para Compor a História da Imigração no Memorial." Section Resgate da História. *Jornal em Revista*, no. 68, January 2002, 13.

"Bunte Fliesen als Element brasilianischer Architektur." *Berliner Morgenpost*, July 21, 1998.

Caetano, Maria do Rosário. "O Poder da Criação dos Excluídos." *Jornal de Brasília*, October 8, 2000, D5.

Caldas, Renata. "Sopro de Qualidade na Cultura." *Jornal de Brasília*, October 8, 2000, D7.

Calligari, Contardo. "Um Teatro, um Centro Comercial e um Monumento." *Folha de S.Paulo*, January 20, 2005, E12.

Cardoso, Mônica. "Região Central Terá Dois Novos Espaços Cultuais até 2011." *O Estado de S. Paulo*, October 21, 2008, C10.

Carvalho, Mario Cesar. "Rodin à Baiana." *Folha de S.Paulo*, July 8, 2009, E1.

Cattassini, Lais. "Praça das Artes Já Tem Investidores." *O Estado de S. Paulo*, May 11, 2009, C5.

"Centro de Educação e Cultura KKKK Será Inaugurado Amanhã." *Jornal Regional*, January 25, 2002.

"Condephaat Autoria "Corte" da Argos para Ampliação da José do Patrocínio." *Jornal da Cidade*, August 30, 1994, 3.

"Condephaat Estuda Tombamento da Argos." *Jornal de Jundiaí*, February 12, 1994, 7.

Constantin, André. "Museu do Tijolo: Sempre Surge, Por estes Desertos Urbanos, Algum Sopro de Delicadeza." Section Cultura e Tendências. *Pioneiro*, November 22, 2019. https://bit.ly/2Rb5XfO.

Costa, Jacqueline. "Um Ícone para Copacabana." *O Globo*, August 7, 2009, 18.

"Curtas e Finas – Primeiro do País." *O Tempo*, July 15, 2008, 4.

Cypriano, Fabio. "Escultura de Amilcar de Castro Causa Impacto em Berlim." *O Estado de S. Paulo*, October 22, 2006, D8.

Diniz, Laura. "Juíza Proíbe Grupo Silvio Santos de Construir Shopping ao Lado do Oficina." *O Estado de S. Paulo*, January 19, 2007, C10.

Diniz, Laura. "Oficina: Zé Celso e Silvio Santos em Paz." *O Estado de S. Paulo*, January 19, 2005, C10.

Diniz, Laura. "Oficina: Zé Celso e Silvio Santos Ensaiam Acordo." *O Estado de S. Paulo*, January 16, 2005, C7.

Ditchum, Ricardo. "O Novo Carlos Gomes." *Diário do Grande ABC*, June 20, 1999, 2.

Dittmann, Ingeborg. "Lateinamerikanisches Flair in der Platte." *Neus Deutschland*, April 9, 1997.

Dobberke, Cay. "Brasilien-Flair Am Plattenbau." *Der Tagesspiegel*, no. 16.074, August 18, 1997, 11.

Editorial. "Reforma Tributária." *O Estado do Paraná*, no. 15.547, November 23, 2002, 4.

"Ein Stück Brasilien in Hellersdorf – Südamerikanishe Künstler gestalten Plattenbau-Fassaden neu." *Der Tagesspiegel*, April 9, 1997.

"Esperando Godot." *Folha de S.Paulo*, December 8, 2006, E10.

"Espetáculo Multimídia Usa Politeama." *Jornal de Jundiaí Regional*, June 14, 1994, 17.

Faria, Ângela. "O Espaço do Encontro." *Estado de Minas*, December 17, 2005, 1.

Faria, Ângela. "Reforma Devolve Vida ao Mercado Municipal." *Estado de Minas*, January 28, 2006, 25.

Faria, Ângela. "Útil e Belo." *Estado de Minas*, December 17, 2005, 3.

Fernandes, José Carlos. "Mil Rotações por Minuto: Mais de 600 Operários Correm Contra o Tempo para Finalizar a Obra no Centro Cívico." *Gazeta do Povo*, November 16, 2002, 1.

Fernandes, José Carlos. "No Cenário de Niemeyer." *Gazeta do Povo*, November 23, 2002.

Fernandes, José Carlos. "Um Alfabeto Escrito em Concreto: Novo Museu Funciona Como Pequeno Inventário das Inovações Criadas por Brasileiros." *Gazeta do Povo*, November 16, 2002, 1.

Fioratti, Gustavo. "Praça das Artes Quer Requalificar o Centro." *Folha de S.Paulo*, December 5, 2012, E4.

Folgato, Marisa. "Silvio Santos Terá de Renovar Área." *O Estado de S. Paulo*, May 3, 2006, D1.

Fraga, Olívia. "Conceito Brasileiro." *O Estado de S. Paulo*, September 14, 2008, 1, 10-13.

Freitas, Iole de. "A Precisão do Risco." *Folha de S.Paulo,* June 11, 1998, 10.

Frias Filho, Otavio. "Brasileiros Ganham Concurso em Berlim." *Folha de S.Paulo*, April 17, 1997, 3.

Gama, Maria. "Brasileiros Latinizam "BNH" Alemão." *Folha de S.Paulo*, October 13, 1998, 5.

Gioia, Mario. "Livros Debatem Identidade Nacional." *Folha de S.Paulo*, January 23, 2006, E4.

Gioia, Mario. "Museu no Interior Gaúcho Ganha Prêmios de Arquitetura." *Folha de S.Paulo*, January 18, 2009, E6.

Gioia, Mario. "Museu Rodin Bahia Ganha Prêmio de Exposição Geral." *Folha de S.Paulo*, December 11, 2007, E9.

Gioia, Mario. "Rodin Bahia Será Aberto no Fim do Ano." *Folha de S.Paulo,* June 14, 2006, E7.

Girão, Eduardo Tristão. "Arte do Cotidiano." *Estado de Minas*, May 18, 2006, 3.

Gonçalves Filho, Antonio. "País Pega Fogo e Paris Alucina por Krajcberg." *O Estado de S. Paulo*, March 31, 1998, D1.

"Governador Participa de Inauguração do KKKK." *Jornal Regional*, January 18, 2002.

"Governo em Crise, Cultura Paralisada." *O Estado de S. Paulo*, June 22, 2005, D3.

"Grafite de Osgemeos Some de Prédio no Vale do Anhangabaú." *Folha de S.Paulo*, February 15, 2012, C8.

Grillo, Cristiana. "Mostra Leva Versão Miniatura ao Rio." *Folha de S.Paulo*, October 9, 2000, E4.

Guerra, Sabrina. "Amigos e Farinha em Homenagem a Lina." *Correio*, December 7, 2004, C2.

Haus. "MON Está de Aniversário! Conheça Detalhes e Curiosidades do Projeto Histórico." *Gazeta do Povo*, November 21, 2018. https://bit.ly/2K4y4J4.

Heathcote, Edwin. "São Paulo: Museum of Modernism." *Financial Times*, April 5, 2013, 15. https://on.ft.com/2CneeEK.

Heathcote, Edwin. "Architecture: Built in Brazil." *Financial Times*, March 28, 2014. https://on.ft.com/2r3cgrf.

Henrique, Klecius. "Por Dentro do Centro." *Correio do Brasil*, October 12, 2000, 3.

"IAB Premia Arquitetura do Polytheama." *Jornal da Cidade*, June 19, 1997, 16.

"Ich War Angetan Vom Umfassenden Städtebaulichen Ansatz…" *Mieter Journal*, 1998.

"Inauguração do Conjunto Arquitetônico KKKK Marca a História de Registro." *Jornal Regional*, January 18, 2002.

"Indianer-Copyright. Ersmals Respektiert." *Berliner Zeitung*, no. 167, July 21, 1998.

"Kassab Projeta Praça das Artes." *Folha de S.Paulo*, January 5, 2008, E2.

"Kiss: O Grande Timoneiro da Argos." *Jornal de Jundiaí*, August 8, 1993, 2.

"KKKK Abrigará Circuito Gestão da Secretaria da Educação." Section Resgate da História. *Jornal em Revista*, no. 68, January 2002, 19.

"KKKK Renasce das Cinzas." Section Resgate da História. *Jornal em Revista*, no. 68, January 2002, 1.

"'KKKK Trará um Futuro Brilhante', Diz Samuel." Section Resgate da História. *Jornal em Revista*, no. 68, January 2002, 10.

Klintowitz, Jacob. "A Cultura Brasileira em Berlim Oriental." *Jornal da Crítica* 1, no. 4, January 1997.

Kröck, Susanne, and Anka Seyfert. "In Hellersdorf Bauen Auch Die Indianer." *Berliner Kurier*, June 20, 1998. https://bit.ly/2Cn3CWs.

Lage, Amarílis. "Sinagoga Será Transformada em Museu." *Folha de S.Paulo*, March 28, 2005, C5.

Lee, Ji Min. "Casa da Lagoa." *Deco Journal,* v. 289, August 2019, 104-115.

Lichote, Leonardo. "Um Nordeste High-Tech no Cais do Recife." *O Globo*, October 17, 2013. https://glo.bo/2PgSoZt.

Machado, Ivan Marcos. "Jundiaí Reforma o Polytheama." *O Estado de S. Paulo*, March 21, 1996, C6.

Machado, Ivan Marcos. "Polytheama Ressurge Asa Vésperas dos Cem Anos." *O Estado de S. Paulo*, December 11, 1996, C4.

Machado, Renato. "Espaço Abrigará Escola e Coral, num Projeto de Resgate da Cinelândia." *O Estado de S. Paulo*, June 2, 2008, C6.

Machado, Renato. "Instituição Luta para Ficar no Centro." *O Estado de S. Paulo*, June 2, 2008, C6.

Maciel, Nahima. "Endereço das Artes." *Correio Brasiliense*, October 11, 2000, 20.

Mariz, Juliana. "Legomania em Mobiliário Verde e Amarelo." *Valor Econômico*, December 10, 2002.

Martí, Silas. "Arquitetos Tentam Criar 'Gramática de Museus' no País." *Folha de S.Paulo*, January 21, 2011, E3.

Martí, Silas. "Arquitetura da Reconstrução." *Folha de S.Paulo*, January 24, 2013, E1.

Martí, Silas. "Sesc Pompeia Contrasta Obras de Artistas e Arquitetos em Mostra." *Folha de S.Paulo*, May 24, 2012, E3.

Martín, Azahara. "Um Shopping para Silvio Santos e um Teatro para Zé Celso." *O Estado de S. Paulo*, July 25, 2005, C1.

Martins, Régis. "O Passado em Busca de um Presente." *A Cidade*, January 17, 2016, 1.

Medeiros, Jotabê. "Azulejos Cadiueus Enfeitam Bairro Reformado de Berlim." *O Estado de S. Paulo*, June 16, 1998, D7.

Medeiros, Jotabê. "Histórias de um Criativo Escritório Chamado Brasil." *O Estado de S. Paulo*, October 22, 2005, D3.

Medeiros, Jotabê. "Intervenção Visionária Pode Mudar Feições de Salvador." *O Estado de S. Paulo*, August 29, 2010, D3.

Medeiros, Jotabê. "Mar Aberto." *O Estado de S. Paulo*, August 29, 2010, D1.

Medeiros, Jotabê. "Museu Rodin da Bahia Já Tem Projeto e Curadora." *O Estado de S. Paulo*, August 3, 2002, 63.

Medeiros, Jotabê. "Museu Rodin da Bahia Será Aberto em Novembro." *O Estado de S. Paulo*, March 1, 2003, 45.

Medeiros, Jotabê. "Nova Joia Brilha na 'Princesinha do Mar.'" *O Estado de S. Paulo*, August 29, 2010, D3.

Medeiros, Jotabê. "Praça das Artes Ataca a "Quadra Maldita."" *O Estado de S. Paulo*, November 11, 2009, D3.

Medeiros, Jotabê. "Um Museu Ancorado na Paisagem." *O Estado de S. Paulo*, August 29, 2010, D3.

Menchen, Denise. "Arquitetura Pode Ajudar, Mas Não É a Penicilina." *Folha de S.Paulo*, August 17, 2009, C6.

Menchen, Denise. "MIS Terá Projeto Inspirado em Burle Marx." *Folha de S.Paulo*, August 11, 2009, C6.

Menchen, Denise. "Paisagem e Biquini Inspiram Projetos de Novo Museu no RJ." *Folha de S.Paulo*, August 7, 2009, C4.

Menezes, Maria Eugênia de. "Mais Espaço para o Municipal." *O Estado de S. Paulo*, August 15, 2012, D1, D3.

Menezes, Maria Eugênia. "Vida Nova Para o Municipal." *O Estado de S. Paulo*, December 5, 2012, D6.

Merten, Luiz Carlos. "Vera Cruz Vai Ressurgir das Cinzas em 1997." *O Estado de S. Paulo*, September 28, 1996, D12.

Michele, Katia. "Lerner e FHC Desprezam Custos do NovoMuseu." *Folha de Londrina*, November 23, 2002, 1.

Michele, Katia. "Para FHC Custo do NovoMuseu é Irrelevante." *Folha de Londrina*, November 23, 2002, 1.

Michelle, Katia. "Novo Museu Deve Ficar Pronto em Novembro." *Folha de Londrina*, November 14, 2002, n.p.

Michelle, Katia. "O Olho de Vidro de Niemeyer." *Folha de Londrina*, November 14, 2002. https://bit.ly/36PRtHN.

Molina, Camila. "Edifício Histórico Vira Centro Educacional." *O Estado de S. Paulo*, January 26, 2002, D10.

Montaner, Josep Maria. "Paraíso Urbano em el Río Grande del Sur." *La Vanguardia*, July 23, 2008, 16-17.

Montaner, Josep Maria. "Rehacer São Paulo." *La Vanguardia*, September 25, 2013, 22-23.

Moraes, Angélica de. "Arte Afro-Brasileira é Ilha de Excelência." *O Estado de S. Paulo*, May 14, 2000, D10.

Moraes, Angélica de. "Museu de Curitiba Afirma Identidade Brasileira." *O Estado de S. Paulo*, November 21, 2002, D7.

Moretzsohn, Carmen. "Arte Popular." *Jornal de Brasília*, October 8, 2000, D3.

Moretzsohn, Carmen. "Essa Gente Brasileira." *Jornal de Brasília*, October 8, 2000, D2.

Moretzsohn, Carmen. "Vazios de Ferro." *Jornal de Brasília*, October 11, 2000, D1.

Mota, Denise. "Em SP, Secretaria da Cultura Quer Reativar Vera Cruz." *Folha de S.Paulo*, January 9, 1997, 4-10.

Mota, Denise. "Parabéns Para Quem?" *Folha de S.Paulo*, February 22, 2000, 1.

"Museu Rodin Bahia Terá Novo Nome e Funções." *Diário Oficial da Bahia*, May 29, 2007.

Muxí, Zaida. "Museu do Pão." *Hoje em Dia*, July 9, 2008, 18.

Naim, Maria Cecília. "Bixiga Ganhará um Shopping e o Teatro Oficina Não Será Demolido." *Gazzetta d'Italia* 14, no. 168, January 2005, 3.

Navarro, Paulo. "Os Projetos." *O Tempo*, July 15, 2008, 4M.

Navarro, Paulo. "Tóquio Mon Amour." *O Tempo*, December 20, 2008, 4M.

Néspoli, Beth. "Debate Esquenta na Pista do Oficina." *O Estado de S. Paulo*, January 16, 2006, D6.

Néspoli, Beth. "Dez Câmeras Para Filmar os Sertões." *O Estado de S. Paulo*, February 23, 2007, D5.

Néspoli, Beth. "O Palco da Polêmica." *O Estado de S. Paulo*, July 8, 2007, D1.

Niemeyer, Oscar. "O Novo Museu." *Folha de S.Paulo*, November 22, 2002, A3.

"Notas & Breves – Zé Celso Convida Silvio Santos Para Celebrar Encontro no Oficina." *O Estado de S. Paulo*, April 18, 2005, D6.

Novaes, Teresa. "Zé Celso Aceita Projeto de Silvio Santos." *Folha de S.Paulo*, January 15, 2005, E6.

Novaes, Teresa. "Zé Celso Quer Ampliar Debate Sobre o Teatro." *Folha de S.Paulo*, February 26, 2005, E3.

"O Decreto que Autorizou Funcionamento do KKKK." Section Resgate da História. *Jornal em Revista*, no. 68, January 2002, 9.

Oliveira, Cida. "Estátua de Aço Fará Homenagem a Japoneses." *O Estado de S. Paulo*, October 31, 2000, 20.

"Outras Opiniões – Bixiga, Teatro e TV: Zé Celso e Silvio Santos." *Jornal do Brasil*, March 6, 2005, A11.

"Paris Elogia Projeto de Museu Rodin BA." *O Estado de S. Paulo*, August 10, 2002, D10.

Pascowitch, Joyce. "Depois de Repaginarem o Bairro Hellesdorff, em Berlim, os Arquitetos Marcelo Ferraz e Francisco Fanucci Armam Agora Projeto de Recuperação dos Estúdios Vera Cruz, em São Bernardo do Campo." *Folha de S.Paulo*, September 8, 1998, D2.

"Patrimônio Restaurado." *Jornal Regional*, January 25, 2002.

Perrotra-Boch, Francesco. "Elementos Vazados São a Pele e a Face do Museu Cais do Sertão, no Recife." *Folha de S.Paulo*, April 30, 2019, C3.

"Personalidades Serão Homenageadas Durante a Inauguração do KKKK." Section Resgate da História. *Jornal em Revista*, no. 68, January 2002, 16.

Pires, Roberto. "Rodin nos Trópicos." *A Tarde*, February 11, 2003, 1.

Pires, Walter. "Conselho Libera Shopping de Silvio Santos." *Folha de S.Paulo*, December 8, 2006, C6.

"Plattenviertel Mit Brasilianischem Flair – Lateinamerikanishe Architekten Frischen Neubausiedlung Auf." *Berliner Beitung*, no. 82.53, April 9, 1997.

"Polyhteama Impressiona Benassi." *Jornal da Cidade*, August 22, 1996, 9.

"Polyhteama. Cartas ao Prefeito Pedem a Conservação do Fosso." *Jornal da Cidade*, July 8, 1996, 22.

"Polytheama Renasce Como Espaço Cultural." *Gazeta Mercantil*, October 19, 1998, 6.

"Polytheama. Inauguração Será em 22 de Novembro." *Jornal da Cidade*, September 12, 1996, 13.

"Polytheama. Incepa Doa 66 Peças Sanitárias." *Jornal da Cidade*, August 25, 1996, 5.

"Polytheama. Miguel Haddad Consegue R$ 1,5 Milhão Para a Restauração." *Jornal da Cidade*, December 6, 1995, 8.

"Polytheama. Obras na Reta Final." *Jornal da Cidade*, October 27, 1996, 17.

"Polytheama. Reta Final." *Jornal da Cidade*, August 18, 1996, 8.

"Polytheama. Vai Começar a Contagem Regressiva." *A Tribuna Jundiaí*, July 27/August 1, 1996.

"Por Aí... Exposição." *Diário da Tarde*, May 18, 2006, 5.

"Praça das Artes Ganha Prêmio Internacional." *O Estado de S. Paulo*, December 7, 2013, A35.

"R$ 3,5 Milhões para o Politeama." *Jornal da Cidade*, November 12, 1995, 3.

Rezende, Marcelo. "NovoMuseu Abre Dia 22 com Sete Mostras." *Folha de S.Paulo*, November 18, 2002, E4.

Rezende, Marcelo. "O Anti-Guggenheim." *Folha de S.Paulo*, November 18, 2002, E1.

Ribeiro, Jô. "Contagem Regressiva Para a Entrega." *Jornal da Cidade*, September 10, 1996, 8.

Risério, Antonio. "É Preciso Dar Vida ao Museu Rodin." *A Tarde*, December 10, 2007, 3.

Rodrigues, Alexandre. "A Arte de Encaixar um Museu num Postal." *O Estado de S. Paulo*, August 7, 2009, C16.

Rosão, Vânia. "Que Maravilha!!! Tarcísio Meira e Glória Menezes Se Encantam Com o Polytheama." *Jornal da Cidade*, October 24, 1996, 8.

Rossi, Clóvis. "Berlim, Luzes e Cores." *Folha de S.Paulo*, March 26, 1997, 1.

"Rotas e Passeios no Vale do Ribeira." *Jornal Regional,* February 22, 2008, 16.

Sabbag, Ricardo. "Curitiba Ganha o Maior Museu da América Latina." *Gazeta do Povo*, November 23, 2002, 3.

Sabbag, Ricardo. "FH Participa da Abertura do NovoMuseu." *Gazeta do Povo*, November 22, 2002, 1, 6.

Sabbag, Ricardo. "Olhar de Desconfiança." *Gazeta do Povo*, November 22, 2002, 1, 4-5.

Saiki, Lyrian. "FHC e Lerner Inauguram Museu de US$ 14 Milhões." *O Estado do Paraná*, November 23, 2002, 1.

Saiki, Lyrian. "Novo Museu de Olho na Revolução Cultura." *O Estado do Paraná*, November 23, 2002, 12.

Sallum, Érika. "Polytheama Renasce em Dezembro." *Folha de S.Paulo*, November 16, 1996, 4-12.

Segawa, Hugo. "Entre o Tijolo e o Concreto." *Folha de S.Paulo*, September 10, 2006, 8.

Shiguti, Aldo. ""O KKKK É um Documento de Arqueologia Industrial", Diz Arquiteto." *Jornal do Nikkey*, January 19, 2002.

Shiguti, Aldo. "|このは知事ら迎え落成式旧海興精米工場を改築." *Jornal do Nikkey*, February 2, 2002, 5.

Shiguti, Aldo. "KKKK "Volta À Vida" Para Resgatar a Autoestima da Comunidade." *Jornal do Nikkey*, January 29, 2002.

Shiguti, Aldo. "Memorial da Imigração Deve Receber 10 Mil Visitantes." *Jornal do Nikkey*, February 2, 2002, 6.

Shiguti, Aldo. "Memorial da Imigração Japonesa Será Inaugurado no Dia 26." *Jornal do Nikkey*, January 17, 2002.

Shiguti, Aldo. "Show de Lica Cecato Marca Inauguração do Memorial." *Jornal do Nikkey*, January 25, 2002.

Shiguti, Aldo. "日本移民記念作が完成." *Jornal do Nikkey*, March 17, 2002, 7.

Shiguti, Aldo. "日本移民記念館盛大に開所式." *Jornal do Nikkey*, March 17, 2002, 7

"Shopping do Silvio Santos Pronto Para Sair do Papel." *Gazzetta d'Italia* 14, no. 168, January 2005, 1.

"Siron Franco É o Dono da Bola de 98." *Folha de S.Paulo*, October 13, 1998, 4.

Solza, Vanilda. "Arquitetos Mineiros Vão Restaurar Berlim." *Estado de Minas*, June 7, 1997, 26.

Souza, Márcio. "Ilópolis Mostra História Para o Mundo." *O informativo do Vale*, October 18, 2007.

"Tanze Samba Mit Mir!" *Mieter Jounal*, no. 10, 1998.

Tim, Nadia. "Revitalizar É Destacar o Que É Bom." *O popular*, October 19, 1999.

Uzêda, Eduarda. "Museu das Irregularidades." *A Tarde*, May 30, 2007, 7.

Veiga, Edison. "Em Sertãozinho um Velho Engenho Se Tornara Museu." *O Estado de S. Paulo*, August 25, 2013, A24.

"Vera Cruz pode Voltar Aos Tempos de Glória." *São Bernardo Hoje*, April 3, 1994.

"Vida Urbana – Proposta de Novos Usos Para o Velho Patrimônio." *Diário de Pernambuco*, June 4, 2010, C4.

Viegas, Camila. "Brasileiros Vencem Concurso Alemão." *O Estado de S. Paulo*, April 17, 1997, D2.

Viertel, Gelbes. "Mieterbeirat Macht Weihnachtspause." *Mieter Journa*l, no. 24, 1997.

Werneck, Felipe. "Novo MIS Terá Projeto Inspirado em Burle Marx." *O Estado de S. Paulo*, August 11, 2009, C10.

Weschenfelder, Josiane. "Ilópolis Prepara o Museu do Pão." *Zero Hora*, October 5, 2007, 58.

Weschenfelder, Josiane. "Museu do Pão Sai do Forno em Ilópolis." *Zero Hora*, February 22, 2008, 47.

Wisnik, Guilherme. "Davi x Golias no Bexiga." *Folha de S.Paulo*, March 19, 2007, E2.

Zibordi, Marcos Antônio. "A Cultura Como Espetáculo." *Gazeta do Povo*, January 27, 2002, 1.

Websites

Baratto, Romullo. "AD Brasil Entrevista: Brasil Arquitetura." *ArchDaily Brasil,* August 3, 2015. https://bit.ly/36HelDF.

Batista Jr., João. "Praça das Artes Será Construída no Segundo Semestre." *Folha Online*, May 11, 2007. https://bit.ly/2PZZvrv.

"Brasil Arquitetura: Fazenda Rio Verde, Conceição do Rio Verde, MG." *Arcoweb,* January 13, 2020. https://bit.ly/2vhipli.

"Brasil Arquitetura: Instituto Socioambiental (ISA), São Gabriel da Cachoeira, AM." *Arcoweb*. https://bit.ly/2oWKECS.

Cabral, Marina. "Arte Preserva Memória. Teatro Engenho Central." *Galeria da Arquitetura*. https://bit.ly/33ye09Y.

"Cais do Sertão Museum / Brasil Arquitetura." Translated by Diego Hernández. *ArchDaily*, January 13, 2019. https://bit.ly/33xp5YF.

"Casa Dom Viçoso / Brasil Arquitetura." *ArchDaily Brasil*, August 2015. https://bit.ly/2NT9lc5.

"Casa na Lapa / Brasil Arquitetura." *ArchDaily Brasil*, August 2015. https://bit.ly/2WQZ9og.

"Casa Pepiguari / Brasil Arquitetura – Pepiguari House / Brasil Arquitetura." Translated by Victor Delaqua. *ArchDaily Brasil*, June 19, 2014. https://bit.ly/34DR0pZ.

Delaqua, Victor. "Teatro Erotídes de Campos – Engenho Central / Brasil Arquitetura." *ArchDaily Brasil*, October 31, 2012. https://bit.ly/2WY9XBl.

"Encontro Trata de Projeto Brasileiro para Bairro da Cidade; Artistas Criticam Tratamento Recebido pelos Alemães. Debate Discute Reurbanização de Berlim." *Folha Online*, May 06, 1999. https://bit.ly/2RLB68a.

Farias, Nuri. "Flora Nativa. Instituto Socioambiental – ISA." *Galeria da Arquitetura*. https://bit.ly/2Q34SGi.

Gonçalves, Marcos Augusto. "Praça das Artes." *Folha Online*, November 19, 2012. https://bit.ly/2ClGCY1.

Helm, Joanna. "Outras Ações na Cidade: Praça das Artes." *ArchDaily Brasil*, November 1, 2013. https://bit.ly/2rmBwly.

"Ilopolis Bread Museum / Brasil Arquitetura. *Archdaily*, July 09, 2008. https://bit.ly/33vH01Y.

"Inspire. Conheça os 8 Projetos Mais Premiados da Arquitetura Brasileira." *Galeria da Arquitetura*. https://bit.ly/2PZXdsn.

"Instituto Socioambiental – ISA / Brasil Arquitetura." *ArchDaily Brasil*, October 24, 2016. https://bit.ly/2WRqQxv.

Jordana, Sebastian. "AD Round Up: Cultural Projects in Brazil." *ArchDaily*, September 7, 2010. https://bit.ly/32tdfgT.

Lalueta, Inés. "Praça das Artes by Brasil Arquitetura." *Metalocus*, February 28, 2014. https://bit.ly/34Ko2Vv.

Lichote, Leonardo. "Um Nordeste High-Tech no Cais do Recife." *O Globo*, October 17, 2013. http://moglobo.globo.com/integra.asp?txtUrl=/cultura/um-nordeste-hight-tech-no-cais-do-recife-10398049.

Mahfuz, Edson. "Museu do Pão, Ilópolis, RS." *Blog Falando de Arquitetura*, April 12, 2008. https://bit.ly/2Q2rc2J.

Melendez, Adilson. "Brésil / A São Paulo, L'art du Béton Selon Brasil Arquitetura." *Le Courrier De L'architecte*, June 5, 2013. http://www.lecourrierdelarchitecte.com/article_4613.

Mello, Tais. "Volumes, Rampas e Vazios Fundem-Se Às Ruas." *Galeria da Arquitetura*. https://bit.ly/2p2VF5H.

"Museu do Pão / Brasil Arquitetura – Ilopolis Bread Museum / Brasil Arquitetura." Translated by Soledad Sambiasi. *ArchDaily Brasil*, November 29, 2011. https://bit.ly/2pQ5e8w.

"Museu Rodin Bahia / Brasil Arquitetura." *ArchDaily Brasil*, February 7, 2019. https://bit.ly/32rP9Dg.

Pereira, Matheus. "Bahia Rodin Museum / Brasil Arquitetura." *ArchDaily*, February 8, 2019. https://bit.ly/2RzVNUz.

Pereira, Matheus. "Casa da Lagoa / Brasil Arquitetura." *ArchDaily Brasil*, June 26, 2019. https://bit.ly/33C6zyB.

Pereira, Matheus. "Girassol Pavilion / Brasil Arquitetura." *ArchDaily*, March 23, 2019. https://bit.ly/3676CCM.

Pereira, Matheus. "New Headquarters of the Shalom Community / Brasil Arquitetura." *ArchDaily*, April 22, 2019. https://bit.ly/2Rwc394.

Pereira, Matheus. "Nova Sede da Comunidade Shalom / Brasil Arquitetura." *ArchDaily Brasil*, March 25, 2019. https://bit.ly/2NpB30Q.

Pereira, Matheus. "Pavilhão Girassol / Brasil Arquitetura." *ArchDaily Brasil*, March 27, 2019. https://bit.ly/2JUvZ2v.

Perrotta-Bosch, Francesco. "Elementos Vazados São Pele e Face do Museu Cais do Sertão, no Recife." *Folha Online*, April 29, 2019. https://bit.ly/2RkK8tN.

"Praça das Artes / Brasil Arquitetura." *ArchDaily Brasil*, February 18, 2013. https://bit.ly/2rnJTnn.

"Praça das Artes / Brasil Arquitetura." Translated by Nico Saieh. *ArchDaily*, April 9, 2013. https://bit.ly/2pKIDKI.

Provoste, Nicolas. "Brasil Arquitectura: Una Obra Inspirada en su Propio País." *Inhaus – arquitectura, vanguardia, experiências*, June 3, 2019. https://bit.ly/2tlUpa8.

Silva, Matheus O. "Teatro Polytheama – Patrimônio Material de Jundiaí." *InRoutes Travel Blog*. https://bit.ly/34KgySs.

Singhal, Sumit. "Dom Viçoso House in Brazil by Brasil Arquitetura." *AECCafe Blogs*, September 23, 2015. https://bit.ly/3cWVGfB.

Singhal, Sumit. "Cais do Sertão Museum in Recife, Brazil by Brasil Arquitetura." *AECCafe Blogs*, October 14, 2019. https://bit.ly/39Qxmdn.

Singhal, Sumit. "House in Lapa, São Paulo – Brazil by Brasil Arquitetura." *AECCafe Blogs*, September 6, 2015. https://bit.ly/39MRQUw.

Singhal, Sumit. "Praça das Artes Performing Arts Centre in São Paulo, Brazil by Brasil Arquitetura." *AECCafe Blogs*, July 14, 2015. https://bit.ly/2Wi5PNU.

Souza, Eduardo. "Lajes Impermeabilizadas Com Água? Entenda a Solução Desenvolvida por Brasil Arquitetura." *ArchDaily*, May 22, 2019. https://bit.ly/2RyNY1w.

Souza, Eduardo. "The Possibilities of Pigmented Concrete: 18 Buildings Infused with Color." *ArchDaily*, February 18, 2019. https://bit.ly/2JYz0Pl.

Souza, Eduardo. "Roof Waterproofing With Water: A Solution by 'Brasil Arquitetura.'" *ArchDaily*, May 28, 2019. https://bit.ly/30Buihy.

"Teatro Polytheama É Patrimônio Histórico." *O Estado de S. Paulo*, August 22, 2012. https://bit.ly/2K3KCAr.

"Tomie Ohtake Faz Obra para Registro." *Folha Online*, November 1, 2000. https://bit.ly/2X19ZrX.

Vada, Pedro. "Brasil Arquitetura Reveals How Building Recovery Is About Meeting the Real Demands of Society." Translated by Guilherme Carvalho. *ArchDaily*, April 5, 2018. https://bit.ly/2K4xRph.

Vada, Pedro. "Museu Cais do Sertão / Brasil Arquitetura." *ArchDaily Brasil*, December 17, 2018. https://bit.ly/36GDJig.

Papers Delivered at Academic Events and Catalogs

Associação das Comunidades Indígenas da Reserva Kadiwéu – ACIRK. *Von der Körperbemalung im Mato Grosso zur Fassadenfliese in Berlin*. Exhibition catalog. Berlim: Staatliche Museen, 2002.

Bastos, Maria Alice Junqueira. "1960-2010: Meio Século de Distância." In *Annals of X Seminário Docomomo Brasil "Arquitetura moderna e internacional: conexões brutalistas – 1955-75."* " Curitiba: PUC-PR, 2013. https://bit.ly/2CrDp9n.

"Brasil Arquitetura – Plaza de las Artes." In *Catálogo da Bienal de Arquitetura de Santa Cruz – BASC*. Santa Cruz de la Sierra, Colégio de Arquitetos de Santa Cruz, March 2018, 169-171.

"Brasil Arquitetura / Francisco de Paiva Fanucci, Marcelo Carvalho Ferraz e Marcelo Suzuki – Fábrica Grisbi Nordeste S/A." In *Catalog of II Bienal Internacional de Arquitetura de São Paulo*. São Paulo: Fundação Bienal de São Paulo, Instituto de Arquitetos do Brasil, 1993, 78.

"Brasil Arquitetura / Francisco de Paiva Fanucci, Marcelo Carvalho Ferraz e Marcelo Suzuki – Bairro Amarelo, Casa Ubiracica e Casa Tamboré." In *Catalog of III Bienal Internacional de Arquitetura de São Paulo. São Paulo: Fundação Bienal de São Paulo*, Instituto de Arquitetos do Brasil, 1997, 301.

"Cais do Sertão." In *Catalog of Prêmio de Arquitetura AkzoNobel 2018*. São Paulo: Instituto Tomie Ohtake, 2018, 76-81.

Camargos, Marcia, and Dan Fialdini (cur.). *"O Conservatório na Praça das Artes."* Exhibition catalog (opening December 5, 2012). São Paulo: Praça das Artes, 2012.

"Casa Pepiguari, Casa da Lapa, Comunidade do Bamburral, Praça das Artes e Cais do Sertão." In *Catalog of W Award*. São Paulo: Instituto São Paulo de Arte e Cultura, Ministério da Cultura, FAAP, Instituto Ethos, 2014, 79; 101; 106; 132-133; 138.

Cavalcanti, Lauro. "Museu do Pão e Escola de Padeiros." In Cavalcanti, Lauro, ed. *Razão e Ambiente*. Exhibition catalog. São Paulo: MAM/SP, 2011, 102-104.

Chiarelli, Silvia Raquel, Ruth Verde Zein, and Maria Isabel Villac. "Um Pavilhão na Vila." In *Annals of XIV Seminário de Arquitetura Latino-Americana*. Campinas: UNICAMP, 2011.

Ferraz, Marcelo Carvalho. "DO! Material." In Lassila, Anssi, ed. *DO! Catálogo do 13th International Alvar Aalto Symposium 2015*. Jyväskylä: 2015, 166-173.

Ferraz, Marcelo Carvalho. "Um Presente para São Paulo." In *Espaço Cultural BM&F*. Exhibition catalog of BM&F's art collection. São Paulo: January 2002, 6-7.

"Francisco Fanucci – Centro Cultural e Comercial do Bixiga." In Catalog of *VI Bienal Internacional de Arquitetura de São Paulo*. São Paulo: Fundação Bienal de São Paulo, Instituto de Arquitetos do Brasil, 2005, 306.

"Francisco Fanucci – Marcelo Ferraz, Brasil." In *Annals of Mundaneum – V Reunión Internacional de Arquitectura*. San José: June 2007, 30-31.

"Francisco Fanucci e Marcelo Ferraz – Centro Cultural e Comercial do Bixiga." *In Catalog of IV Bienal Internacional de Arquitetura e Design de São Paulo*. São Paulo: Fundação Bienal de São Paulo, Instituto de Arquitetos do Brasil, 2005, 306.

Governo do Estado de Pernambuco. *Cais do Sertão*. Exhibition catalog. Recife: Companhia Editora de Pernambuco, 2013.

Grossman, Luis. "Menciones – El Molino de Ilópolis – Molinio Colognese, Museo del Pan y Escuela de Confiteros." In *Premio Cubbio 2009 – Sección América Latina y Caribe*. Exhibition catalog. Buenos Aires: Buenos Aires Ciudad, 2010, 70-71.

Guerra, Abilio. "Museu de Igatu – Brasil Arquitetura." In Guerra, Abilio, ed. *Arquitetura Brasileira: Viver na Floresta*. Exhibition catalog (Instituto Tomie Ohtake, São Paulo, June 15 – August 1, 2010; Palácio das Artes, Belo Horizonte, April 8 – May 8, 2011). São Paulo: Instituto Tomie Ohtake, 2011, 128-131.

Guerra, Abilio. "Visión Panorámica de la Arquitectura Brasileira Contemporánea." In OLEAS Serrano, Diego, and Abilio Guerra, ed. *Brasil – Documentos del Colegio de Arquitectura de la UFSQ*. Annals of X Foro Internacional de Arquitectura – Brasil, March 27-28, 2009. Quito: El Colegio de Arquitectura de la Universidad San Francisco de Quito, 2010, 22.

Katinsky, Julio. "Casa Jardim Santo André, Brasil Arquitetura, Santo André SP 2006." In Katinsky, Julio, ed. *Arquitetura Brasileira: O Coração da Cidade – A Invenção dos Espaços de Convivência*.

Exhibition catalog (Instituto Tomie Ohtake, São Paulo, April 20 – July 3, 2011; Palácio das Artes, Belo Horizonte, February 1 – March 18, 2012). São Paulo: Instituto Tomie Ohtake, 2012, 128-131.

"Libros Selecionados / Francisco Fanucci, Marcelo Ferraz – Brasil Arquitectura." In *Catalog of V Bienal Iberoamericana de Arquitetura y Urbanismo, Montevidéu*. Madri: Ministerio de Vivienda de España, 2014, 234.

"Lo que No Se Vio." In *Catalog of Bienal de Arquitetura de Santa Cruz – BASC*. Santa Cruz de la Sierra: Colégio de Arquitetos de Santa Cruz, March 2018, 224-225.

"Marcelo Carvalho Ferraz & Francisco de Paiva Fanucci – Museu Rodin Bahia." In *Catalog of VII Bienal Internacional de Arquitetura de São Paulo*. São Paulo: Fundação Bienal de São Paulo, Instituto de Arquitetos do Brasil, 2007, 235.

Marques, Claudio, and Graça Mendes. "A Palavra dos Premiados." In Mendes, Graça, Léa Scatrut, and Tadeu Gonçalves. *Prêmio Rodrigo Melo Franco de Andrade*. Catalog. Brasília: IPHAN, 2008, 13-15.

"Menções Honrosas." In Serapião, Fernando. "Prêmio IAB/SP." *Premiação Exigente Se Divide Entre o Público e o Privado*. Catalog of 2006 Premiation. São Paulo: IAB/SP, January 2007, 15.

Moimas, Valentina. "Brasil Arquitetura – Museu Rodin." In Cinqualbre, Olivier, ed. *Collection Architecture – La Collection du Centre Pompidou: Musée National d'Art Modern – Centre de Création Industrielle*. Paris: Centre Georges Pompidou, 2016, 95.

"Museu do Pão – Moinho Colognese." In *Catalog of VII Bienal Iberoamericana de Arquitectura y Urbanismo, Medellín*. Madri: Ministerio de Vivienda de España, 2010, 70-77.

"Museu Rodin Bahia." *In Catalog of VI Bienal Iberoamericana de Arquitectura y Urbanismo, Lisboa*. Madri: Ministerio de Vivienda de España, 2008, 18-25.

"Passagem da Cidadania." In Diretoria de Comunicação da Escola da Cidade. *Escola da Cidade*. Course catalog. São Paulo: Associação Escola da Cidade Arquitetura e Urbanismo, 2008, 17.

Pellegrini, Ana Carolina, and Carlos Eduardo Comas. "O Futuro do Pretérito e a Invenção do Patrimônio: O Museu do Pão em Ilópolis." In *Annals of XII Seminário de História da Cidade e do Urbanismo*. Porto Alegre: UFRGS, 2012.

Pellegrini, Ana Carolina. "O Patrimônio Projetado." In *Annals of Encontro da Associação Nacional de Pesquisa e Pós-Graduação em Arquitetura e Urbanismo – IV Enanparq*. Porto Alegre: UFRGS, 2016. https://bit.ly/34O53JA.

Pellegrini, Ana Carolina Santos. "Pretérito Mais Que Perfeito?" In *Annals of Arquimemória 4 – Encontro Internacional Sobre Preservação do Patrimônio Edificado*. Salvador: UFBA, 2013.

Perrone, Carlos. Vertentes – *Interiores Brasileiros Contemporâneos*. Exhibition catalog. São Paulo: Ministério das Relações Exteriores/FAAP, 2008, 100-101.

Pino, Andrés, and Leonardo Coloma. "Praça das Artes." In *Catalog of Bienal Panamericana de Arquitectura de Quito – BAQ*. Quito: Colegio de Arquitectos del Ecuador, Pichincha, 2018, 94-105.

Pino, Andrés, and Leonardo Coloma. "Teatro Engenho Central." In *Catalog of Bienal Panamericana de Arquitectura de Quito – BAQ*. Quito: Colegio de Arquitectos del Ecuador, Pichincha, 2018, 116-121.

"Praça das Artes." In *Catalog of IX Bienal Iberoamericana de Arquitectura y Urbanismo, Rosario*. Madri: Ministerio de Fomento de España, 2014, 124-133.

"Praça das Artes, São Paulo, Brazil, Phase 1, 2013; Phase 2, ongoing." In Ryan, Raymund, ed. *Building Optimism: Public Space in South America*. Exhibition catalog (The Heinz Architectural Center, Pitsburgo, September 10, 2016 – February 13, 2017). Pitsburg: Carnegie Museum of Art/Carnegie Institute, 2016, 6-27.

"Premio Bienal – Teatro Polytheama." *XI Bienal de Arquitetura de Quito*, 1999, 72-75.

"Produtos e Consumidores – Moinho Colognese." In Dornellas, João (ed.). Nestlé – *Responsabilidade Social Corporativa da Nestlé Brasil*. Business catalog. São Paulo: 2008, 46-47.

"Proyecto Seleccionado – Plaza de las Artes." In *Catalog of Premio Oscar Niemayer para la Arquitectura Latino Americana – Premio 'ON'*. Cidade do México: Red de Bienales de Arquitectura de América Latina – REDBAAL, Taller General, 2016, 62.

"Sala Especial Francisco de Paiva Fanucci e Marcelo Carvalho Ferraz – Centro de Capacitação de Professores – KKKK, Terminal Rodoferroviário de Santo André e Museu Rodin Bahia." In *Catalog of V Bienal Internacional de Arquitetura e Design de São Paulo*. São Paulo: Fundação Bienal de São Paulo, Instituto de Arquitetos do Brasil, 2003, 190.

Secretaria de Estado da Educação de São Paulo. *KKKK – Kaigai Kogyo Kabushiki Kaisha*. Institutional brochure. São Paulo: Governo do Estado de São Paulo, 2002.

"Teatro Polytheama, Jundiaí, Brasil." In *Catalog of I Bienal Iberoamericana de Arquitectura y Ingeniería Civil*. Madri: Electa, 1998, 195.

"Teatro Polytheama." In Catalog of *XI Bienal de Arquitectura de Quito*. Quito: Colégio de Arquitectos del Ecuador, Pichincha, February 1999, 72-75.

"Terreiro Òsùmàrè. Interpreting History Through the Layering of Walls. Architects Brasil Arquitetura, Location Salvador – BA." In Kozlowski, Gabriel, Laura González Fierro, Marcelo Maia Rosa, and Sol Camacho. *Muros de Ar / Walls of Air*. Catalog of Brazilian Pavillion at 16th International Architecture Exhibition at La Biennale di Venezia 2018 (Venice, May 26 – November 25, 2018). São Paulo: Bienal de São Paulo, 2018, 414-415

Awards

1979

Paço Municipal, Cambuí MG – winner, public competition.

1985

Câmara Municipal e Centro Cultural, Varginha MG – winner, public competition.

1993

Vila Operária Grisbi, Pirapora MG – highlight, category Works, II Bienal Internacional de Arquitetura de São Paulo, Fundação Bienal de São Paulo/Instituto de Arquitetos do Brasil, São Paulo SP.

1994

Faculdade de Odontologia da Universidade Braz Cubas, Mogi das Cruzes SP – winner, public competition.

1996

Teatro Polytheama, Jundiaí SP – Rino Levi Prize, IAB-SP Prize, Instituto de Arquitetos do Brasil, São Paulo SP.

1997

Requalificação do Bairro Amarelo, Berlim, Alemanha – winner, private international competition.

1998

Teatro Polytheama, Jundiaí SP – finalist, best design, I Bienal Iberoamericana de Arquitectura e Ingeniería Civil (current Bienal Iberoamericana de Arquitectura y Urbanismo), Madrid, Spain.

Teatro Polytheama, Jundiaí SP – winner, category Architectonical Rehabilitation, XI Bienal Panamericana de Arquitetura, Quito, Ecuador.

Terminal Rodoferroviário, Santo André SP – winner, category Buildings, IAB-SP Prize, Instituto de Arquitetos do Brasil, São Paulo SP.

2000

Exhibition Brasil 500 Anos Artes Visuais, São Paulo, Rio de Janeiro e Brasília – honorable mention, category Interior Architecture, IAB-SP Prize, Instituto de Arquitetos do Brasil, São Paulo SP.

Monumento aos Imigrantes e Migrantes do Estado de São Paulo, São Paulo SP – honorable mention, public competition.

Requalificação do Bairro Amarelo, Berlim, Alemanha – winner, Projeto Global, Expo 2000, Hannover, Germany.

2002

KKKK Complex, Registro SP – winner, category Buildings Revitalization, IAB-SP Prize, Instituto de Arquitetos do Brasil, São Paulo SP.

KKKK Complex, Registro SP – finalist, best design, III Bienal Iberoamericana de Arquitectura e Ingeniería Civil (current Bienal Iberoamericana de Arquitectura y Urbanismo), Santiago, Chile.

2005

Jewish Museum, São Paulo SP – honorable mention, private competition.

Villa Isabella, Finland – winner, private competition.

2006

Centro Educacional Jardim Santo André, Santo André SP – winner, category Built Work / Commercial Building / Institutional, V Bienal de Arquitetura de Brasília, Brasília DF.

Book Francisco Fanucci e Marcelo Ferraz: Brasil Arquitetura – honorable mention, category Written Works / Publications, IAB-SP Prize, Instituto de Arquitetos do Brasil, São Paulo SP.

Rodin Bahia Museum, Salvador BA – second place, category Works with more than 1.000m², Prize Iberoamericano a la Mejor Intervención en Obras que involucren el Patrimonio Edificado, Centro Internacional para la Conservación del Patrimonio / Sociedad Central de Arquitectos, Buenos Aires, Argentina.

Rodin Bahia Museum, Salvador BA – winner, category Intervención en el Patrimonio Edificado, XV Bienal Panamericana de Arquitetura, Quito, Ecuador.

Rodin Bahia Museum, Salvador BA – winner, category Built Work / Heritage, V Bienal de Arquitetura de Brasília, Brasília DF.

Paço Municipal, Hortolândia SP – highlight, public competition.

2007

Living Steel For Sustainable Housing, Recife PE – finalist, international competition.

Rodin Bahia Museum, Salvador BA – winner, category Built Work, VII Bienal de Internacional de Arquitetura de São Paulo, Fundação Bienal de São Paulo / Instituto de Arquitetos do Brasil, São Paulo SP.

Nova Sede da Comunidade Shalom, São Paulo SP – winner, private competition.

2008

Ateliê Shirley Paes Leme, São Paulo SP – winner, category Offices with no more than 500m², Prize O Melhor da Arquitetura, magazine *Arquitetura & Construção*, São Paulo SP.

Bread Museum, Ilópolis RS – finalist, Prize World Architecture Festival, Barcelona, Spain.

Bread Museum, Ilópolis RS – winner, category Buildings of Mixed Use, Prize O Melhor da Arquitetura, magazine *Arquitetura & Construção*, São Paulo SP.

Bread Museum, Ilópolis RS – winner, category Preservation of Movable and Immovable Assets, Rodrigo Melo Franco de Andrade Prize, Instituto do Patrimônio Histórico e Artístico Nacional, Brasília DF.

Bread Museum, Ilópolis RS – winner, Rino Levi Prize, IAB-SP Prize, Instituto de Arquitetos do Brasil, São Paulo SP.

Rodin Bahia Museum, Salvador BA – finalist, best design, VI Bienal Iberoamericana de Arquitectura y Urbanismo – BIAU, Lisbon, Portugal.

Vila Nova Esperança, Salvador BA – winner, category Social Housing / Public Production, IAB-SP Prize, Instituto de Arquitetos do Brasil, São Paulo SP.

2009

Bread Museum, Ilópolis RS – honorable mention, Gubbio Prize, Section Latin America and Caribbean.

2010

Bread Museum, Ilópolis RS – finalist, best design, VII Bienal Iberoamericana de Arquitectura y Urbanismo, Medellin, Colombia.

2012

Dom Viçoso House, Dom Viçoso MG – winner, category Country House with no more than 300m², Prize O Melhor da Arquitetura, magazine *Arquitetura & Construção*, São Paulo SP.

Igatu Museum, Andaraí BA – winner, category Institutional Buildings – Unbuilt Designs, AsBEA 2012 Prize, Associação Brasileira dos Escritórios de Arquitetura, São Paulo SP.

Praça das Artes, São Paulo SP – winner, category Work of Architecture, APCA Prize, Associação Paulista de Críticos de Artes, São Paulo SP.

Central Mill Theater, Piracicaba SP – winner, category Built Architecture, IAB-RJ Prize, Instituto de Arquitetos do Brasil, Rio de Janeiro RJ.

Central Mill Theater, Piracicaba SP – winner, category Historical Heritage – Requalification and Restoration, Antonio Luiz Dias de Andrade Prize – Janjão, IAB-SP Prize, Instituto de Arquitetos do Brasil, São Paulo SP.

Central Mill Theater, Piracicaba SP – winner, IAB-RJ Special Prize, Instituto de Arquitetos do Brasil, Rio de Janeiro RJ.

2013

International Olympic Committee – IOC, Lausanne, Switzerland – finalist, internacional competition.

Escritório Brasil Arquitetura – winner, Mérito Cultural Serafino Corso, Prefeitura de Piracicaba e Secretaria da Ação Cultural.

Praça das Artes, São Paulo SP – winner, category Building of the Year, Icon Awards, magazine *Icon Magazine*.

Praça das Artes, São Paulo SP – winner, category Cultural Buildings, Prize O Melhor da Arquitetura, magazine *Arquitetura & Construção*, São Paulo SP.

2014

Praça das Artes, São Paulo SP – finalist, best design, IX Bienal Iberoamericana de Arquitectura y Urbanismo – BIAU, Rosário, Argentina.

Praça das Artes, São Paulo SP – finalist, Mies Crown Hall Prize – MCHAP.

Praça das Artes, São Paulo SP – finalist, Prize Designs Of The Year 2014, Museu de Design, London, England.

2016

Socioambiental Institute – ISA, São Gabriel da Cachoeira AM – honorable mention, Latinoamericano de Arquitectura Rogelio Salmona Prize, Rogelio Salmona Foundation, Bogota, Colombia.

2018

Cais do Sertão, Recife PE – winner, category Valuing Heritage by Tourism, Prize Nacional do Turismo, Ministério do Turismo, Brasília DF.

Cais do Sertão, Recife PE – winner, category Requalification and Restoration – Built, Prize IAB-SP 2018 – 75 years Special, Instituto de Arquitetos do Brasil, São Paulo SP.

Cais do Sertão, Recife PE – selected, Oscar Niemeyer Prize, Red de Bienales de Arquitectura de América Latina – REDBAAL.

Cais do Sertão, Recife PE – finalist, V Prêmio de Arquitetura Instituto Tomie Ohtake Akzo Nobel, São Paulo SP.

Terreiro de Òsùmàrè, Salvador BA – selected, XVI Mostra Internacional de Arquitetura, Brazilian Pavilion at Venice Biennale, Venice, Italy.

Escritório Brasil Arquitetura – winner, category Contribution to Brazilian Culture, APCA Prize, Associação Paulista de Críticos de Artes, São Paulo SP.

2019

Praça das Artes, São Paulo SP – winner, Prêmio Gubbio, Section Latin America and Caribbean.

Cais do Sertão, Recife PE – winner, Prize Obra do Ano, website *Archdaily Brasil*.

Cais do Sertão, Recife PE – highlight, Gubbio Prize, Section Latin America and Caribbean.

Pampa Museum, Jaguarão RS – winner, category Requalification and Restoration – Built, IAB-SP Prize, Instituto de Arquitetos do Brasil, São Paulo SP.

Bamburral, São Paulo SP – winner, category Social Housing – Unbuilt, IAB-SP Prize, Instituto de Arquitetos do Brasil, São Paulo SP.

Exhibitions

Architectures by São Paulo
Projects: KKKK Complex and Terminal rodoferroviário em Santo André
Berlageweg, Holland, 2002.

Architectures by São Paulo
Projects: KKKK Complex and Rodoviária de Santo André
Technische Universität Delft
Delft, Holland, 2002.

Arquitetura Brasileira em Berlim – a recaracterização do Bairro Amarelo
Project: Instituto Goethe
São Paulo, Brasil, May 6 – June 4, 1999.

I Bienal Iberoamericana de Arquitectura e Ingeniería Civil (current Bienal Iberoamericana de Arquitectura y Urbanismo)
Project: Theatro Polytheama de Jundiaí
Madrid, Spain, October 5-10, 1998.

III Bienal Iberoamericana de Arquitectura e Ingeniería Civil (current Bienal Iberoamericana de Arquitectura y Urbanismo)
Project: KKKK Complex
Santiago, Chile, October 1-6, 2002.

V Bienal Iberoamericana de Arquitectura y Urbanismo
Book: *Francisco Fanucci, Marcelo Ferraz – Brasil Arquitectura*
Montevideu, Uruguay, December 4-8, 2006.

VI Bienal Iberoamericana de Arquitectura y Urbanismo
Project: Rodin Bahia Museum
Lisbon, Portugal, April 28 – May 2, 2008.

VII Bienal Iberoamericana de Arquitectura y Urbanismo
Project: Bread Museum – Colognese Mill
Medellín, Colombia, October 11-17, 2010.

IX Bienal Iberoamericana de Arquitectura y Urbanismo
Project: Praça das Artes
Rosário, Argentina, October 13-18, 2014.

2ª Bienal Internacional de Arquitetura de São Paulo
Project: Fábrica Grisbi Nordeste S.A.
São Paulo, Brasil, August 8 – September 5, 1993.

3ª Bienal Internacional de Arquitetura de São Paulo
Projects: Gelbes Viertel Requalification, Ubiracica House, and Tamboré House
São Paulo, Brasil, November 9-30, 1997.

4ª Bienal Internacional de Arquitetura de São Paulo
Exhibition of the IAB-SP 98 Prize (itinerant exhibition Arquitetura para a Cultura) – Projects: Teatro Polytheama and KKKK Complex
São Paulo, Brasil, November 20, 1999 – February 6, 2000.

5ª Bienal Internacional de Arquitetura e Design de São Paulo
Special Room Francisco de Paiva Fanucci and Marcelo Carvalho Ferraz – Projects: Centro de Capacitação de Professores – KKKK, Terminal Rodoferroviário de Santo André, and Rodin Bahia Museum
São Paulo, Brasil, September 14 – November 2, 2003.

6ª Bienal Internacional de Arquitetura de São Paulo
Project: Centro Cultural e Comercial do Bixiga
São Paulo, Brasil, October 22 – December 11, 2005.

7ª Bienal Internacional de Arquitetura de São Paulo
Project: Rodin Bahia Museum
São Paulo, Brasil, November 11 – December 16, 2007.

10ª Bienal de Arquitetura de São Paulo
Project: Praça das Artes
São Paulo, Brasil, October 12 – December 1, 2013.

IX Bienal de Arquitectura de Quito
Project: ESAN
Quito, Ecuador, November 9-14, 1994.

XI Bienal de Arquitectura de Quito
Project: Theatro Polytheama de Jundial
Quito, Ecuador, November 16-20, 1998.

XIII Bienal de Arquitectura de Quito
Project: KKKK Complex
Quito, Ecuador, November 18-22, 2002.

XVI Bienal Panamericana de Arquitectura de Quito
Project: Bread Museum – Colognese Mill
Quito, Ecuador, November 17-21, 2008.

XIX Bienal Panamericana de Arquitectura de Quito
Project: Praça das Artes
Quito, Ecuador, November 17-21, 2014.

Brazilian Architect Tribute
Brasil Arquitetura
Sydney, Australia, December 13-15, 2018.

Building Optimism: Public Space in South America
Project: Praça das Artes
The Heinz Architectural Center
Pitsburgo, Estados Unidos, 10 set. 2016 – 13 fev. 2017.

Copyright by Kadiwéu
Ethnologisches Museum Dahlern
Berlin, Germany, June 9 – October 6, 2002.

Expo 2000
Project: Gelbes Viertel Requalification
Hannover, Germany, June 1 – October 31, 2000.

Exposição Infinito Vão – 90 Anos de Arquitetura Brasileira
Casa de Arquitectura
Matosinhos, Portugal, 28 set. 2018 – 28 abr. 2019.

Exhibition retrospectiva dos projetos da Brasil Arquitetura e da Marcenaria Baraúna
Universidade de Washington
Saint Louis, United States, April 2006.

Exhibition retrospectiva dos projetos da Brasil Arquitetura e da Marcenaria Baraúna
Escola da Cidade
São Paulo, Brasil, 2006.

Exhibition retrospectiva dos projetos da Brasil Arquitetura e da Marcenaria Baraúna
Tokyo Art Museum
Tokyo, Japan, November 1 – December 28, 2008.

Exhibition retrospectiva dos projetos da Brasil Arquitetura e da Marcenaria Baraúna
Museo Andersen
Rome, Italy, February 26 – May 2, 2010.

Exhibition retrospectiva dos projetos da Brasil Arquitetura e da Marcenaria Baraúna
Casartac La Giardinera
Turin, Italy, July 1-25, 2010.

Exhibition retrospectiva dos projetos da Brasil Arquitetura e da Marcenaria Baraúna
Loftmt 55
Vicenza, Italy, October 24-30, 2010.

Exhibition retrospectiva dos projetos da Brasil Arquitetura e da Marcenaria Baraúna
Space Callot – ENSA Paris-Malaquais
Paris, France, November 25 – December 17, 2010.

Exhibition retrospectiva dos projetos da Brasil Arquitetura e da Marcenaria Baraúna
Bienal Panamericana de Quito
Quito, Ecuador, 2010.

Exhibition VI Prêmio de Arquitetura Instituto Tomie Ohtake Akzo Nobel
Project: Praça das Artes
Instituto Tomie Ohtake
São Paulo, Brasil, October 18 – December 1, 2019.

L'Amazonie en Construction: l'architecture des fleuves volants
Maison du Brésil Cité Universitaire
Paris, France, July 19 – August 30, 2019.

16ª Mostra Internacional de Arquitetura
Projeto: Terreiro de Òsùmàrè
Pavilhão do Brasil na Bienal de Veneza
Veneza, Itália, 26 mai. – 25 nov. 2018.

Museu Rodin Bahia e Projetos selecionados 1980-2008
AsBEA – Associação Brasileira de Escritórios de Arquitetura de Santa Catarina
Florianópolis, Brasil, March 26 – April 8, 2008.

Território de Contato, Módulo 1: Cao Guimarães e Brasil Arquitetura
Curators: Marta Bogéa and Abilio Guerra
Sesc Pompeia
São Paulo, Brasil, May 24 – June 10, 2012.

Monte Mor House under construction, with three *taipa de pilão* walls with earth colors

List of Works

black: built
gray: not built

1979

City Hall (with José Sales Costa Filho, Marcelo Suzuki, Tâmara Roman and Robinson de Moraes, competition), Cambuí MG.

Vila Operária Grisbi (with Marcelo Suzuki), Pirapora MG.

Cambuí House (with José Sales Costa Filho e Marcelo Suzuki), Cambuí MG.

1980

Grisbi Indústrias Têxteis (with Marcelo Suzuki), Camaçari BA.

1981

Itupeva House (with Marcelo Suzuki), Itupeva SP.

1982

Jardim São Francisco House (with Marcelo Suzuki), São Paulo SP.

Acoustic Shell (with Marcelo Suzuki), Colina SP.

1983

Island House (with Marcelo Suzuki), Guapé MG.

1984

Ibiúna House (with Marcelo Suzuki), Ibiúna SP.

Acoustic Shell (with Marcelo Suzuki), Mongaguá SP.

1985

Council and Cultural Center (with Eneida Carvalho Ferraz Cruz and Marcelo Suzuki, competition), Varginha MG.

Baleia House (with Marcelo Suzuki), São Sebastião SP.

Benedito Calixto Square (with Marcelo Suzuki, competition), São Paulo SP.

1986

Paúba House (with Marcelo Suzuki), São Sebastião SP.

Prof. Dantés School (with Marcelo Suzuki), Igarapava SP.

Star Point Store (with Marcelo Suzuki), São Paulo SP.

Sahy Houses (with Marcelo Suzuki), São Sebastião SP.

1989

Tamboré House (with Marcelo Suzuki), Barueri SP.

Cachoeira House (with Marcelo Suzuki), Cachoeira BA.

Aldeia da Serra House (with Marcelo Suzuki), Barueri SP.

1990

Escola Superior de Administração e Negócios (with Marcelo Suzuki), São Paulo SP.

Santa Bárbara House (with Marcelo Suzuki), Santa Bárbara MG.

Cemitério São Paulo Funeral Home (with José Rollemberg de Mello Filho, Marcelo Suzuki and Tereza Herling), São Paulo SP.

1992

Coronel Joaquim José School (with Marcelo Suzuki), São João da Boa Vista SP.

1994

Blue Wall House (with Marcelo Suzuki), São Paulo SP.

Braz Cubas University Dental School (with Guilherme Paoliello, competition), Mogi das Cruzes SP.

Federation of the Indigenous Organizations of Rio Negro – FOIRN (with Marcelo Suzuki), São Gabriel da Cachoeira AM.

Socioambiental Institute – ISA Researchers House (with Ricardo Caruana and Marcelo Suzuki), São Gabriel da Cachoeira AM.

São Paulo Art Museum – MASP Store, São Paulo SP.

1995

Polytheama Theater (with André Vainer, Marcelo Suzuki and Roberval Guitarrari), Jundiaí SP.

1996

Ubiracica House, São Paulo SP.

Alto de Pinheiros House, São Paulo SP.

KKKK Complex, Registro SP.

Vera Cruz Studios, São Bernardo do Campo SP.

1997

Expedicionários Square (with Lina Harumi Shimuzu and Kunihiko Takahashi), Registro SP.

Vera Cruz Cultural Center, São Bernardo do Campo SP.

Gelbes Viertel Requalification (with Pedro Moreira and Nina Nedelikov, competition), Berlin, Germany.

Expo Lisboa 1998 Brasil Pavillion (with Judith Cortesão and José Roberto Aguilar, competition), Lisbon, Portugal.

Beira Rio Park (with Koiti Mori, landscape), Registro SP.

Pedra Branca Hotel, Rio das Pedras SP.

Graziela Valentinetti Apartment, São Paulo SP.

1998

Vila Mariana House, Cambuí MG.

BankBoston Branch (with Raul Pereira, landscape), Paulista Avenue, São Paulo SP.

Ateliê Rico Lins, São Paulo SP.

Fapesp New Headquarters (competition), São Paulo SP.

Sagarana House, São Paulo SP.

Cotia House, Cotia SP.

Bus and Train Terminal (with Henrique Zanetta, landscape), Santo André SP.

1999

São Francisco Xavier House, São Francisco Xavier SP.

Abrigo-mirante, São Francisco Xavier SP.

Morumbi House, São Paulo SP.

Tamboré House, project 3, Santana do Parnaíba SP.

Cineteatro de Variedades Carlos Gomes, Santo André SP.

Darcy Ribeiro Foundation, Rio de Janeiro RJ.

Vitrine da Cidade – Infobox, Santo André SP.

2000

Socioambiental Institute – ISA (coordinator Anderson Freitas and Pedro Barros), 1.083m², São Gabriel da Cachoeira AM.

Mantiqueira House, São Francisco Xavier SP.

Nações Indígenas Monument (with Siron Franco), Aparecida de Goiânia GO.

Afro-Brasileira Art Exhibition – Brasil 500 Anos Artes Visuais, São Paulo SP.

A Estética do Cangaço Exhibition – Brasil 500 Anos Artes Visuais, Rio de Janeiro RJ.

Arte Popular Exhibition – Brasil 500 Anos Artes Visuais, Brasília DF.

TELEMAR Telephone Museum (competition), Rio de Janeiro RJ.

SP Immigrant and Migrant Monument (competition), São Paulo SP.

2001

Trajetória Ayrton Senna Exhibition, São Paulo SP.

Tamanás House (renovation), São Paulo SP.

Atibaia House, Atibaia SP.

Commercial Building, Brasília DF.

Anima Building, Brasília DF.

Rio das Antas Park and Urban Plan, Cambuí MG.

City Museum, Cambuí MG.

Market Square, Cambuí MG.

Escola da Vila (renovation), São Paulo SP.

Grupo Corpo (competition), Belo Horizonte MG.

2002

Rodin Bahia Museum (with Raul Pereira, landscape; coordinator Cícero Ferraz Cruz), 3.055m², Salvador BA.

Tacaruna Cultural Center (competition), Recife PE.

Takano School (renovation), São Paulo SP.

Emanoel Araújo House, São Paulo SP.

Oscar Niemeyer Museum, existing building (renovation in collaboration with Oscar Niemeyer), Curitiba PR.

Uma História do Sentar Exhibition, Curitiba PR.

Porto Seguro Museum, Porto Seguro BA.

Central Mill Park, Piracicaba SP.

2003

Federation of the Indigenous Organizations of Rio Negro – FOIRN (coordinator Cícero Ferraz Cruz), project 2, 785m², São Gabriel da Cachoeira AM.

Casa das Rosas Reading Center, São Paulo SP.

Room at V Bienal Internacional de Arquitetura, São Paulo SP.

CESA Jardim Santo André School (with Vera Lucia A. Paiva Ribeiro, landscape), Santo André SP.

2004

Girassol Pavillion, 441m², São Paulo SP.

Afro Brasil Museum, São Paulo SP.

Bixiga Cultural and Commercial Center (with Marcelo Suzuki), São Paulo SP.

2005

Bread Museum – Colognese Mill (with Anselmo Turazzi), 660m², Ilópolis RS.

Villa Isabella (coordinator Cícero Ferraz Cruz, competition), 330m², Finland.

Public Market, Cambuí MG.

Beth el Jewish Museum (competition), São Paulo SP.

Bacopari House, São Paulo SP.

Pinacoteca Benedito Calixto (with Anselmo Turazzi and Vinícius Spira), Santos SP.

Forte de Itapema, Guarujá SP.

Goethe Institute, São Paulo SP.

Bixiga Viaduct, São Paulo SP.

São Gall House, São Paulo SP.

Ateliê Emanoel Araújo, São Paulo SP.

2006

Praça das Artes (with Marcos Cartum, architecture; Fábio Oyamada, structure; coordinator Luciana Dornellas), 28.500m², São Paulo SP.

Prague National Library (competition), 57.000m², Prague, Czech Republic.

Trabalho e Trabalhadores no Brasil Exhibition, travelling exhibit, São Paulo SP, São Bernardo do Campo SP, Belo Horizonte MG, Rio de Janeiro RJ, Recife PE, Brasília DF, Fortaleza CE, Salvador BA, Belém PA, Porto Alegre RS.

São Miguel Paulista Square, São Paulo SP.

Central Area Urban Plan (with Studio Gang Architects), Várzea Paulista SP.

Ubatuba House, Ubatuba SP.

Cotia House, project 2, Cotia SP.

Viva Agency, São Paulo SP.

Instituto do Patrimônio Histórico e Artístico Nacional – IPHAN Headquarters (with João Xavier, competition), Brasília DF.

City Hall (competition), Hortolândia SP.

2007

CESA Santo Antônio Jardim Irene School, Santo André SP.

Vila Nova Esperança, Salvador BA (under construction).

Living Steel For Sustainable Housing (competition), Recife PE.

Estação Natureza (with Apiacás Arquitetos), São Paulo SP.

Shalom Community Building (competition), São Paulo SP.

Railroad Open Museum, São Paulo SP.

Serviço Social do Comércio – Sesc Cultural Center (competition), Glória building, Vitória ES.

Madalena House (renovation), São Paulo SP.

Hotel Central, São Paulo SP.

1000 Mulheres Pela Paz Exhibition, traveling exhibit, São Paulo SP, Brasília DF.

Congregação Israelita Headquarters, Curitiba PR.

Museu da Cidadania (with Chão Arquitetos), São Paulo SP.

Armando Arruda Pereira Pavillion (renovation), parque Ibirapuera, São Paulo SP.

Barueri House, Barueri SP.

Emanoel Araújo House, project 2, São Paulo SP.

Nestlé Kitchen, São Paulo SP.

2008

São Bartolomeu (coordinator Cícero Ferraz Cruz), 55.700m² (2.700m², reference center; 2.000m², nursery; 51.000m², housing), Salvador BA.

Igatu Museum (coordinator Luciana Dornellas), 570m², Andaraí BA.

Bamburral Housing, São Paulo SP (under construction).

Cotia House, project 3, Cotia SP.

Caropá House (renovation), São Paulo SP.

Commercial Building (with Fábio Mosaner), project 2, Brasília DF.

Passagem da Cidadania, São Paulo SP.

Ateliê Shirley Paes Leme, São Paulo SP.

Federation of the Indigenous Organizations of Rio Negro Exhibition, São Gabriel da Cachoeira AM.

USP Leste Swimming Pool (with Fábio Mosaner), São Paulo SP.

Unipalmares, São Paulo SP.

Cantina Famiglia Facin, Porto Alegre RS.

Castaman Mill, Arvorezinha RS.

Pantanal Museum, Corumbá MS.

2009

Cais do Sertão (with Fábio Oyamada, structure; coordinator Pedro Del Guerra), 8.500m², Recife PE.

Museum of Image and Sound of Rio de Janeiro – MIS RJ (coordinator Gabriel Grinspum, competition), 7.000m², Rio de Janeiro RJ.

Central Mill Theater (coordinator Gabriel Grinspum), 2.850m², Piracicaba SP.

Cidade Baixa (with Roberto Pinho, Maurício Chagas, Alexandre Prisco, Nivaldo Andrade, and Sérgio Ekerman), 700ha, Salvador BA.

Lapa House (coordinator Anne Dieterich), 360m², São Paulo SP.

Pampa Museum (coordinator Vinícius Spira and Gabriel Grinspum), 1.880m², Jaguarão RS.

Marighella Exhibition, travelling exhibit, São Paulo SP, Rio de Janeiro RJ, Salvador BA.

Sugar Cane Museum, Sertãozinho SP.

Cine Dom José, São Paulo SP.

Transversal Art Galery, São Paulo SP.

UNICAMP Science Museum (with Studio Gang Architects, competition), Campinas SP.

Museé des Beaux Arts (competition), Quebec, Canada.

Museum of Archeology and Botany, São Leopoldo RS.

Casa das Retortas Museum (with André Vainer, competition), São Paulo SP.

2010

Work and Workers Museum, (with Fábio Oyamada, structure; Raul Pereira, landscape; coordinator Cícero Ferraz Cruz), 5.000m², São Bernardo do Campo SP (under construction).

Jaguarão Market (coordinator Luciana Dornellas), 1.735m², Jaguarão RS.

Dom Viçoso House, 240m², Dom Viçoso MG

Bohemia Beer Museum (competition with Miguel Góes and Yacoff Sarkovas), Petrópolis RJ.

Câmera de Dirigentes Lojistas, Porto Alegre RS.

Juquiá House (renovation), São Paulo SP.

Wine Museum, Bento Gonçalves RS.

City Hall Plan, São Bernardo do Campo SP.

Centro Paulicéia, São Bernardo do Campo SP.

Acoustic Shell, São Bernardo do Campo SP.

Rua Marechal Deodoro (with Luciano Margotto), São Bernardo do Campo SP.

Department of Health, São Bernardo do Campo SP.

Pedra Opala Museum, Pedro II PI.

Dalle Mill, Anta Gorda RS.

Marca Mill, Putinga RS.

2011

Pepiguari House (coordinator Laura Ferraz), 295m², São Paulo SP.

Praça da Matriz (with Raul Pereira, landscape), São Bernardo do Campo SP.

Papelaria Papel Design, São Paulo SP.

Iquitos House, São Paulo SP.

Renova SP (competition), São Paulo SP.

Fecomercio (competition), Porto Alegre RS.

Área Central Várzea Paulista (competition), Várzea Paulista SP.

Badra Housing (with Vittorio Garatti), São Paulo SP.

COHAB Ipiranga Housing, Ipiranga Avenue, São Paulo SP.

Maestro Elias Lobo House (renovation), São Paulo SP.

Miranhas House (renovation), São Paulo SP.

2012

Democracy Memorial (coordinator Victor Gurgel), 21.220m², São Paulo SP.

Bar Aamam, São Paulo SP.

Vila Kanan, Canela RS.

Idea Zarvos Building, São Paulo SP (under construction).

Ministro Rocha Azevedo Apartment, São Paulo SP.

Palácio Pereira (with Mario Figueroa and Marcus Damon, competition), Santiago, Chile.

Poetry Museum, Rio de Janeiro RJ.

2013

International Olympic Committee – IOC (with Rui Furtado, engineer; competition), 9.500m², Lausanne, Switzerland.

Holocaust Museum and Memorial (coordinator Felipe Zene), 4.192m², São Paulo SP.

Fábrica Boyes Complex, Piracicaba SP.

Trancoso House, Porto Seguro BA.

Cinepolis Shopping Batel, Curitiba PR.

Santa Produtora, São Paulo SP.

Fundação Casa de Rui Barbosa (competition), Rio de Janeiro RJ.

Leão Coroado Apartment, São Paulo SP.

2014

Mission Museum (with Carlos Eduardo Comas, coordinator Victor Gurgel), 8.571m², São Miguel das Missões RS.

Sexual Diversity Museum (competition), São Paulo SP.

Polytheama Theater Annex, Jundiaí SP.

Centro das Artes, Jundiaí SP.

2015

Rio Verde Farm (coordinator Gabriel Mendonça), 42.250m², Conceição do Rio Verde MG.

Pure and Applied Mathematics Institute – IMPA (with Rui Furtado, engineer; competition), 15.525m², Rio de Janeiro RJ.

Brick Museum, 577m², Arvorezinha RS (under construction).

Beco do Batman Square, São Paulo SP.

CEU Alvarenga School, São Bernardo do Campo SP.

Delfina Building (renovation), São Paulo SP.

City Museum, Pelotas RS.

Losso Neto Municipal Theater (renovation), Piracicaba SP.

Ferrovia Paulista S. A. – FEPASA Complex, Jundiaí SP.

2016

Lagoa House, 174m², Florianópolis SC.

Marighella Memorial, 391m², Salvador BA.

Lima Art Museum – MALI (with Pedro Ivo Freire, competition), 6.524m², Lima, Peru.

Japonese Immigration Museum (coordinator Felipe Zene and Julio Tarragó), 680m², Registro SP (under construction).

Los Andes University Civic Center (with Mauricio Rojas, competition), Bogota, Colombia.

Cidade Jardim House, São Paulo SP.

CEU Orquídeas School, São Bernardo do Campo SP.

Orós House (renovation), São Paulo SP.

Sumaré Gas Station, São Paulo SP.

2017

Villa Carolina, 230m², Finland (under construction).

Terreiro de Òsùmàrè (coordinator Roberto Brotero), 4.020m², Salvador BA.

New Rheingantz Complex (with Rafael Grantham), Rio Grande RS (under construction).

Sesc Limeira (competition), Limeira SP.

Barra do Sahy House, São Sebastião SP.

Ipiranga Museum (with Apiacás Arquitetos, competition), São Paulo SP.

Jardins House (renovation), São Paulo SP.

Ipojuca House (renovation), São Paulo SP.

JK Apartment, São Paulo SP.

2018

Araucaria Museum (coordinator Luciana Dornellas), 1.005m², countryside of Rio Grande do Sul.

Sesc Registro (coordinator Cícero Ferraz Cruz), 13.300m², Registro SP (under construction).

Monte Alto Farm, Guaxupé MG.

Marteli House, Anta Gorda RS.

São Vicente Apartment, São Paulo SP.

Monte Mor House, Monte Mor SP (under construction).

Bird House, Manaus AM.

2019

Dom Viçoso Chapel, 15m², Dom Viçoso MG.

Casa Domingos Montagner Foundation, São Paulo SP.

Gregório Paes de Almeida House (renovation), São Paulo SP.

Pôr do Sol House (renovation), São Paulo SP.

Nova Lima House, Nova Lima MG.

Murundu House, São Bento do Sapucaí SP.

Bertioga Pavillion, Bertioga SP.

Piauí Apartment, São Paulo SP.

Galeria das Cobras, Instituto Butantã, São Paulo, SP.

Saúde Pública Emílio Ribas Museum, Instituto Butantã, São Paulo SP.

Museu da Casa Brasileira Annex, São Paulo SP.

architects

2019
2017
2015
2013
2011
2009
2007
2005
2003
2001
1999
1997
1995
1993
1991
1989
1987
1985
1983
1981
1979
francisco fanucci
marcelo ferraz
marcelo suzuki
josé sales costa filho
tâmara roman
marco antonio machado
roberval guitarrari
giancarlo latorraca
adilson lima
hermann tatsch
desirée pierro
cícero ferraz cruz
anderson freitas
maurício imenes
adriana carneiro
pedro barros
carlos ferrata
carmem ávilla
cláudia schneider
gabriel grinspum
fernando nigro rodrigues
juliana antunes
bruno levy
albert sugai
yuri de oliveira
rodrigo izecson
mônica esmanhotto
luciana dornellas
anne dieterich
vinícius spira
pedro del guerra
anselmo turazzi
fabiana paiva
carol silva moreira
victor gurgel
felipe zene
márcio targa
sérgio ekerman
kristine stiphany
gabriel mendonça
beatriz marques
fred meyer
laura ferraz
julio tarragó
william campos
hayako ohba
juliana ricci
roberto brotero
pedro renault
harold ramirez
andré villas boas
guega rocha carvalho
heloisa oliveira
karina irino
francielle lopes
rodrigo sena

interns

1979 · 1981 · 1983 · 1985 · 1987 · 1989 · 1991 · 1993 · 1995 · 1997 · 1999 · 2001 · 2003 · 2005 · 2007 · 2009 · 2011 · 2013 · 2015 · 2017 · 2019

heloisa
lucas isawa
nivaldo gomes
paulo campos
andré goldman
duk jun lee
luiz bessa
orlando lobosco
plínio ferraz
otaene de souza
cristiana rodrigues
marcia porto
clarissa ballario
luciana dab dab
ulisses santiago
adriana levyski
fernanda barbara
bárbara conte
simone carneiro
stefania abakerli
fábio mosaner
francisco rocha
danielle klintowitz
roberto corrêa
juliana huet
ana paula prado
karine madsen
trine pedersen
maira costa
virginia lambert
carolina cagno
moracy almeida
paula granado
fabricio
michel do vale
paloma agramonte
thomas kelley
pedro vannucchi
rebeca grinspum
andré carvalho
guilherme tanaka
jacky dahan
gabriel biselli
laura peters
marina patrocínio
vinicius rigonato
catalina hosiasson
gabriel carvalho
giulia lucente
isabella abbatepaulo
caroline grácio-juhué
antônia romer
anna laura prado
bruno veiga
alice ravelo de tovar
karen moreno
lucas martins
vitor lima
victor maitino
mably rocha
diogenes victor da silveira filho
luiza azevedo silva
matheus garcia

Brasil Arquitetura
Francisco Fanucci, Marcelo Ferraz
projects 2005/2020

editors
Abilio Guerra
Marcos Grinspum Ferraz
Silvana Romano Santos

critic essays
Abilio Guerra
Guilherme Wisnik
Marta Bogéa

graphic design
Victor Nosek

photographic essays
Nelson Kon
Daniel Ducci
Leonardo Finotti

projects texts
Francisco Fanucci
Marcelo Ferraz

editorial staff
Abilio Guerra
Fernanda Critelli
Silvana Romano Santos

editorial assistant
Jennifer Cabral

image research
Juliana Ricci

research assistant
Mably Rocha

text revision
Ana Mendes Barbosa
Abilio Guerra

translation
João Luiz Teixeira de Brito

CAD drawings
André Marques
Brasil Arquitetura
Carlos Amadeo Arellano Rivera
Eduardo Martorelli
Fred Meyer

image editing and printing
Ipsis

Image credit

photographers
Alexandre Lepoldino p. 228 (left down)
André Falleiros Heise / Taipal Construções em Terra p. 248, 251
Beto Ricardo p. 44 (down), 45 (down)
Cassio Zanetti p. 181
Daniel Ducci p. 45 (up), 46 (up), 47, 48, 49, 51, 60, 61 (up), 61 (down), 62 (down), 63 (up), 63 (left down)
Eduardo Beltrame p. 202, 203 (down), 205 (down)
Efraim Silva Cruz p. 114 (down)
Fafá M. Araújo p. 212, 215 (left down)
Fred Jordão p. 116
Gsé Silva / DiCampana Foto Coletivo p. 89 (down)
Igor Vilela Rotundo p. 189 (down)
Isabella Cabral p. 81 (up), 81 (down)
Joana França p. 115 (down), 117
Leonardo Finotti p. 58 (down), 65 (down), 72 (up), 76, 77, 78, 79 (up), 83, 88, 90 (right up), 134 (down), 135, 137, 138, 139
Ives Padilha p. 99 (down), 100 (middle), 100 (down)
Marcelo Ferraz p. 8, 9, 10, 11, 12, 13 (right up), 13 (down), 15 (right), 16, 17 (right), 18, 19, 32, 33, 37 (left down), 38, 39 (left), 41, 64, 74, 79 (down), 92 (down), 112 (left up), 123 (left down), 141, 142 (up), 143 (up), 144 (up), 145, 146 (up), 146 (right down), 147 (down), 149 (up), 152, 153, 156 (up), 157, 162, 163 (up), 163 (left down), 199, 200 (right), 201
Nelson Kon p. 20, 34, 35, 36, 37 (left up), 37 (right), 39 (right), 40 (left), 42, 53, 54, 55, 57, 58 (up), 59, 66, 67, 68 (down), 69, 71, 72 (down), 73, 84, 85, 87, 89 (up), 90 (left up), 90 (down), 91, 92 (up), 93, 107, 109, 110 (up), 110 (left down), 112 (right up), 112 (down), 113, 114 (up), 115 (up), 123 (up), 123 (right down), 125, 126, 127, 143 (down), 146 (left down), 158, 159 (up), 159 (down), 161, 164, 165, 167, 168, 169, 186, 187, 189 (up), 190, 191, 229, 230
Pedro Vannucchi p. 250
Renato Martelli Soares / ISA p. 50 (down)
Ronaldo Azambuja p. 203 (up), 205 (up)
Sylvia Masini p. 40 (right)
Willian Lopes de Abreu p. 228 (up), 228 (right down)

archives
Brasil Arquitetura p. 13 (left up), 14, 15 (left), 17 (left), 21, 22, 23, 24, 25, 26, 27 (left), 28, 29, 30, 43, 44 (up), 44 (middle), 52, 61 (middle), 63 (right down), 65 (up), 68 (up), 80, 81 (middle), 82, 86 (up), 94, 95 (down), 98, 99 (up), 100 (up), 101, 102, 103, 105, 106, 110 (right down), 111 (up), 118, 119, 122, 130, 131, 132, 134 (up), 140, 144 (down), 148, 149 (down), 151, 154, 155 (down), 159 (middle), 163 (right down), 170 (left), 175 (middle), 177 (middle), 179 (down), 180, 193 (left down), 195, 197 (up), 197 (down), 198, 200 (left), 206, 207, 208, 211 (up), 213, 214 (middle), 214 (down), 215 (up), 215 (right down), 216, 217, 218, 219 (up), 219 (middle), 220 (up), 220 (middle), 221, 222, 223, 225, 226, 227, 249, 252, 253
Marcelo Ferraz p. 27 (right)

CAD drawings
André Marques + Brasil Arquitetura p. 46 (middle), 46 (down), 50 (up), 50 (middle), 56, 62 (up), 70, 75, 86 (middle), 86 (down), 96, 97 (down), 104, 108, 120 (middle), 120 (down), 124, 136, 142-143, 150 (middle), 150 (down), 156 (down), 160, 166, 172, 176, 184, 185 (down), 188, 194, 196-197, 204, 210 (up), 210 (middle), 214 (up), 219 (down), 220 (down), 224
Carlos Amadeo Arellano Rivera p. 95 (up), 97 (up)
Eduardo Martorelli p. 209, 210 (down), 211 (down)
Fred Meyer p. 111 (middle), 111 (down), 120 (up), 121, 132-133, 142 (down), 147 (up), 150 (up), 155 (up), 170 (right), 171, 173, 174, 175 (up), 175 (down), 177 (up), 177 (down), 178, 179 (up), 182, 183, 185 (up), 185 (middle), 192, 193 (up), 193 (right down), 196 (down)
Fred Meyer / Visualize p. 128, 129

Romano Guerra Editora

Editors
Abilio Guerra
Silvana Romano Santos
Fernanda Critelli

Romano Guerra Editora
Rua General Jardim 645 conj. 31
01223-011 São Paulo SP Brasil
Tel: 55 11 3255.9535
rg@romanoguerra.com.br
romanoguerra.com.br
/romanoguerraeditora

SERVIÇO SOCIAL DO COMÉRCIO
Regional Management in São Paulo State

President of the Regional Board
Abram Szajman

Regional Director
Danilo Santos de Miranda

Editorial Board
Ivan Giannini
Joel Naimayer Padula
Luiz Deoclécio Massaro Galina
Sérgio José Battistelli

Edições Sesc São Paulo
Manager
Iã Paulo Ribeiro
Deputy Manager
Isabel M. M. Alexandre
Editorial Coordination
Francis Manzoni, Clívia Ramiro,
Cristianne Lameirinha
Editorial Production
Simone Oliveira
Graphic Coordination
Katia Verissimo
Graphic Production
Fabio Pinotti
Communication Coordination
Bruna Zarnoviec Daniel

Edições Sesc São Paulo
Rua Serra da Bocaina, 570 – 11º andar
03174-000 São Paulo SP Brasil
Tel: 55 11 2607.9400
edicoes@edicoes.sescsp.org.br
sescsp.org.br/edicoes
/edicoessescsp

Printed in Brazil 2020
Legal deposit was made

Internacional Cataloging in Publication (CIP)

Brasil Arquitetura: Francisco Fanucci and Marcelo Ferraz, projects 2005-2020 / edited by Abilio Guerra, Marcos Grinspum Ferraz and Silvana Romano Santos; critic essays by Marta Bogéa, Abilio Guerra and Guilherme Wisnik. – São Paulo: Romano Guerra, Edições Sesc São Paulo, 2020.

256 p., Il.
Bibliography.
ISBN: 978-65-87205-00-7 (Romano Guerra Editora)

1.Arquitecture – Brasil – 20th Century
2.Brazilian architects – 20th Century I.Guerra, Abilio II.Ferraz, Marcos Grinspum III. Santos, Silvana Romano IV. Bogéa, Marta V. Wisnik, Guilherme VI. Fanucci, Francisco VII. Ferraz, Marcelo

CDD – 724.981

Card catalog elaborated by librarian
Dina Elisabete Uliana CRB/8-3760

About the editors

Abilio Guerra is an architect (FAU PUC--Campinas, 1982), master and PhD in History (IFCH UNICAMP, 1992 and 2002), adjunct professor at FAU Mackenzie (undergraduation and graduation). With Silvana Romano Santos, is editor of Romano Guerra Editora and of Vitruvius Portal. Author of the books *Architecture and Nature / Arquitetura e Natureza* (Romano Guerra, 2017, CICA Awards 2017); and editor of two volumes of *Textos Fundamentais sobre História da Arquitetura Moderna Brasileira* (Romano Guerra, 2010); among others. Curator of the exhibition *Arquitetura Brasileira: Viver na Floresta* (Instituto Tomie Ohtake, 2010, CICA Awards 2011) and of the series of three exhibits *Território de Contato* (with Marta Bogéa, Sesc Pompeia, 2014).

Marcos Grinspum Ferraz is jornalist, graduated in Social Sciences by University of São Paulo (FFLCH USP, 2010). Worked at the newspaper *Folha de S.Paulo* (2009-2012), writing about music and theater; also worked at magazines *Brasileiros* and *ARTE!Brasileiros* (2012-2016), writing about literature, music, visual arts, and architecture. In 2015, integrated the research team for conceptual content design of Mission Museum. Lived for a year in Lisbon, where studied anthropology (Universidade Nova de Lisboa) and worked as researcher for the series *A Cidade no Brasil*, held by Sesc TV. In 2019, resumed working at *ARTE!Brasileiros*. Over the years collaborated with other magazines, like *Super Interessante* (Portugal), *Harper's Bazaar,* and *Host & Travel*.

Silvana Romano Santos is architect (FAU PUC-Campinas, 1983). With Abilio Guerra, is editor of Romano Guerra Editora and of Vitruvius Portal. Coordinated the edition and publishing of several architectural books, among them: *Arquitetura: Uma Experiência na Área de Saúde* (João Filgueiras Lima, 2012, Jabuti Prize 2013); *Ministério da Educação e Saúde, Ícone Urbano da Modernidade Brasileira* (Roberto Segre, 2013, Jabuti Prize 2014, CICA Awards 2014, IAB/RJ Prize 2013, ANPARQ Prize 2014); *Lina Bo Bardi, Sutis Substâncias da Arquitetura* (Olivia de Oliveira, 2006, IAB Prize 2006, RIBA International Book Awards finalist 2007, Jabuti Prize 2007); *Quarenta Anos de Prancheta* (Marcello Fragelli, 2010, Jabuti Prize finalist 2011); *David Libeskind, Ensaio sobre as Residências Unifamiliares* (Luciana Tombi Brasil, 2007, IAB/SP Prize 2008); *Taipa, Canela Preta e Concreto* (Lia Mayumi, 2008, Rodrigo Melo Franco de Andrade Prize finalist, IPHAN 2009).

This book was composed in Frutiger and Helvetica Neue, and printed in paper Eurobulk 150 g/m^2 by Ipsis Gráfica e Editora for Romano Guerra Editora and Edições Sesc São Paulo, in 2020.

FSC www.fsc.org
MISTO
Proveniente de fontes responsáveis
From responsible sources
FSC® C011095